T0322892

WHY POLITICIANS LIE ABOUT TRADE

Dmitry Grozoubinski

First published by Canbury Press 2024
This edition published 2024

Canbury Press
Kingston upon Thames, Surrey, United Kingdom
www.canburypress.com

Printed and bound in Great Britain
Typeset in Athelas (body), Futura PT (heading)

This is a work of non-fiction

FSC® helps take care of forests for future generations.

ISBN:
Hardback 9781914487118
Ebook 9781914487125

WHY POLITICIANS LIE ABOUT TRADE

...and What You Need to Know About It

Dmitry Grozoubinski

Canbury

Contents

For Eldina, Vera, and Jade

I am not worthy but I'm trying

Chapter 1
I'm Sorry You Have to Care

I am very sorry. I once led a trade negotiation so impenetrably dull and infuriating that my boss said our top priority was to ensure he never had to explain it to our trade minister. I am fully aware the average human being would rather eat a broken glass salad than read about the small print of a World Trade Organization tariff schedule. I get it. Unfortunately, trade *is* important and important people keep lying to us about it. In fact, the very fact that important people lie to us about it proves its importance, and its importance is probably what compels those people – let's call them politicians, though that does leave some liars out – to lie about it.

As technology speeds up the global flow of goods, services, money and ideas, trade policy is growing in importance. Growing, too, is the role of trade in politics where it is increasingly used as a bludgeon to batter the opposition, or as a magical unicorn that can be ridden to peace and prosperity at no cost to any voter. Tragically, the truth of all this is that while you may have chosen to take little interest in trade policy, trade policy is increasingly taking an interest in you. In the 2020s, trade touches on almost every aspect of our lives and almost all of our passions. Understanding this web of trading connections and the debate over how governments should organise it may no longer be optional.

The good news is that participation in the public debate on trade's contribution to the things you care about (such as, say, your industry, business, wealth, food, health and our air, rivers and climate) doesn't require you to be a tenured professor of international economics or to have adopted a favourite treaty footnote.

Instead, to have a working idea of international trade and its critical role in your life and in the affairs of your nation, you need only an awareness of the general shape of matters:

- How do things work?
- Who are the players?
- What are the competing interests?
- What questions should I be asking?

So while you don't need to know the details, you need to know that there are details, and how they could be important. That shields you from opportunistic politicians relying on the density of the subject matter to peddle easy answers, simple narratives and misleading twaddle. Moreover, it can also equip you with the right questions to puncture the inflated rhetoric of political chancers. That's what I hope to achieve with this book.

I'm still sorry, though.

Trade Policy, Not Trade Economics

Some books superbly explain the economics of international trade through supply and demand graphs, comparative advantage analysis and currency fluctuations. This is not one of them. Instead, our focus will be on trade policy – the meeting point of governments and international business – and how such policy is talked about, sold and abused by politicians (them again).

Other books argue for a specific set of trade policies, by authors ranging from libertarian open marketers, who say it's vital nothing interferes with their right to import an Apache Helicopter Gunship for personal use, to protectionists who think every imported potato is treasonous. This isn't one of those books either. My goal is not to advocate for any one ideology, but to sufficiently explain the debates and the issues so that you have a functioning bullshit detector.

Pay Attention (*Wait, No, Not Like that*)

Trade experts sometimes ruefully remark we are the dog that caught the car. For years we moaned and complained that no one was taking an interest in our work; that trade was a wonky, technocratic field of interest only to nerds and a handful of civil society groups who hated it. Then, through President Trump, the Brexit debate, and the re-emergence of geopolitical tensions and their ensuing trade wars we rediscovered what it looks like when politicians kick your job into the headlines. It hurt. Badly.

It turns out the only thing worse than being ignored by the world is being noticed by charlatans.

Politicians best tell lies and half-truths when reality is confusing or counterintuitive. Where 'common sense' suggests the world faces one way, when it actually faces another. This is not a phenomenon unique to trade. When discussing the national budget, politicians calling for cuts love nothing more than to liken the government to a family that must live within its means. Anyone familiar with how government finances actually work will tell you this analogy is easily understood... and completely wrong. Yet politicians persist in evoking it year after year precisely because it *sounds* correct.

Trade is especially vulnerable to this kind of demagoguery. Although it is confusing and technical, with many knock-on effects that only happen further down the line, trade is also the sort of topic people feel like they intuitively 'get'. This leaves them open to confidently spouted rubbish disguised as plain spoken common sense. Trade rhetoric is inflated with this hot air.

Politicians offer up the intuitive upsides of a policy choice, but obscure its less obvious downsides. They bamboozle with numbers that have another meaning. So while tariffs feel like they are taxes on foreign producers, they are actually also taxes on local buyers. Shutting out foreign products or workers may feel like it will create jobs, but it can actually kill productivity, growth and innovation. You might think scrapping a 10% tariff would lower supermarket shelf prices by 10%, but it will hardly alter them at all. Over and over again, the natural and intuitive assumption is wrong.

Politicians are relentless in exploiting this counter-intuitiveness – mining trade policy for cheap applause lines and populist prescriptions that appear to have no losers. They make grand promises of free national transformations. Every generation breeds a new firebrand who comes up with the idea that keeping out foreign goods will boost local factories, or limiting immigration will increase employment. Every generation hears that 'slashing red tape at the border' will catapult their country into a world of plenty or that only a quick win-win trade agreement with a distant ally stands between the average citizen and prosperity.

Trade wonks are not blameless here, either. The technical nature of the field combined with the apparent political consensus (and political apathy) that formed around its core tenets in many countries atrophied our public policy debate muscles. With some phenomenal exceptions we lost, or never developed, the art of condensing complexity into punchy soundbites, brawling on a debate show, or crafting an accessible analogy that resonates. We were unprepared for the bullshit tsunami and found ourselves unable to help lift the public discourse out of its foul waters. That's on us.

Trade Policy is Actually Quite Complicated

While this book isn't here to take sides in the various heated debates about trade, I hope it helps illustrate why there are debates. So I will not be telling you what to think, but I will be making a case for why you should think – and ask you to reject those who suggest trade issues can be zapped with a magic wand without solid evidence or deep consideration. The notion that easy answers are available if only our leaders had the gumption to execute them is attractive, but almost always wrong. It's also dangerous.

Trade is complicated because it involves politics, business, and competing interests – often each with a valid and logical case to make. Any decision on intervening in interstate commerce, including the decision not to intervene at all, benefits some at the expense of others and requires choosing between their competing claims. Even where there is an expert or scientific consensus, it is almost always answering a narrower question than the one facing policymakers. Even where all the policy implications have been fully thought through, a technically optimal decision could be wrong for political, cultural or equity reasons. Trade policy is a balancing act, where competing priorities and interests must be weighed against one another. Understanding what's on the scales is critical.

And here we should give some grudging credit to those dastardly politicians. Introductory trade economics focuses almost exclusively on maximising efficient distribution of resources, optimally producing the highest number of the highest value goods and services to meet demand. But of course that is not the stated objective of any government. Which aspiring political leader promises voters to achieve 'maximally efficient global factor of production resource allocation?' (Answer: an unsuccessful one.)

As a rule, politicians focus on tangible, dynamic-sounding goals like job creation, increasing innovation, and developing a technical advantage over international rivals. Achieving these objectives is invariably far more complicated than just pulling whichever policy lever causes the biggest spike in GDP. This book can't summarise the political tensions of every aspect of trade, but it will not ignore how some issues tend to play out publicly because it is so often there, in the politics, that we find the true motivations of policymakers.

My Priors

I will do my utmost to introduce these complexities to you without staining them with my own biases. In the interests of transparency, however, let me share my general philosophy. I believe:

1. Trade and capitalism more generally work well when the profit incentive aligns with socially desirable outcomes, or can be made to do so through government regulation.
2. Where the profit incentive can't be neatly channelled toward good outcomes, a government should intervene.
3. Governments should not get between a buyer in one country and a seller in another without a compelling reason to do so.
4. Sometimes, there are compelling reasons.
5. Climate change is real, imminent, dangerous and anthropogenic – even if it weren't, greening our production, consumption and lifestyle would still be important.
6. While it's true that trade can contribute to climate change, it must also be part of the solution.

Hopefully, none of the above make you want to throw this book in a nearby fire (if so, please consider recycling it instead!). I also welcome robust and intellectually honest debate. Much as I disagree with both libertarians and communists on most trade issues, I value their relentless scrutiny and critique of the role of the state and private capital, respectively. I hope that despite my own biases both you and they find what I have to say useful.

I should also be transparent about the limits of my knowledge. Though journalists have sometimes referred to me as a 'trade expert' by way of shorthand, international commerce is far too vast and diffuse for that to be an accurate label – at least for me. I am an enthusiastic generalist, with experience in some areas of trade policy (interstate negotiations, mainly) who makes a living explaining a vastly larger world of complexity quickly and accessibly. There are far greater experts than I on every individual topic covered in this book, and I will frequently pause in the narrative to encourage you to seek them out if you want to go deeper.

Finally in this soul-baring section of the introduction, allow me to clarify what I mean when I say that politicians are 'lying' about trade. It's not a word that I use lightly – and I use it knowing full well that many that media outlets often shy away from it, arguing they can't definitively and provably state that the speaker knew what they were saying to be false, only that it was. For the purpose of this book, I reject that dichotomy. The people lying to you about trade are overwhelmingly well-staffed, well-resourced and doing so into microphones they know will reach millions. A trade minister or senior official choosing not to learn the basics before spouting off untruths is just as wilfully deceiving the public as if they learned and then said the opposite. I'm going to call that lying whether the *New York Times* would or not.

What We're Trying to Do Here

This book's goal is to arm you against deception, both accidental and deliberate. More specifically, I want to better equip you to judge policies and ideas – ways in which politicians claim they'll make your life better through trade. In my experience, the best way to do so is to understand the motivations and forces behind policy. If you can understand what the people who shaped a decision were trying to achieve and what they were trying to avoid, you can assess how well they did, or how well they're likely to do when their desires clash with those of others. My mantra is that calling someone a dangerous idiot is more satisfying and impactful when it comes from a place of understanding. 'I can see where you want to get, but you're still steering us off a bridge.'

On Twitter, I am sometimes asked why I bother engaging with policies espoused by bad-faith actors who are clearly lying about their objectives, motivations and reasoning. Why engage when a proposal is the drunken brainwave of a knave playing to the tabloids, an opinion-for-hire paid for by corporate donors or a pandering bit of populism by a grifter farming engagement from their followers. My answer is that it's important to illustrate why a silly idea is misguided or self-defeating, regardless of its proponents' character, intellectual track record or possible ulterior motivations. A daft policy you defeat by unmasking its proposer as a liar risks returning again with a more virtuous champion or at least one with better marketing. Only by demonstrating why an idea itself is foolish can you hope to dispatch it once and for all.

Finally, it's also important to have some strategic empathy for both the proponents of a course of action and its detractors. Making milk cheaper is a win for families, but a loss for farmers. Keeping out foreign steel protects smelting jobs, but drives up the cost of manufacturing. Carbon regulations may be good for the planet, but could mean job losses and factory closures in developing countries unable to raise the capital or source the technology to meet high foreign standards. A new category of visas for bright young IT professionals is a boon to their prospective employers, but a potential blow to home-grown graduates. Some choices are easy and others are hard, but whichever way you pull the trade policy lever, some will think they have won and others that they have lost – and we neither can nor should expect the latter to take that without protest. Trade policy is notorious for having narrow, acute pain points and diffuse, disaggregated and difficult to perceive benefits. Those hurting are going to raise a cry.

How the Book Works

The book you're holding is divided into two parts. We begin in Part 1 with an exploration of how trade policy came to be, its principles, and how it's negotiated in modern times. In some places, just describing how things actually work will be enough to highlight the most egregious political lies. In others I will pause and go through them one by one. I admit this will be as much for my catharsis as for your interest.

Having looked at these 'core trade issues,' we can consider in Part 2 trade's interplay with some of the pivotal issues of our lifetimes, from job creation to national security and climate change. In each of these, I will do little more than jet-ski across a vast lake of knowledge and complexity, with three aims:

1. Revealing the existence of the lake
2. Giving you a sense of its hidden and treacherous currents
3. Helping you detect if politicians are lying about catching its fish

If by the end of any chapter in this book you feel like you understand trade's role in key debates, its main actors, and the general thrust of their arguments, then I will be able to sleep soundly knowing I have not entirely wasted your time.

Part 1
How Trade Works

Chapter 2
Why is Trade Policy?

How You Can Think About it – *If You Absolutely Must*

A little like municipal plumbing, trade policy is something most people prefer not to think about. It chugs along somewhere behind the scenes, safely ignored until it goes wrong, leaving us in the lurch because a supertanker got wedged in the Suez Canal, an export ban has left a quarter of the world's grain supplies trapped in a foreign country, or visa restrictions have left hospitals without nurses. It is the impact of trade policy, rather than trade policy itself, which tends to interest people. Therefore, and assuming you are not using this book to conceal a graphic novel or Nintendo Switch, let's dive deeper into how trade affects the things you care about by dashing through its history.

Trade between humans has existed since we first climbed down from the trees and one of us realised she could exchange her well-crafted club for a warm fur, rather than just braining the owner to steal it. Fast forward a few thousand years and a kid in Beijing is exchanging something called 'Dogecoin' for a Silicon Valley-minted smart contract conferring ownership of an internet link that displays a crudely drawn cartoon ape. The principle is the same.

What is Trade Policy?

While trade is ancient, trade policy is newer and arises from governments taking an active and interventionist role in transactions between their citizens and those notoriously tricksy people called foreigners. As governments of all types became increasingly capable of securing the borders of their territory, they also started to police the movements of people and goods crossing them. For hundreds of years thereafter, they mostly confined themselves to raising revenue by taxing such crossings. Ports, bridges, city gates and other tollbooths charged traders for passage, swelling the government's coffers and creating exciting new job opportunities for smugglers and corrupt officials.

That made sense at the time. The cost of bringing anything across long distances meant trade was overwhelmingly in products local people could not or did not make themselves. No one was going to bother filling a wagon with their goods and driving it over bumpy, bandit-haunted roads for days or even weeks only to arrive and find themselves competing on price with locals who make exactly the same thing without those transport costs. Trade gave locals the opportunity to buy things they couldn't acquire locally, and so rather than restrict it, governments just skimmed a little revenue off the top.

As shipping became quicker and other factors made moving goods around the world easier, foreign producers began competing directly with locals on price and quality. More alarmingly for some governments, their citizens did not do their patriotic duty to eschew foreign-made temptations in favour of inferior or more expensive domestic goods. Instead, irritatingly, they tended to buy whatever they wanted at the best value they could find regardless of its origin.

For farmers and agricultural landowners, this saw plummeting prices and increased competition as improved logistics and reduced transport costs made direct competition in even basic staple crops possible. Meanwhile and not unrelatedly, all this coincided with a dramatic relocation of people from villages to cities, where the availability of jobs depended on the commercial viability of factories. Faced with unemployment and discontent in both rural farming communities and urban manufacturing districts, some governments began looking afresh at trade policy for solutions.

The problem as some governments saw it was rooted in foreign goods just being too darn competitive. Imports were reducing prices for consumers, and perhaps generating some revenue for the treasury through import taxes, but they were also driving down farm revenues and pushing factories out of business. Governments could have tried to fix this problem by making their own farms and factories more efficient, but this would be a long term and potentially uncertain project likely involving multi-decade investments in infastructure, education and logistics as well as complex regulatory and tax reforms. The problem was seen as far too pressing for that kind of long-termist thinking alone. Instead, governments decided to attack the problem directly at the border, by raising their import taxes high enough to alter the competitiveness of foreign imports against what was being made at home. If a foreign-grown potato is 20 per cent cheaper than a locally made one, then a 30 per cent tax at the border should raise its price to the point where locals will once again start buying domestic produce. This is the essence of what we now call 'protectionist' policy – a policy deliberately designed to change the market in favour of local goods.

An immediate challenge these policies precipitated was a cycle of escalation and retaliation. Upsetting foreigners by locking them out of your market may not cost you many votes at home, but it does tend to upset your neighbours, who may naturally respond in kind. If I'm a French factory owner that suddenly finds that the government of

Finland is erecting barriers to keep Finns from buying my products, I'm going to want France to fight back on my behalf. France can throw money at me, to make my products even cheaper in the hopes of helping me compete in Finland despite the Finnish trade barriers, but Finland is likely to respond by just raising even higher barriers – and so are other countries I export to where French government money has suddenly made me even more competitive. France could also simply retaliate in kind, raising trade barriers against Finnish exports to keep them out of the French market and hopefully offset any job losses in France. Of course this will no doubt generate calls for help from those Finnish industries impacted, all leading to an ever-escalating cycle of higher subsidies and trade barriers.

This cycle of several major governments trying to outdo one another in bullying their shoppers into buying local actually happened, and indeed peaked in the early 1930s as panicking politicians faced with mass unemployment tried to create jobs at home by making it more difficult to import goods. In the US this saw the passage of the Smoot-Hawley Tariff Act in 1930 and in the British Empire the agreement of the Imperial Preference system of 'home producers first, empire producers second and foreign producers last' in 1932. Only a few years later the US seemed to realise an escalating cycle of tariffs was only pouring fuel onto the fire of a potential world war and by 1934 had passed the Reciprocal Tariff Act authorising the President to try to sign bilateral tariff reduction deals, but it was probably already too late. Escalating tariffs and protectionism only seemed to fuel unemployment, contributing to the Great Depression and the rise of fascism across Europe.

After World War II, leaders in the West were faced with (among many others) three challenges. First, how to rebuild a European continent ravaged by the cataclysm. Second, how to prevent another cycle of economic depression, followed by protectionism, followed by war. Third, how to strengthen a sense of unity against what they saw as an existential threat in the Soviet Union. A solution they landed on toward achieving all three was a system of legally binding international treaties amongst themselves that would provide the banks, companies and industrialists they were trying to coax into making big, long-term investments that international trade policy would not again slide into protectionism and tit-for-tat barrier erection. Such agreements would be designed to last well beyond any specific leader or government, encouraging trading links and international enterprises to take root throughout the West.

Trade agreements did not however end protectionism, merely somewhat constrain a sub-section of its most blatant manifestations. For the past 70 years politicians of all hues have continued to adopt protectionist policies as an economic pick-me-up, an arm of foreign policy, or simply a form of patriotic signalling. 'Keep out foreign junk so we can create good honest jobs here at home,' is a shiny accessory that never goes out of fashion. Every few years some ambitious firebrand picks it up off the rack, polishes it up a bit by aiming it at the foreign devils *de jour* and waves it on the stump to collect applause, votes, and money.

In the West, this kind of populist appeal is especially strong because it glides across traditional party lines. More recently it has become a powerful rhetorical weapon in the fight for the votes of so-called 'working-class voters' in the US 'rust belt' or the English 'red wall'. To vastly oversimplify an area of political science that has spawned innumerable books and opinion pieces following the 2016 UK Brexit referendum and US Presidential election, some voters are said to feel that the job security and prosperity previously available to factory workers and farmers have been eroded by a combination of factors, including trade. Specifically that cheap imports from lower-wage developing countries like China have pushed economies in the West away from having opportunities for non-college educated workers, especially outside major cities.

I am not going to debate the legitimacy of these voter grievances or the accuracy of their diagnosis. The only thing more complicated than the global economy are its people, and voter behaviour can rarely be distilled down to a single sentiment. What's significant for our purposes is that there is a subset of voters who are at least perceived to be swayable by protectionist proposals, which means that inevitably there will be political aspirants who make them. This naturally brings us to a key question, which remains as relevant today as it was in the 1940s....

Is Protectionism Bad?

Economic theory tells us that in the absence of government intervention the market should become efficient. Higher value offerings find buyers and lower value ones do not, eventually leading the former to thrive and the latter to die, with the labour and resources tied up in those that don't succeed moving into other, more efficient or lucrative pursuits. So, if we want to make as many of the things consumers want at the prices they're willing to pay for them, we should just get governments out of the way and let the natural selection of the marketplace cull the weak and reward the strong. This is fine in theory, but more complicated in practice.

Governments are supposed to enhance the welfare of the people living under them, and that involves choosing between competing interests. Not everyone agrees that this exclusively consists of maximising the efficiency of resource allocation, production and value for consumers.

Let's imagine an autoplant in your country is on the verge of closing, unable to compete with better value imports. The owners, management and the union representing the workers there come to the government pleading for help. They point out that their factory has been around for decades, that it's the largest employer in an already struggling region, and that dozens of other businesses up and down the supply chain rely on it to make ends meet. They push the government to implement an increased tax on imported cars, thus prioritising this factory and its jobs over consumers, or to give them a subsidy, prioritising the factory over other budget priorities. Should the government give in? On the one hand, this might prop up an inefficient producer, setting a negative precedent and making car ownership more expensive nationwide, on the other, it might save hundreds or even thousands of jobs. Declaring that there are simple answers to such questions is easy in an academic classroom or well-financed think tank piece, but far harder in Cabinet during an election year, or at a town hall full of worried families staring at a jobless future.

Workers and farmers are not resources in a video game, that can simply be relocated from one productive task to another if the former proves inefficient. Nor can they reasonably be expected to pick up and move from one side of the country to another in search of jobs like buffalo migrating to greener pastures. People have specialisations, local community links, families with children in school and spouses with local jobs, homes they grew up in or have borrowed to finance and a thousand other constraints. The free market may sometimes open a window when it closes a door, but not everyone locked out will be able to climb through it.

Making things even murkier is the fact that the economy is not a carefully controlled experiment in which firms rise and fall exclusively based on their competence, value proposition and innovation. It's messy and chaotic, making it hard to tell at a glance who is 'playing fair' when it comes to competing abroad. It is one thing to have your factories or farms imperilled because they have been outcompeted, it is perhaps quite another for jobs to be lost because governments overseas are putting their fingers on the scales of international commerce. Telling the difference however, isn't always straightforward.

Above, I mentioned two ways governments can tip the scales of the market in a firm's favour – taxes at the border and direct cash subsidies, but there's a big grey area of state help for competing products or services that's not as easy to categorise. If your factory is producing cars of the same quality as mine, but you are doing so 20 per cent cheaper because you streamlined your production line, invested in new machinery, and signed good-value deals with suppliers, most economists would agree that you have gained a legitimate competitive advantage. You deserve to kick my ass up and down the market. But what if that's not how you achieved your edge?

Let's start at the extremes. Your factory is cheaper than mine because it has exploited a government programme to replace its salaried workers with unpaid prison labourers or political prisoners. Even a free market libertarian may recoil from suggesting that your lack of scruples about forced labour should give you an acceptable advantage. If I demanded my government either ban your goods entirely or bring in a tariff to level the playing field, I would be seeking government protection and few would blame me. Suppose instead of building your factory in a slave-labour-permitting hellscape you instead put it in a site where smart government investments in electricity infastructure a decade ago now sell you power so cheaply it brings that same 20 per cent advantage? Would I be equally justified in begging my government to price you out of my market? Intuitively, most of us would say there is a difference between forced labour and good infastructure. We consider some advantages to be more legitimate than others. But many other examples are more nuanced. What if your country simply has significantly lower wages than mine and doesn't allow any kind of unionisation or collective bargaining? If it has laxer environmental regulations, allowing you to cut costs by disposing of waste products irresponsibly? Are these subsidies unfairly boosting your producers, or legitimate regional differences that should drive us to each specialise in areas of our comparative advantage?

Things get murkier still when you enter into indirect state interventions and financing. Is your advantage legitimate if all the shiny robots and machines that are outperforming my factory were financed by a below-market rate loan from a government-owned bank? What if you were able to make these long-term investments because the government guaranteed you a lucrative order to restock the national fleet of vehicles through an uncompetitive tender process?

In virtually all the above cases, the consumer ultimately receives a cheaper and potentially higher-value product, at least in the short term. Government intervention may stifle innovation and competition in the long run, ultimately hurting tomorrow's shoppers, but in the here and now a car drives the same regardless of whether the carbon produced in making it was captured. Is it protectionist to demand the government intervene to protect environmentally responsible producers who pay more to capture the carbon? What about mandating only to demand transparency, so that vendors must inform consumers of the carbon footprint or labour ethics of their products? I raise these questions to illustrate that while 'protectionism' is a dirty word for many economists, the actual role of government in the market is wrapped in shades of grey. Even when deliberately intervening to support local firms against a competitor, governments may be operating on impulses purer than those of an unscrupulous moustache-twirling capitalist fat cat lobbying for state protection.

When is Protectionism Protectionism?

As the above demonstrates, the debate about whether protectionism is good or bad comes alongside a debate about which policies are actually protectionist. Ostensibly, governments have several valid reasons to change how goods and services flow across their borders. Most would agree it's reasonable for a country to want to know what and who is entering it, to protect consumers from dangerous chemicals, or to combat money laundering. Yet, while seemingly justifiable, all of these policies can and do impose costs and restrictions on foreign firms. Are they all protectionist?

A simple test of *deliberate* protectionism is whether at any point in the design of a policy, giving domestic firms an advantage over their foreign rivals was a specific objective. If it was, then that policy is at least partially protectionist. If not, then any protection is incidental and inadvertent. Consider labelling requirements. Many governments require that food sold on their territory lists ingredients in the official or dominant language. This tells customers what they're about to put in their bodies and helps those with allergies. At the same time, it increases costs for foreign firms who must create, print and affix labels specifically for the market in question (which might be small).

Now, it is unlikely that the mandatory local-language labelling requirement was introduced with the aim of boosting local producers. It's just common sense that consumers should be able to read the basic details on the label of a product for sale on their local store shelf and that firms should not be able to skimp by shipping goods labelled only in a foreign tongue. Or is it? Even a simple question like this can be argued in different ways. Some would say that for the vast majority of consumers, a government decision to force, say, toilet paper, to be relabelled in the local language does nothing but needlessly drive up costs. They would urge the government to stay out of it, leaving the choice of whether to pay a tiny bit more for toilet tissue with localised labeling up to the consumer. Yet this too raises questions. Should those with allergens be forced to gamble on products they can't read? Should the government decide, on a product by product basis which products should be locally legible and which can risk retaining their foreign language stickers?

The above illustrates some of the debates in trade policy, and their habit of manifesting in what one might be forgiven for believing to be infertile ground for argument. What's significant for us at the moment however, is that even a policy devised in good faith and on the basis of sound reasoning can be nakedly protectionist if one is conniving enough in its implementation. The devil can lurk in the detail. Were I so inclined, for example, I could mandate that in order to be approved for sale in my country any foreign product purporting to have been relabelled in my country's language has to receive approval for the wording of each label from the Ministry of Grammar and Punctuation. The Ministry would employ precisely two staff, accept submissions exclusively in courier delivered hard-copy, charge an arm and a leg for an approval certificate, and consider each application for at least a month to ensure it didn't miss a stray comma. By contrast, anything made locally would automatically be assumed to be correctly labelled because their creators would have benefited from my country's unparalleled education system. Hip hip hurray!

Consider another example. A case of bovine spongiform encephalopathy (sometimes called mad cow disease) breaks out on the other side of the world. My imperative is to protect both my cows and my citizens so I ban all meat imports, of any kind, from anywhere. While this almost certainly achieves my objective of ensuring that none of my restaurants ever serves a contaminated sirloin, it's also a protectionist policy that completely shields my livestock farmers from all competition, including that from animals incapable of carrying the disease, or from beef sourced in countries that have never had so much as a suspected case in the region.

Though these examples are exaggerated, anyone familiar with government and bureaucracy can tell you that milder versions come into force worldwide daily. Whether through deliberate planning, accident, or as a result of corruption and incompetence, even measures genuinely intended to meet legitimate and completely unrelated objectives can end up skewing the market in the favour of domestic producers. This makes defining exactly what constitutes protectionism a challenge. It is, as was so famously said of pornography, something that defies exhaustive definition but which one invariably recognises when one sees it.

You may be wondering at this point why the question of identifying and categorising measures as deliberately versus incidentally protectionist even matters. After all, a business locked out of a market by accident or unfortunate collateral damage is no better off than one locked out by design. The truth is, it may not... except in identifying the best approach to the implementing government on behalf of such a business. A government may be willing to alter or redesign an inadvertently protectionist policy in a less commercially disruptive way, provided it can still achieve its other, underlying purpose. By contrast, changing an overtly protectionist measure requires convincing the implementing government that the protectionism itself is undesirable.

At this point in our historical narrative, there was at least partial consensus among Western policymakers that beyond a certain point, deliberate protectionism or just the possibility of it, was undesirable. It led to waste, corruption and made global markets too uncertain for long-term investors to be comfortable with long-term capital commitments.

Back to History – What is to be Done?

Imagine you're a leader considering all this in 1946. You know that:

1. Rampant deliberate protectionism can lead to a tit-for-tat retaliatory cycle that leaves everyone poorer.

2. Protectionism will always appeal politically to people on the basis that it creates jobs among their countrymen and women at home at the expense of faraway foreigners.

3. Your government may want to enact some policies that could be seen as containing an element of protectionism, but which you still consider necessary, such as those protecting the health of humans and animals.

4. Despite points one and two above, you may sometimes want to deploy overtly protectionist policies for protectionist ends, and do not wish to give up that power entirely.

5. Your counterparts in other countries will be subject to the same pressures and protectionist impulses, and that unilateral disarmament may fail. Protectionist policies may be a double-edged sword, but you don't want to be the only one laying down your weapon.

So what, then, do you do with all these facts? The answer, for late 1940s policymakers at least, was to lay the foundations of a modern trading system governed by rules. We've been torturing students into learning about it ever since.

The Rules Based Trading System

The trade policy community is famously bad at naming things, so it should come as no surprise that the 'Rules Based Trading System' is really nothing of the sort. If trade policy is the sum of the decisions governments make that affect international commerce, the rules-based trading system is the network of promises exchanged by countries about what those decisions won't be. These promises are mutually agreed guard rails against temptation and protectionism, which don't pinpoint what a policy must be, but do set some boundaries which a government must stay within to abide by its commitments to others. Two things entice a government into making such an arrangement.

Most prominently, the promises they'll receive from other governments help ensure predictability and market access for its own exporters. Secondly, issuing a binding promise not to enact certain policies somewhat insulates a government from internal pressure to do so. 'We can't because we have made a legally binding international treaty commitment not to' is a stronger rebuff to an industry's special pleading than: 'We can, but we just don't want to.'

Weighed against these benefits is the flipside. Promises and treaty obligations at least theoretically limit what a government and its successors can do, with varying degrees of risk and consequence for disregarding them. Governments have therefore sought to strike a balance, securing maximum commitments from others while seeking to strictly and tactically minimise their own. This is a balance government representatives continue to aim for in every negotiation to this day.

In the case of leaders in 1947, this led to the eventual negotiation and signature of the General Agreement on Tariffs and Trade, known simply as 'the GATT.' The GATT was an attempt by the

23 signatories[1] to dismantle some of the protectionism seen in the US and Europe prior to World War II, agree a minimum level of access to each other's markets, and begin a process of negotiations toward even more liberalisation, bringing down trade barriers over time. This kind of collective journey toward liberalisation was also intended to make sure no one felt they were the only ones moving away from protectionism unilaterally, and to create a kind of mutually reinforcing momentum in that direction. With the devastation of World War II still fresh on everyone's minds, and a vast rebuilding challenge ahead, leaders wanted to assure investors and businesses that they could invest in export industries knowing that trade policy would not be turned against them by importing countries at the first sign of a global slump.

As if to illustrate my earlier point about the difficulty of striking the right balance, the GATT was actually something of a post-mortem organ harvesting exercise from a much broader, more ambitious project called the 'International Trade Organization' or ITO. This was a body that would have gone considerably further than the GATT (a treaty that had been intended to be just one of its component parts) in terms of constraining potential protectionism among its parties, but was ultimately scuppered by the US Senate despite the ITO being a US initiative in the first place. By the time the ITO reached the US legislature, enthusiasm for building global institutions had somewhat cooled and senators of the time baulked at the potential restrictiveness of the proposed commitments. With the ITO's creation thus thwarted, the parties salvaged what they could in the form of the more modest but also more politically palatable GATT. Do not forget to raise a glass to me if this ever comes up at Trivia Night.

Like most later trade agreements, the GATT had three components:

---

[1] Since you asked, the signatories to the WTO were: Australia, Belgium, Brazil, Burma, Canada, Ceylon, Chile, China (specifically the Republic of China, with the post-revolutionary People's Republic of China not joining until 2001), Cuba, Czechoslovakia, France, India, Lebanon, Luxembourg, Netherlands, New Zealand, Norway, Pakistan, Southern Rhodesia, Syria, South Africa, United Kingdom and the United States – though Syria and Lebanon would leave just a few years later.

- The horizontal 'commitments' all signatories would make about how they treated each other;
- The unique 'commitments' each would make to the others as their 'price of admission'; and
- Institutional provisions describing how the treaty would work, how it could be expanded in the future, and how any disputes might be resolved.

You'll notice immediately we talk about commitments here. In most cases, these are commitments not to do things. With rare exceptions, the bulk of an international trade agreement is a long list of things a country or trade bloc promises not to do any more to avoid harming the trading interests of other countries.

Examples include:

- Not charging import taxes (tariffs) more than five per cent on cars made in another country;
- Not using an immigration or visa regime to keep legal professionals from another country from competing in yours;
- Not subsidising products just because they are for export; or
- Not allowing exporting industries to flout your environmental or labour regulations.

If you take all the romance out of it (which is easily done) a trade negotiation is a conversation between two deeply suspicious and paranoid groups as they work together to agree a binding and lasting agreement. Each is asking the same questions:

'I have committed to giving you a certain level of access to my market. What tricksy manoeuvre or legal loophole will you try to sneak into this deal that gives your firms more access than I thought I was providing?'

'You have committed to allowing a certain level of access to your market. How are you planning to ensure my firms receive less access than that in practice?'

The sneaky tricks being alluded to here are broad and varied. Governments have a big box of tools from hygiene regulations to how they administer their borders that can be either legitimate, or an underhanded way to make the lower tariffs they've offered to another country unusable in practice. I wouldn't blame you for finding that nasty, suspicious and legalistic. It also hardly fits the spirit of governments collaborating to create a shared prosperity. What I'd beg you to keep in mind, however, is that treaties are intended to last decades, if not in perpetuity, and so those drafting them must reckon not only with the character and good faith of those they are negotiating with today, but that of every government and official who will follow them. Today the other side may champion free trade, but tomorrow they may be protectionists. Every loophole must be closed.

In the 1947 GATT, the signatories were prepared to keep tariffs on entire categories of products below certain thresholds to allow foreign goods to compete in their domestic markets, providing other GATT parties promised to do the same, albeit on their own lists of goods and thresholds. They were, however, deeply suspicious. Therefore in addition to simply negotiating acceptable exchanges of duty reductions, they also negotiated rules to ensure they were actually getting the level of access trading partners promised, as well as a range of exceptions that meant they could still intervene in the market if necessary.

In addition to lowering tariffs, the GATT tried to introduce more predictability for goods trade among its membership. Two key rules it adopted included:

The **Most Favoured Nation Rule** said that if a GATT member had a tariff on a certain product, they had to charge that tariff on products of that type regardless of which GATT member they came from. In other words, it prevented having bespoke tariff arrangements for each individual GATT member, and did not allow you to tweak tariffs for one member without also doing so for all the others. This was intended to both create a level playing field among potential exporters, and to create predictability.

The **National Treatment** rule obliged a GATT member to treat any product it imported from another no differently than it did its own versions, once it was across the border. You could screen a foreign made car at the border, but you could not insist it be serviced more often or paid a 'foreign car levy' for the duration of its life. This aimed to limit behind the border regulations being used to punish consumers for, or to prevent them from buying foreign goods.

In coming decades, the GATT would expand with new signatories and new liberalisations. Eventually, in 1994, new treaties covering services, intellectual property, agriculture and investment made up the new World Trade Organization. Remarkably, this was pretty much the last time trade ministers made a big, significantly liberalising global agreement.

No World Police *(Interpol Doesn't Count)*

The brief history above spends a lot of time talking about rules and international treaties, as if these are ironclad and immutable facts of the universe. This is of course not the case, and I think it's worth pausing for a moment to talk about what we mean by 'trade law' and how the rules and agreements we'll be talking about for the rest of the book actually work.

Consider law, and specifically criminal law as we know it domestically. In exchange for our place in a functioning society, we are bound by laws that govern our behaviour. These laws do not automatically prevent illegal actions, but rather establish a code of societal expectations and create consequences for their violation. By making the theft of trousers illegal, society has signalled that such behaviour is undesirable. While it's frankly unlikely a police officer will be on hand to physically stop me from stealing a pair of trousers from a clothes line, the legal consequences and societal frowning may deter me anyway.

As someone with an immensely punchable face, I benefit very much from a society where laws (such as those against punching faces) are followed. But not everyone feels like this. Society is not a harmonious, unified whole. If I were a member of a criminal gang, my view on the desirability of breaking the law might be very different to that of a law-abiding citizen. So no matter how strong the societal signal that a behaviour is unacceptable, or how punitive the punishment, the law can only ever dissuade, not fully prevent. Instead, you can think of legal compliance as an equation. On one side are the direct benefits you'll gain from the violation itself; the reasons a particular crime is attractive (a new pair of trousers). On the other side are the societal signals against the crime, any investment in the law as a value, and the likelihood and severity of likely consequences or punishments.

Crimes like jay-walking or illegally downloading an episode of *Game of Thrones* are relatively common because society is fairly relaxed in its condemnation of them. Neither offence is likely to lead to anarchy, and so the odds of a jay-walker or media pirate being prosecuted are low and the punishments are mild. By contrast, much more serious, rarer crimes that society finds abhorrent, such as kidnap or murder, are prosecuted energetically and with heavy sentences. This same 'equation' logic holds in international law, albeit with some modifications.

First, an international agreement, like a domestic law, is a form of signalling. Signing a treaty is a way of saying: 'We are so certain that this is how the world should work that we are prepared to offer our government's commitment in writing.' Dozens of countries signing the same treaty can signal a broad consensus about what is acceptable. Of course, that doesn't guarantee compliance, or even agreement among non-signatories. Much as the views of an individual citizen might differ from society as a whole, so too might a country differ from the prevailing views of the international community. Moreover, there can be advantages in being in a minority that breaks norms or laws. Hitmen can charge a premium for their services because so few individuals are willing to kill others for money. Similarly, governments willing to circumvent rules on trading with pariah states can profit handsomely as a result.

Second, the strong incentives of a rules-based approach to international relations can often outweigh any potential benefits from individual violations. Governments benefit from a world of predictable policies and trustworthy countries. A general expectation that governments will largely abide by most international treaties they've signed fosters widespread collaboration and cooperation.

Where international law differs most from domestic law, however, is in the consequences of breaking the rules. Unlike in a country's own legal system, nobody is truly empowered to enforce international law. Neither the United Nations nor the World Trade Organization can, on their own, meaningfully punish a member for violating the rules. The United Nations Secretary General cannot deploy helicopter-borne shock troops to kick in the door of a rogue parliament or arrest an international law-breaking President. In the rare cases where international law has been enforced, such as arrests made under International Criminal Court warrants or United Nations forces deployed, the situation invariably owed far more to individual decisions by select member states than the institution itself.

In many cases, even the most 'robust' trade treaties don't include 'enforcement mechanisms' but rather have 'dispute settlement procedures'. This distinction is significant. The polite fiction behind 'dispute settlement' is that every signatory to a treaty will always try to abide by its terms – and will only break them if it has a different view about what they actually mean. Dispute settlement procedures are therefore politely imagined not as scourges of the wicked, but as genteel umpires at Wimbledon, helping players resolve good faith disagreements about which side of the line the ball fell on. Even if you, quite sensibly, discard these diplomatically rose coloured glasses, you are left with 'enforcement mechanisms' that fall far short of those in domestic criminal law. In fact even in domestic civil law, the power of the state may eventually be deployed to enforce a ruling in a way that it likely won't be in international law.

The consequences for violating a trade treaty are almost always entirely confined to the treaty itself. In other words, the worst thing that can be done to you for failing to honour the commitments you made in a treaty with others is that they will cease honouring the commitments they made to you in the same treaty. If the maximum punishment that could be levied against someone for attacking someone was losing legal protection against being assaulted themselves, then big well-trained fighters would be tempted to break the rules with impunity. I leave you to draw your own obvious comparisons with the behaviour of economic and military superpowers. This context is important when thinking about what leaders are actually doing when they enter into an international treaty. By signing an agreement between states that makes certain policy choices 'illegal' they aren't stopping those policies from ever being adopted, merely adding something to the negative side of the cost/benefit equation other governments use to determine their own policy choices. Just as in the case of criminal or civil penalties, the results are likely to vary. Unlike in criminal and civil cases the consequences are often quite limited.

Framing Your Thinking About Trade Policy

If you do not work in this field every day, it can be easy to get lost in the complexity as commercial, legal, practical and political considerations bob up and down on a soup of acronyms, badly named concepts and grandiose philosophies. No one has time for all that. While either the history lesson above or the guilt from skipping it is fresh in your mind, let me end this chapter with some suggestions on a mental framework you can use as shorthand to consider trade policy and international trade rules.

When you strip away everything else, fundamentally trade policy is a set of policy levers which states can pull in various directions, and at various strengths, to get what they want. This is just as true for governments today as they seek to tackle climate change or outmanoeuvre geopolitical rivals in technology as it was when they were mostly interested in collecting revenue from trading caravans.

My recommendation when considering any aspect of trade policy is to focus your attention on the stated objective, the proposed method, and the likely impact at the coalface, while ignoring all the pretty words and grand platitudes woven around them.

First, the objective. This is often the easiest to identify, as politicians will tend to shout it from the rooftops – but even so they are often irritatingly vague about what precisely they're hoping to achieve. Is it job creation? Smuggling prevention? Lower prices on the supermarket shelf? Protecting the public from dangerous chemicals? Increasing investment? Increasing wages? Attracting skilled workers from abroad? What would a win actually look like?

Having established what a trade actor hopes to achieve or prevent, you can cut through a tremendous amount of the highfalutin babble that follows by waiting for them to pause and politely ask which lever of power they're proposing to pull, in which direction, and how hard. What does their vision look like when filtered through the actual powers wielded by governments? There are four such powers:

- Legislation: Laws passed by politicians
- Regulation: Rules created by agencies within those laws
- Procedures and Enforcement: How the laws and regulations are applied in practice, the steps a business must follow to navigate them, and how compliance is enforced
- Spending: Budget allocations

Anyone whose argument boils down to 'someone ought to do something' without an identifiable *whom* or a plausible *what* is expressing a dream or a grievance, not proposing a policy. Meanwhile, anyone who can identify exactly which lever they want the government to pull should be able to explain why that's feasible, effective, and what the costs and unintended consequences might be. They should be able to identify who has the power and authority to make the changes they want to see, and at least sketch out a realistic path toward their doing so.

They also have to have some idea of how the changes they're proposing will look on the ground. How will whatever someone is proposing change trading in practice? What is the current experience, what will change, and why will the new approach yield the desired outcomes? How will the new vision manifest itself in the requirements, paperwork, scrutiny or finance of cross border trade? The best way to rid a conversation of nonsense is to reveal how a proposal would work on the factory floor, at the docks, or at the border.

Finally, because trade policy does not occur in a vacuum, it's worth considering the likely reaction from other countries. How will they react to the levers of power being pulled, and how will the international business community adjust to the new realities created on the ground? Will it make your country a more, or less attractive prospect for investors and those building international supply chains? How well does the proposal fit within the letter of your government's binding commitments, and how well into the spirit? What are the consequences likely to be, commercially, reputationally, and perhaps even systemically, for rules-based trade as a whole? If this sounds like a lot of questions, remember that you probably do not need to ask them all. In most cases, simply asking what the government hopes to do, how it plans to do it, and what will change for traders will suffice. Loading your analytical quiver with three arrows will separate chancers from policymakers and identify emperors lacking clothes.

As a cheat sheet, my questions in descending order of importance to most normal people:

- What is a trade actor (a government, industry body or business) trying to achieve or trying to prevent?

- What specific changes do they want to make to legislation, regulation, spending or procedure? Are they feasible, politically palatable and are those empowered to make them likely to do so?
- What will these changes mean, in practice, for those conducting trade across borders? What is the status quo, and how will it be altered by the proposals?
- What is the likely reaction of the international community and business?
- Could these changes run foul of the letter or the spirit of international agreements? With what consequences?

Chapter 3
What is Trade Policy?

Since Absolutely No one Asked

There may be nothing more human than believing any field other than your own to be straightforward while ceaselessly rattling off the endless litany of complexities and nuances that terrorise one's own specialty. My one line guide to evaluating candidates for political office is to find the ones suggesting historically intractable problems can be easily fixed if we 'just got on with it' – and vote for their opponents. I appreciate the irony that this rule massively oversimplifies the complexities of political science – as the kids say on social media, 'don't @ me.'

This book exists in large part because trade policy, where selling across borders meets government policy, procedure and regulations, is ludicrously vulnerable to rhetorical handwaving. It can feel, intuitively, like something which just should not be that hard. Fill a container, ship it, maybe pay some taxes at the border, and bing bang boom little Tyler has the new Lego pieces your bare feet will be stepping on in the dark for the next decade.

Politicians, either knowingly or because they share the misconception that things really are so simple, feed into this by talking about anything 'red tape at the border' as if all the forms were just work invented by bureaucrats to keep busy. They brandish the flavour of the month digital innovation, from drones to blockchain, as the miracle solution to all border friction. They describe any agreement they've signed, no matter how practically inconsequential, as the sun around which the trading universe will orbit for the better.

Trade is complex but unlike some other pursuits many people feel they instinctively understand it. Most people will accept it is hard to build a rocket, perform brain surgery, or cook French cuisine in a way that doesn't make Pierre remark, '*Alors*, it is precious how you allow your toddler to experiment in the kitchen, I am sure he will improve in time, *non*?' The same is not true of trade policy which simply does not feel like it should be so difficult.

Good News, None of Us Know What We're Doing

If there are elements in this chapter you find surprising or simply new, you're not alone. While universally slandered with the catch-all term 'trade expert' even the majority of those that work in the field truly understand only a subsection. At the highest level most fall into either being experts on:

International Trade Policy

The way governments regulate trade and the agreements that constrain them.

Typically, practitioners include negotiators and officials from Ministries of Trade or Commerce who help shape the rules, and economists who measure their impact and suggest ways they could work better. It is entirely possible to spend an entire career working in this sub-sector of the field and never directly interact with an actual shipment or anyone trying to freight one. It is to the business of trade what being a FIFA executive is to scoring a goal on the pitch.

International Trade Law

Interpreting, advising on and litigating the rules created by the policy community.

When questions or even disagreements arise about what the rules actually mean in practice, and how to apply them, we turn to international trade law experts. When confronted with a question of legality, these lawyers, litigators, and legal scholars interpret the text of international agreements, consider how arbitration panels have judged similar matters in the past, and very occasionally and with great reluctance even apply some basic common sense, all to arrive at advice or a persuasive position. The vast majority of those working in this field are in compliance, helping firms stay on the right side of the law, or in fields like anti-dumping (more on this later). A smaller number work in arbitration and international dispute settlement, hearing cases or representing clients and governments in their formal disputes over what the rules mean.

In our football metaphor they are the referees, the wildly gesticulating team captains arguing for a ruling their way, and the bespectacled advisors in the locker room explaining for the ninth time the legal implications of handing out methamphetamines to players at half-time.

International Trade Practice

The practical work involved in selling goods and services across borders, and navigating the bureaucracy thereof.

The vast majority of people working in trade aren't in Geneva discussing international trade rules at the World Trade Organization or in government ministries establishing regulations – they're out in the world implementing or navigating the government policies around moving goods, services and capital. This vast catch-all includes specialists in regulation, customs formalities, taxation, sanctions compliance, export finance and insurance and port procedures. They are the players, specialising in their own role when it comes to making sure the ball keeps moving in the desired direction, circumventing obstacles in its way. They (mostly) operate within the rules set by FIFA and the judgment calls made by the referees, but that still leaves plenty of scope for creative play and tactical mastery.

You could be forgiven for thinking these three groups are in constant dialogue, given the natural complementarities of their work. They are not. The policy wonks and lawyers mix a little, with the latter often being brought in to test ideas against existing laws, or to ensure a new draft treaty text created by eager-but-not-legally-trained policy negotiators doesn't accidentally outlaw hats or oblige a country to invade Greenland, but a wall of separation exists even there. Lawyers grumble that policy folk are cavalier lunatics, willing to scribble anything into a legally binding international agreement if it gets them one step closer to a signing ceremony. Policy folk for their part will moan that the legal eagles are forever slowing things down by being obsessively paranoid nudniks, imagining impossible legal disputes and insane interpretations of any proposed text by largely hypothetical future legal panels.

Practitioners for the most part are far too busy taking the world as it is to engage too closely with policy makers or lawyers. Just as many policy wonks have never held a customs declaration form in their hands, most people filling out that form have never studied the international agreements that set rules about what the form is allowed to ask. Practitioners may seek legal advice or representation on individual questions, or raise a concern about an egregious bit of policy, but for the most part they operate on their own, taking the world as it is.

All three groups contribute to the football match in their own way. My job, in addition to torturing you with increasingly strained metaphors, is to weave their worlds together into a tapestry that is at once sweeping enough for you to see the entire landscape and yet intricate enough for you to appreciate the depth of detail in every corner and pattern. I also plan to mock trade lawyers a lot because it's not punching down if the target drives a Porsche.

Chapter 4
Trade's Policy Drivers

Trade is Political – Always

The most boring but probably accurate way to describe public policy is 'governments making choices between competing interests'. Any decision a government makes, from where to open an embassy to which artillery system to buy for the armed forces, invariably advantages specific groups or priorities over others.

This is not unique to trade policy. The decision to fund a hospital over a bridge has both winners and losers. A new procedure to approve medications for public use will benefit some and likely disadvantage others. Every call, from zoning to selecting designs for a new stamp, inevitably upsets someone.

Even when a policy seems to have negligible opposition or even none at all, it is still almost certainly a choice between competing interests. Those disadvantaged by it may have decided to keep their powder dry by not campaigning against the decision or complaining about it too loudly, but that doesn't mean they weren't there. Shutting down my kitten-powered factory is certainly against my interests, but

I may let that one go because it's not a fight I can win or a battle I will look good waging.

In representative democracies (as opposed to direct ones) we elect leaders and legislators whom we trust to make these tradeoffs. Even election campaigns fought on the basis of extremely detailed and all-encompassing manifestos are ultimately about giving voters a flavour of the decision-making approach of a candidate or party. 'These are my values and how I will approach the choices I'll be asked to make in office,' is the unspoken message of electioneering. A candidate couldn't possibly anticipate and outline in a manifesto or campaign every decision they'll have to make during their term and so must provide voters with a window into how they make decisions instead.

Direct democracies like Switzerland put options to the people directly through referendums or other mechanisms. In dictatorships or one-party states, decisions are made by leaders who may not be directly answerable to the people in a democratic sense but still have to balance factions, priorities and sentiment among the public or the elites. Regardless, the choices are still there, the only thing that changes is the people making decisions and whose input or interests they must heed.

There are Always Losers

While not the subject of this book I hope you'll allow me to add here that whenever a politician, lobbyist or interest group attempts to sell you a policy choice as having no losers at all they are almost always either lying, or encouraging you to dismiss as irrelevant the interests of those their preferred policy choice would disadvantage. Politics is hard and it's about choices, and anyone who pretends otherwise is a prime candidate for charlatanism.

This is not to say that the winners and losers from policy, especially complex policy, are always immediately obvious. Consider for example a ban on television and billboard advertising for cigarettes.

While it feels like the major losers of such a decision would be major tobacco manufacturers, that's not necessarily the case. After all, they have big established brands and loyal customers. It could well be that an advertising ban would actually benefit these firms by making it incredibly difficult for any new market entrant to establish name recognition or a brand identity. An advertising ban may hurt the tobacco industry as a whole, but it's a potential boon to the big players already in it. That's not to say such a policy isn't worth implementing, only that the wailing and gnashing of teeth you may hear about it from Philip Morris may not be entirely sincere.

The world of international supply chains makes discerning exact winners and losers even more complex. More and more often the things we're bringing in across our borders are actually components or so-called 'intermediate goods'. These can be complex microchips or simple screws, but either way they are vital to the production process and the ability to source them from the best value suppliers abroad is imperative for one's own domestic industry to remain competitive.

That means that what seems like a straightforward decision to side with either workers, management, or consumers, is in fact probably a decision to favour one group of workers over another – and that's before you factor in the complexities of international or public ownership structures which make even identifying the players a challenge.

The reason I bring up, and some would say belabour this point, is the perception within the public imagination that trade policy discussions are far more driven by economics, modelling and statistics, than they tend to be in practice. It's an entirely understandable misconception. Trade policy deals with billion-dollar questions of international commerce and the media understandably talks about it by throwing around a lot of numbers, percentages and statistics. So one can be forgiven for assuming trade policy discussions take place in a data-driven and scientific way.

The truth is that while economic modelling and analysis have a role to play in trade negotiations, it's not as large as you might expect. In some negotiations this is so much the case that economists are only truly brought in at the very end, once a deal has been finalised, to run the sums and provide some numbers on the deal's benefits for the inevitable press releases and Ministerial speeches.

What then, if not economic analysis or forecast, determines the positions of the parties in a trade negotiation? Politics, just like everything else. Politics is the lifeblood of trade policy pretty much everywhere except on technical questions so dull to the common man that even tabloid journalists haven't figured out how to mine them for outrage. Everywhere else, politics reigns supreme. It determines whether free trade negotiations happen, with whom, and the so-called 'red lines' which delineate the furthest either side can go on certain issues and still sign the final deal.

For much of the late 20th and 21st Century, in the West at least, the politics of trade was somewhat muted because major parties tended to agree on the basics. Gradual liberalisation and the opening of markets was good, predictability beneficial, and therefore free trade agreements and a 'rules-based trading system' were broadly desirable. There were disagreements of course on where to put the emphasis, and political point scoring over what was and wasn't included in a deal, but a fair degree of consistency otherwise.

At the time of writing, this consensus has splintered somewhat. Smaller economies like Australia, New Zealand, Singapore and Costa Rica still pursue free trade agreements enthusiastically, in part because their own economies are already significantly open.

The European Union, too, is negotiating ceaselessly, but increasingly facing domestic rumbles and hurdles around ratification of deals as national parliaments apply ever greater scrutiny and raise questions about the implications of trade deals for issues like environmental sustainability.

The United States, once seen as the champion of rules-based trade and liberalisation, has under subsequent administrations rather cooled on the whole endeavour. Under President Obama, the US was a leading player in three big trade negotiations: the Transpacific Partnership (TPP), the Transatlantic Trade and Investment Partnership (TTIP) and the Trade in Services Agreement (TiSA).

President Donald Trump pulled the US out of the TPP and ended negotiations on TTIP and TiSA in favour of renegotiating existing US deals with Korea, Canada and Mexico, and initiating trade conflicts with half the world. President Trump was also the first US leader in generations to be openly hostile to the multilateral trading system and World Trade Organization. Of course, you could probably add 'Trump was the first US leader in generations to…' to the front of just about any sentence about him, but for trade geeks it was noteworthy.

President Joe Biden has not at time of writing significantly departed from Trump's approach, even if the rhetoric has improved from when US officials had to check Twitter hourly lest they missed the launch of a new trade war. The Biden Administration has forsworn negotiating new 'traditional' free trade agreements in favour of a 'worker-centric trade policy' (no one seems to know exactly what this means) and a still-emerging set of discussions called the 'Indo-Pacific Economic Framework' about which little is known right now except that it definitely won't cut tariffs (traditionally the most newsworthy part of any trade agreement).

This shift is especially relevant to our discussion because of how clearly it demonstrates the primacy of politics over economics. No academic consensus has emerged saying 'actually, trade deals are bad.' The 'math' behind free trade agreements has remained broadly the same in the last five to six years. Economics is an ever-evolving field and the debate about how to quantify and calculate the exact impacts of trade deals is ceaseless, but I don't believe the field has seen any kind of change in the last decade that could justify such a radical shift in approach.

On the Republican side, the shift toward anti-free trade messaging has been spurred by President Trump's personal convictions and a loss of power by traditional donors and the more pro-corporate wing of the party. The US Chamber of Commerce simply does not have the ear of populist Republicans the way it did their more traditional forefathers.

Meanwhile, on the Democratic side, the decision to shun the more treaty making and trade liberalising approach to trade policy followed by President Obama is also political – born of favouring one set of priorities, interests and talking points over others and avoiding battles with traditional opponents of trade liberalisation among the Democratic base and in swing districts across the electorally crucial battleground states. President Biden came to office with a domestically focused agenda anchored on revitalising American manufacturing, and he does not consider greater American market openness or more commitments that might tie his hands in areas like stimulus or government procurement to be conducive to that objective.

For both parties, the shift also reflects the US government's increasing focus on competition with China because of which it is unwilling to sign away the policy tools it may want to use in the future. You could argue this is less 'political,' but it still represents a shifting of opinion among US leaders from a belief in the power of multilateral institutions to engage China and constrain its state-capitalist impulses to a concern that they are incapable of doing so. It also represents a shifting perception of China's threat to the interests of the United States and a jettisoning of the belief that commercial ties alone will be enough to prevent conflict.

None of this is a criticism of US policy or policymaking. It is entirely legitimate for a country to rethink its priorities and to shape its decision-making accordingly. The US is entirely within its rights, no matter how frustrating that may be for those who preferred a world where the US was a more active, vocal and constructive champion of liberalisation and a rules-based system.

It's Not Enough to be Right

Defining a set of objectives and navigating the gaps and contradictions between the interests accommodated or impeded in pursuit of those objectives is an inherently political exercise, whether in the most direct Swiss-style democracy or the most repressive dictatorship. The stakeholders and deliberation process may vary, but the underlying concept remains the same: trade is political, and there is no way to understand its twists and turns without a political lens firmly lodged in one eye.

As a result, I will often focus on how things *appear* to work and what is intuitively rather than empirically true, or what makes for an effective line on the campaign trail. The future of trade policy will be determined by those who are able to make a compelling political case for their preferred outcome – which may not necessarily be those whose positions are best supported by the academic literature, economic models or wonky editorials in the *Financial Times*. Trade policy will continue to be exploited by carnival barkers and grifters so long as those within the community cling to the belief that just being objectively correct on the substance will always carry the day.

Chapter 5
Goods Trade

The majority of this book will focus on international trade *policy* rather than law and practice, because that's the part of this world I know best – and it's also the part that politicians lie about most. However, I want to build that conversation on a solid foundation grounded in the reality of international trade. To that end, let's begin by talking through what it takes to move goods around – and specifically on how governments get in the way, and why.

Three caveats first:

1. Because we're focused on policy, I am going to stick to the interactions between business and government bureaucracy, without going into pure commerce. Even if international trade were completely unregulated and untaxed, it would still be an immensely complex exercise involving freight providers, port operators, insurance agents and financiers – trying to cover all that would turn this book into an unreadably dense brick and somewhat ironically, drive up its shipping costs.

2. Many firms outsource some or all trade paperwork to specialist third parties like freight forwarders, customs agents, import/ export brokers or global marketplace behemoths like Amazon or Alibaba. What's important for our purposes is knowing that a government hurdle is there, not whether an exporter jumped over it themselves or paid a mega corporation to have its staff jump it for them in between electronically timed bathroom breaks.

3. This is all going to be vastly oversimplified, either skimming over some of the complexities or drawing on the starkest examples to illustrate why a rule exists. Most exporters aren't shipping weapons grade plutonium or endangered rhinos infected with swine flu, but looking at fringe cases helps illustrate why rules and procedures are there and what they can be like to navigate.

With those out of the way, let's dive into the step-by-step journey of a firm trying to export a shipment to foreign lands. At each step, the critical thing to focus on isn't the procedure itself but what it's supposed to do, what it's supposed to prevent, and what complying with it means for businesses trying to trade.

Step 1 – Registering as an Exporter (Plus Several Side Rants)

In most countries, you need permission from the government to be a business that makes money by selling goods to foreigners in other lands. In some countries, this is a largely automatic registration process where you indicate your intention to export, provide some information and receive a pro-forma confirmation that you're now in the government system and can proceed. In others, it can be a more complex or opaque process, with the bureaucracy evaluating your request and deciding if you are worthy of registration. This may involve some bribes. In fact, feel free to mentally add 'this may involve some bribes' roughly every third sentence for the rest of this chapter.

So why is registering as an exporter necessary? Governments like exports. They create jobs, bring foreign capital into the country and are evidence that your economy is succeeding internationally. These are all big positives. Yet most countries still require exporters to be registered, sometimes even making that process onerous or expensive. There are three reasons why.

The first is boring and procedural. Some exporters must submit information or requests to the government, and registration creates a bureaucratic file and identification number. It is similar to how registering with Google or Apple creates a virtual profile you can use for all future interactions with their ecosystems, but with less selling of your private information to advertisers.

The second is also boring. Governments need to know which businesses see themselves as exporters so that they know who to talk to about trade. You can think of this as compiling a mailing list for updates, but it's also about knowing who to survey. If a trade ministry hopes to address problems exporters are facing in a target market, it's helpful to be able to find the relevant ones and ask them.

Many governments are terrible at this part. Faced with the prospect of a trade negotiation with another country, they'll either consult the three or four gigantic businesses whose lobbyists or government affairs professionals they already frequently meet with, send out vast surveys to every export business in the country that are so detailed and onerous to complete that owners ignore them, or hold 'consultations' that amount to sending the entire business community a text saying, 'So... America. Any thoughts?' and produce correspondingly useful results.

The third and slightly less boring reason is control. By limiting exporting to registered traders, governments can control who exports without resorting to individually licensing every shipment. The right to take things out of the country and exchange them for money abroad is potentially lucrative and not all governments are comfortable handing it out to anyone who asks. Governments may be legitimately wary of businesses with clear connections to organised crime becoming exporters. More shadily, the registration process also creates a way to punish political rivals and extort payments, as does the ability to subsequently punitively withdraw registration.

Practically speaking, how onerous registration is for a business will vary wildly from country to country and sometimes even city to city. As with any bureaucratic process, sometimes you can do it online with just a few keystrokes and sometimes you have to deliver 36 documents to 12 different government buildings, none of which seem to communicate with one another, publish their opening hours, or adequately explain the circumstances under which you should have filled out Form 24F-A1 instead of 24F-A2.

Aside: Digitising Government Procedures

While we're here, let's address something that you may be thinking already and will almost certainly be thinking by the end of this chapter: *'This all feels like it could be a lot easier if government computers just talked to each other.'* I know, right? We have become so used to this being an obvious but unrealised option that many of us don't even question it anymore. It's just considered normal that each and every government department we deal with appears to treat our relationship as unique and self-contained, unable or unwilling to draw on the identical answers we gave to their neighbouring department mere moments ago.

In trade, we even have a term for the dream of addressing this: 'single window'. This is the fantasy of a single portal through which a business can simultaneously meet the requirements of all the government departments it needs to satisfy in order to conduct trade. It's logical, intuitive and attractive. Yet in most countries it remains a distant aspiration with apparently decades long work programmes toward its realisation that make at best incremental progress. Understanding the reasons is important to interpreting political bullshit, precisely because this is exactly the sort of challenge politicians love to handwave.

One thing that surprises many officials who move from one government department to another is that the IT systems are completely different – and in many cases clearly not designed to talk to one another. Remember government departments didn't all go out and buy computers and IT solutions together on the same day. In most cases, individual departments digitised themselves one by one, piece by piece at their own pace, depending on when funding was made available and at the whim of their leadership. Subsequently, every upgrade was done piecemeal, to solve individual problems or introduce specific functionalities, again only when there was some spare change left in the treasury.

In many cases these digital projects are overseen and delivered by a combination of civil service generalists with only a vague idea of how computers work, and outside technology consultants with only a vague idea of how governments work. To make things more fun, they are generally delivered alongside the regular functioning of the department, which can't afford to just go offline and stop processing citizen requests except for a very short time. This means every government department ends up with a bespoke software package not built to talk to the software of any other department.

Teaching these disparate computer systems to talk to each other can be an arduous technical challenge and a messy bureaucratic fight.

None of this is to say digitising government procedures is hopeless, or that Single Windows are impossible. There is incremental process being made toward these goals all over the world, and sheer generational momentum means that at some point all these departments will be run by Millennials and Zoomers for whom the idea of IT systems that don't integrate and work with each other is abhorrent. Yet when politicians running for office loudly declaim that their priority will be digitising bureaucracy, building online portals and fixing problems by 'putting it on the computer' they are almost always drastically understating the challenges and woefully underestimating the cost in both money and disruption that their promises entail. You should treat them with scepticism.

Perhaps counterintuitively, building a Single Window from scratch can sometimes be easier in a developing country context than in a rich country because there are fewer legacy systems in place that must be replaced or made mutually compatible.

Step 2 – Checking the Naughty List

Having registered your business as an exporter, it's time to find out how your government feels about you shipping the thing you'd like to put in a big box.

Two factors determine whether your shipment might run into trouble: what you're shipping and where you're shipping it to. Let's start with the products. For obvious reasons, there are certain products your government probably won't let you send abroad for commercial gain, and some that it's not comfortable receiving. Depending on the country this might include illicit substances like drugs or extreme pornography, native or endangered species, religiously prohibited products, or dangerous weapons.

There are certain things, like toilet seats, that governments are generally reasonably relaxed about being exported. An Abrams M1A2 Main Battle Tank or an endangered Javan Rhino however, will probably raise some eyebrows. Of course, there may be legitimate reasons to ship these things, and governments make exceptions from time to time. Narcotics from approved manufacturers for the purposes of medical research, endangered species shipped between zoos or sanctuaries, weapons as part of military procurement contracts and so on. These are the niche cases however, and for the most part not something the average business will ever encounter. With that said, if you find yourself with a contract to ship hyper-graphic hentai to the Australian government, I'm sorry I misled you.

There's also a fascinating category called 'dual-use' which we'll cover once we get to sanctions, which refer to products which may be completely innocent if used in one way, but restricted if used in another.

Beyond these clearly prohibited categories, which for the most part are fairly intuitive, are the much larger range of products which are 'restricted' or 'monitored' without being outright prohibited. These are things you may well be allowed to trade, but for which you require special approval from the sending government, the receiving government, or both, over and above simply being registered as a trader. For example, while India allows you to ship most products without specific authorisation, it does require you to get permission for some products which are intuitive (firearms and ammunition) and some which may not be (sand, soil, seeds, camels, silkworms and vintage cars).

Governments impose these halfway house measures for a variety of reasons. Sometimes they want to control the volume of a product leaving the country, such as a rare national resource or cultural heritage. At other times, the government wants to retain or protect the monopoly of a selected firm, which the state may own. For example, following the Great Depression countries like Canada and Australia set up 'Wheat Boards' which collectively managed grain exports in an effort to prevent food price inflation.

Depending on the context, receiving permission to ship something on the restricted list can be relatively straightforward or frustrating, time-consuming and expensive – and that's just the products themselves. Sources and destinations add further complexities, hurdles and potentially even criminal charges as countries slap sanctions, export restrictions and trade embargoes on each other in ways that feel like they should be straightforward but often aren't.

Sanctions, trade embargoes and even blockades are ancient tools of aggressive foreign policy. In the diplomatic toolkit, denying a country the benefits of trade through sanctions or an embargo is seen as a very big step, while still falling well short of armed conflict. On a spectrum with sending their ambassador a chiding WhatsApp message on one end and carpet bombing their capital city on the other, it lies as close to the latter as one can get without shooting – making it attractive to governments looking to be tough without crossing the line into open warfare.

Increasingly, governments are also imposing export restrictions in areas like high technology microchips and the tools to make them, or rare minerals, not as a sanction, but as a way of trying to maintain a technological or industrial edge over their geopolitical rivals. For business however, whether their trade is illegal because the recipient invaded Crimea or just because the sending country doesn't want them building their own microprocessors, the practical impact is near indistinguishable.

Aside: Do Sanctions Work?

The efficacy and ethics of sanctions is an immense topic, on which there are many books written by far smarter and more expert people. As with much of this book, I would prefer to take the coward's way out and avoid expressing any strong views either way, instead offering a framework for evaluating sanctions which hopefully helps you structure your own thoughts.

In my experience, the debate around sanctions frequently flounders due to a lack of precision in identifying the goal a specific sanction or package of sanctions intends to achieve. Sanctions come with a financial and human cost that often falls on civilians, and any evaluation of their wisdom as a policy must consider this cost in the context of their effectiveness in achieving what they are supposed to achieve. Generally, most sanctions or trade embargoes are motivated by one or more of the following four objectives:

1. Symbolism – To very publicly signal that the sanctioning state finds something so unpalatable that it is willing to resort to measures just short of warfare.

2. Degrading Capacity – To weaken another state or deny it the ability to pursue certain courses of action effectively.
3. Policy Change – To motivate the sanctioned state to change a specific policy or set of policies.
4. Regime Change – To try to weaken a state or anger its common people or elites to the point where they replace the existing government with someone more palatable.

In many cases, the sanctioning state would love to produce all four but doesn't realistically expect to achieve more than a symbolic message and perhaps some degradation of capacity. Most sanctions by smaller states fall into this category. New Zealand is well aware that there are few countries, perhaps with the exception of small Pacific island states, that would be so inconvenienced by being cut off from New Zealand's trade that they would reverse course on a key policy or overthrow their government. In most cases, even significant capacity degradation is probably beyond the reach of a New Zealand sanction package. Yet New Zealand will join larger sanctions efforts anyway because it sees itself as a moral force on the world stage, and wants to signal its opposition to courses of action it finds unconscionable.

Even for major economies or near global sanctions efforts, changing a policy or securing regime change may be a secondary objective, blurring with capacity degradation and symbolism. For example, the United States and its allies would probably very much like to see regime change for the better in North Korea and Iran and for those states to abandon their nuclear weapons programmes, but must mostly accept that the most their sanctions are doing is symbolically backing the non-proliferation regime, raising the costs of pursuing nuclear arms, and degrading the target's capacity to build many nuclear weapons quickly.

The sanctions on the Russian Federation following its reinvasion of Ukraine in 2022 follow a similar pattern. Judged on the standard of whether they have led to the overthrow of Putin's regime or a reversal of his decision to send his armies west they have (at the time of writing) clearly failed. On the other hand, they (to an extent) demonstrated Western solidarity and outrage at a level Russian statecraft didn't seem to anticipate, and from all accounts have meaningfully hurt the ability of the Russian military to resupply and upgrade by cutting them off from parts and machining equipment.

Historically, the track record of sanctions in achieving regime change is fairly dismal. The one example anyone seems to be able to point to for even a tangential connection between sanctions and regime change is the end of South African apartheid, and there were many other factors at play there making the extent of causality difficult to quantify.

Whether sanctions can lead to policy change is a more difficult proposition to evaluate. Certainly there aren't a lot of policies which changed immediately upon sanctions being imposed, but the one data point we'll never have is how many policy ideas were abandoned without ever seeing the light of day for fear that implementing them would lead to sanctions, or because sanctions were threatened.

Hopefully the above is helpful to you in framing some of your own thinking about sanctions, but also in parsing the way political figures talk about them. When politicians vow tough measures, it's worth checking if they are setting their expectations at symbolic gesture, damaging capacity, policy reversal, or regime change, so as not to allow them to wriggle out later and declare victory by lowering their objectives after the event. Similarly, when politicians and other public figures declare sanctions to have failed, it is worth checking that against what the sanctions were expected to achieve.

Whatever the ethics and efficacy of sanctions, businesses must take the world as it is and the world as it is features various sanctions on individuals, firms and states. Sanctions violations are treated as matters of grave concern by departments with absolutely no sense of humour, like the US Treasury, and contrary to what you might expect the list of goods subject to sanctions-related export restrictions to certain destinations isn't always intuitive. Sure, it's obvious that an arms embargo or similar will target machine guns and explosives, but some ordinary civilian goods may have a 'dual-use', such as specific types of aluminium pipe and ball bearings. As the complexity of weapons systems increases, more and more technology components with perfectly legitimate civilian applications, like microchips and processors, are likely to find their way onto dual-use sanctions lists.

Complicating this further are on-selling and secondary sanctions. On-sellers would seem to be an obvious loophole to sanctions but the expectation of most governments which impose sanctions is that you not only abstain from selling prohibited items to a sanctioned state, but also do not sell goods to clients in third countries that clearly intend to sell on or transfer them to the sanctioned state. You can end up in all sorts of financial and legal jeopardy if you sell to someone you knew, or should have known, was acting as a middleman to evade your national sanctions.

Moreover, because secondary sanctions exist, it is not just your own government you have to worry about. Secondary sanctions are punitive measures imposed by a country against firms in a completely different, unsanctioned country that is selling certain goods to a country against which the first country has sanctions but the second one doesn't. In re-reading that sentence I am reminded that for some reason I pride myself on my communication skills. Let's take an example. Canada decides the US is too militaristic, and imposes an arms embargo and sanctions on the US. That means Canadian firms can't sell guns to American customers anymore, and they can't sell them to a Mexican company called 'Boom Booms for Locos Hombres Americanos' either, because of the obvious on-selling risk. However, Canada goes one step further. It announces that it will impose secondary sanctions on any Mexican firm that sells guns to America, even if those guns have no connection to Canada.

For businesses seeking to trade across borders in turbulent times this can mean not only navigating the specialised licensing requirements of their own state, but also doing some research to ensure the buyers are not obviously on-sellers to sanctioned countries, and that they do not accidentally fall foul of the secondary sanctions regime of third countries whose wrath they might wish to avoid. With modern supply chains that can span a dozen countries, scores of sub-contractors and suppliers, and hundreds of components, this can all be easier said than done, with significant financial and criminal consequences for getting it wrong.

Yet even all this is still just the start of the international trade journey because looming up ahead is the border and <ominous music> customs.

Step 3 – Customs: What's in the Box, Then?

Customs officers are officials country deputises to monitor the movement of goods into and out of their territory. It is their job to ensure nothing that shouldn't be leaving the country does so and vice-versa, and that anyone moving goods across a border provides the required information and pays the relevant fees and taxes. This simple statement hides a bottomless well of complexity which has spawned an entire industry of experts solely dedicated to helping businesses navigate its depths. Let's see why.

Put yourself in the shoes of a customs official at a busy port. You have in front of you hundreds of shipping containers, some as large as 300 square feet. Within them are tens of thousands of products, ranging from beef carcases to sex dolls. Your government has ordered you to collect taxes called tariffs on certain products when they enter your territory, but these are different for every product category and sometimes for every product source. You cannot manually open every container, check every product inside and decide the appropriate tariff to levy on it without grinding the port and much of your country's economy to a halt. So what do you do?

Your biggest challenge is to find a way for those wanting to move boxes through your port to be able to tell you and the government what's in them in a format that's usable for you, and doesn't require you to learn the individual brand and product names of every commercially sold item in existence. The solution is a system called 'tariff classification' and it is, depending on your perspective, a fascinating blend of art and science working in which is a non-stop journey of discovery... or a horrific bureaucratic hellscape from which there is no waking or salvation. Where you stand on this question has a close correlation to whether you are being paid by the hour to resolve customs issues, or paying by the hour to have them resolved for you.

Tariff Classification – 10,000 Things I Hate About You

Tariffs are taxes on imports. If you want to bring a product subject to a tariff into the country, you have to pay a tax for the privilege of doing so. In the vast majority of cases, tariffs are levied as a percentage of the value of the incoming good at the time it crosses the border. Therefore, to charge you the right tariff our plucky customs official needs to know the quantity and value of the shipment. Sounds simple enough, until you get into tariff classification.

The reason tariff classification exists at all is that countries don't (generally) charge the same tariff on every good. In fact, most countries try to target their tariffs very carefully, charging high tariffs on some products and no tariffs at all on others. They do this because tariffs are by definition a tax on consumption by their own citizens and businesses – and one they want to deploy judiciously. Economics tells us that if you are to have tariffs at all (some economists think you shouldn't), you ideally want them falling on luxury goods, finished goods, and goods where you are determined to maintain a domestic industry. In most cases economists suggest avoiding charging tariffs on goods poor people need, on goods you don't produce domestically, or on the inputs (like materials and components) needed by your own producers.

Faced with wanting to apply tariffs on some goods but not others, governments came up with a system of 'codes' into which any and all traded products could be classified. These codes are literally numerical sequences that get more specific as they grow longer – with the first six digits generally being pretty standard around the world in line with the tariff codes publised by the World Customs Organizations, but with governments then adding additional numbers to differentiate between sub-categories So a code of 18 covers cocoa and anything made out of it, whereas 18062095 is the European Union's designation for, and I'm not joking here:

Chocolate and other food preparations containing cocoa, in blocks, slabs or bars weighing > 2 kg or in liquid, paste, powder, granular or other bulk form, in containers or immediate packings of a content > 2 kg, containing < 18% by weight of cocoa butter (excl. cocoa powder, chocolate flavour coating and chocolate milk crumb)

This is, of course, to differentiate it from 1806210:

Chocolate and other food preparations containing cocoa, in blocks, slabs or bars weighing > 2 kg or in liquid, paste, powder, granular or other bulk form, in containers or immediate packings of a content > 2 kg, containing >= 31%, by weight, of cocoa butter or containing a combined weight of >= 31% of cocoa butter and milkfat (excl. cocoa powder)

This granularity gives the European Union the ability to micro-target its tariffs, potentially applying a different rate to chocolate slabs with 43% cocoa butter than to chocolate slabs with 13% cocoa butter. Vital stuff and doubtless critical to the continued prosperity of all Europeans. But let's consider what this means in practice for businesses.

If you are contemplating moving a shipment across borders, you are going to have to be able to tell the customs authorities what it is, and you're going to have to do it by tariff code – for every product in every shipment and for every destination . . . and you really don't want to get it wrong. Making a mistake and misclassifying a shipment risks overpaying tariffs, delays at the border, significant fines, shipment confiscation and being entered into customs databases as a troublemaker requiring greater scrutiny moving forward. All varying degrees of bad.

Exactly how big a challenge this is will vary massively from business to business. If you are an oil company whose entire business model is extracting crude oil in Australia and shipping it to Japan then this whole thing is almost a non-issue. You looked up the tariff code Japan uses for crude oil (2709.00) and the tariff they charge on it (0%) and from then on the only thing you have to change on the forms is the volume. Heck, because the tariff is 0% you don't even have to do any math -this entire process is barely an inconvenience.

Except not all export businesses are so simple. To go back to our previous example, if you are a chocolatier shipping to the European Union you have to classify each and every item you send against a selection of more than 20 different tariff categories, many of them with internal sub-categories (filled chocolates yes . . . but do you mean the ones with alcohol inside or not?). Having somehow navigated these, you may find yourself having to redo the exercise when you ship elsewhere, as they may not use the EU's precise sub-categories. You may also find yourself staring incomprehensibly at two categories both of which could, on a plain reading, apply to your goods.

This latter situation occurs so often that customs authorities have set up what are effectively expert panels which issue 'customs rulings' in the case of ambiguities. They do this, it must be said, not out of a desire to make life difficult but precisely to maintain the integrity of their tax code and a level playing field between importers. In customs, when a difference of just two digits in the classification could mean a 20% difference of cost paid at the border, there are very serious commercial implications to imprecision (deliberate or accidental).

Valuation – Somehow also Not Always Straightforward

Most, but not all, tariffs are (thankfully) a simple percentage of the 'value' of the good. You can think of it as a formula that looks like this:

Tariff Rate x Value x Volume = Tariff to be Paid

For example:

If I were bringing in 100 widgets each costing $50, and I was bringing them into somewhere with a 10% tariff rate on widgets, the formula would look like this:

10% (Tariff Rate) x $50 (Value Per Item) x 100
(Number of Items) = $500 (Tariff Due)

This sounds like it should be relatively straightforward once you know what tariff rate applies to your widgets, because you know how many of them you're shipping and how much they cost. You will be completely unsurprised to learn that this, too, can be hard.

There are two causes for this complexity: trust and weirdness. Trust is the more straightforward. Because tariffs are primarily calculated on the value of your goods, you have an incentive to tell customs your goods are worth less than they actually are to minimise the taxes you'll pay on them. Even if you're not being dishonest, calculating the value of something like a sub-component of a larger machine that only you make may not be simple. You know how much the total car costs, but breaking down a fair price for one of the 67 sub-components your factory produces is harder – especially when in a lot of modern goods much of the value lies in the brand's strength, the proprietary technology or the associated software.

Now you might wonder, if this is so complicated and governments are worried about being lowballed by valuations, why don't they just value everything themselves? Imagine a giant Excel spreadsheet that lists, by tariff line, how much every type of good under that tariff line typically costs. Many governments do have one, and some still make extensive use of it, but here they run into a reverse trust issue – other governments don't trust them not to abuse these databases to charge higher tariffs than they promised. If I as a government promised you and all other WTO members I would charge a maximum tariff of 10 per cent on cars, but my customs valuation spreadsheet prices every $10,000 Kia Rio as if it were a $50,000 Mercedes C Class and I charge $5,000 in tariffs (10 per cent of $50,000), I'm making a mockery of my promise. As a result, governments agreed through the World Trade Organization Agreement on Customs Valuation to phase out the use of such spreadsheets and databases as the primary form of evaluating how much something should cost.

Now onto complexity. The EU's 2022 Compendium of Customs Valuation Texts covers a vast cornucopia of possible line-ball calls, edge cases, and assorted weirdness that might factor into properly valuing a product. How do you apportion transport costs? How much are hunting trophies worth? Are free samples shipped with a sale included in the price?

Just like getting the tariff classification of your goods wrong could lead to penalties, delays and greater scrutiny, so too could improperly valuing your shipment. If you value your shipment higher than the government, you may end up overpaying tariffs and disadvantaging yourself against your competitors. If you value your shipment lower, you are committing either wilful or accidental customs fraud.

Preferential Tariffs and Rules of Origin

What probably feels like 600 paragraphs and three years of your life earlier, we discussed how and why countries have lower tariffs on some products than others, spawning the need for tariff codes and tariff classification. Unfortunately for the sanity of those trading across borders, that's not all countries like to differentiate – they also like to apply different tariffs to identical products depending on where they're coming from.

For the most part, the treaties government signed when joining the World Trade Organization limit this kind of differentiation (we'll get into all that later, as a little treat). However, they do allow it under certain circumstances, and over time these have expanded exponentially. They are:

1. Free Trade Agreements
2. 'Preferences' for Developing Countries
3. Anti-dumping Duties and Countervailing Measures

For now, let's focus on the first two. World Trade Organization rules allow a country to charge lower tariffs on goods coming from a specific source under two conditions: a signed free trade agreement, or through 'preferences' which privilege goods coming from developing countries by offering them lower tariff rates. The argument for the latter is that it offers richer countries a way to support poorer ones by creating a competitive advantage for firms producing goods there. In theory, a competitive advantage in being able to sell to wealthy consumers in rich countries will stimulate investment, innovation and growth.

What does this mean for someone actually moving goods across borders? It opens up the possibility that their shipment may be eligible for lower tariff rates. There are over 350 free trade agreements around the world, and many developed economies, and richer developing economies, have broad preferential schemes. If your goods would otherwise pay hefty tariffs, it's worth checking if they're eligible.

There are two stages to this, and the first is generally pretty simple. You already know the tariff code of your goods. So now, you have to check on the website of the relevant customs authority whether that country has an agreement or preference scheme covering goods like yours from the location you're exporting them from – and, if so, what it does. Many free trade agreements and preference schemes reduce tariffs to 0%, but some merely reduce what you'd otherwise pay. That doesn't sound so hard, does it? A quick check on a website for each of your products. What's the big deal? Oh you sweet summer child, welcome to our second stage: Rules of Origin.

If you are trying to use the lower tariff rate of a free trade agreement or preference scheme, Rules of Origin are how governments demand you prove that whatever you are shipping is eligible. Why? Because if governments have a tariff in place they want it to work. If they provide another country a better rate than the one they're charging everyone else then it's for one of two reasons: as part of a free trade agreement through which they also received better access into that country's market, or as a freebie to a developing country. Either way, they don't want anyone else to be able to access it.

That, however, doesn't really capture the subtextual politics and power dynamics at play here. If I have a tariff, that almost certainly means I want to protect my domestic producers of that product from competition. Any request for me to lower that tariff for your producers requires me to make two calculations: will being able to sell into my market with lower tariffs make your producers a threat to my own, and are the benefits I'll be getting in exchange worth it?

In most cases, preference schemes for least developed countries exist because the answer to that first question is 'probably not.' No matter how low tariffs get, it's unlikely that cars from Afghanistan or Tuvalu will flood the market of richer countries, and so giving them access is a 'victimless' act of generosity with few downsides. When you hear politicians bragging about having offered least developed countries full or 97% market access, it's always worth asking what those countries actually export.

Nonetheless, your own producers can get squeezed by meaningful competition they were previously shielded from. This will be painful. Businesses that find themselves staring down the barrel of losing their protection tend to get very vocal, and you can fully expect them to tell any journalist who will listen about factory closures, job losses, redundancies and families left without income. Exactly how big a potential threat their industry is to yours, and how politically organised and powerful the domestic opposition to a tariff cut will be will all come together to help establish the 'price' the other side will need to pay, generally in the form of making politically painful and commercially significant cuts of their own.

Canny observers of the dark arts will likely already be detecting the landmine here. If the determination of whether to lower a tariff for a trading partner is based on an assessment of how threatening their domestic industry is, then no other nation's industry should be able to sneak in and use it. The nightmare scenario for a country that cut its formidable car tariffs for Tuvalu is to suddenly find thousands of South Korean or Japanese cars flooding into their market tariff free after a brief stop in Tuvalu to have their hubcaps attached alongside a shiny 'Made in Tuvalu' sticker. So how do you determine if a car really is 'made in Tuvalu' instead of just assembled or shipped from it? It turns out the answer is: 'hellishly'.

Rules of Origin are the conditions written into every trade agreement and preferential trade liberalisation that determine what a good must be (how local) in order to qualify for its lower tariff rate. For some products, this is relatively simple. If you are shipping bananas, then as long as you can prove they were grown in the eligible country, you're probably OK. As so often in life, matters become exponentially complicated with things that are not a banana. A modern car might be assembled from somewhere between 1,800 and 30,000 parts (depending on how big you think something needs to be to qualify as a 'part'). These might come from up to a dozen different countries before assembly. Is a car assembled in the UK by a British company but with a German engine and French transmission, 'British'? What if the seats are Italian leather? What if the thing that actually makes the car valuable is the one of a kind hand-tooled body made locally, and all the imported components are just cheap off-the-shelf stuff?

Believe it or not, the above only begins to scratch the surface of complexity that traders have to navigate in trying to qualify for reduced or eliminated tariff rates. Every free trade agreement tends to have its own approach to Rules of Origin, and some allow cumulation (including components from other countries the destination country has agreements with or preferences to) while some do not. Rules of Origin look at things like whether the final product has moved between 'categories' within the tariff code (cotton becoming a T-shirt), where the percentage of the 'value-add' was done (where the most expensive manufacturing took place) and the percentage of 'local content' by price (adding up the cost of the local versus foreign parts).

Rules of Origin aren't insurmountable of course, and millions of traders manage to emerge at the promised land of a reduced tariff rate beyond, but they're not easy. Just about every trade agreement and preferential arrangement ever made has a 'utilisation rate' well below 100 per cent as businesses simply opt out of even attempting to meet the labyrinthine rules and continue doing business at the higher tariff. Even that however may be no escape, as sanctions, targeted tariffs, and export restrictions have necessitated the emergence of so-called 'non-preferential rules of origin' to keep honest those trying to slip goods in around barriers.

When politicians talk about the transformational impact of their latest trade deal, it is often niggly details like Rules of Origin that they conveniently skip over. A tariff reduction for which businesses are ineligible, or which is too bureaucratically painful to access, is little better than no tariff reduction at all.

Step 4 – Standards and Regulations

The grand theory of libertarian capitalism says that there should be no need for the government to intervene to protect the general public from dangerous, defective or morally repugnant products – the free market will take care of it. When Evil Corp sells a children's cereal made of toxic woodchips and kids fall ill, word will get out and parents will cease buying Cruncho Pulpies, tarnishing Evil Corp's brand in the process. Evil Corp doesn't want this, and so has a commercial incentive to ensure the woodchips it uses are less toxic. Hurray for capitalism.

Except that's not really how anything works. First, parents would like the comfort of knowing that a cereal is safe to feed their kids and guarantees a little stronger than the logic of the market making peddling poison a poor long-term corporate strategy. Second, relying on market logic alone makes product safety just another variable in a complex equation involving brand management, marketing, costs and elasticity of demand. Enter standards and regulations.

In trade policy, we tend to consider these two concepts as related but distinct. Both refer to the rules which determine whether a product can be sold to the general public, or imported into the country. What makes a regulation distinct is that it has the force of government authority behind it. Many shops, like supermarkets, might have higher *standards* for certain products than the national *regulation*. For example, they may require that all their coffee come from plantations certified as ethical producers by a body like FairTrade International. This would be a standard rather than a regulation because it's not a government requirement, just something a supermarket has stipulated. If a government were to step in and say that all coffee sold in the country had to be FairTrade International certified, then that would make this requirement a regulation.

Regulations come in all shapes and sizes, with the toxic woodchip example above being one extreme example. Chances are if you walk into any shop in your area, you'll find a strong uniformity to the information packaging contains. It will all be in the official language of your country, it will list ingredients, it may list caloric data or the energy rating of the appliance, and it will do so regardless of whether that information is likely to be a selling point or not. Left to their own devices, the producers of unhealthy foods would probably be happy to leave off their packaging that a spoonful of their product has more sugar than Willy Wonka's factory, but the government compels them to present that information, and to do so in the same standardised, comparable and easy to digest format as everything else on the shelf.

As a general rule, most governments err on the side of more heavily regulating products which are potentially dangerous, such as food, cosmetics, or medicine. In trade we tend to bifurcate regulations into those relating to human, animal or plant health (sanitary/phyto-sanitary) and those relating to everything else (technical), but these distinctions aren't hugely important outside nerd circles and I mention them only for the sake of completeness. What truly matters is whether, and how, a product being imported into the country can demonstrate it meets the regulations.

A government will define not only what meeting a regulation looks like, but also what proof is needed. Importing a new medication into the country might require undergoing a certification process that takes months and costs hundreds of thousands, while a toilet brush may not be regulated at all. Some products such as meat will find themselves regulated at multiple stages, with the premises where they are made, abattoirs for example, requiring certification separate and additional to that required of any given shipment. Regulators will in some cases accept a certification issued by another government, or a test conducted in a foreign laboratory, and in other cases demand examinations right at the border by their own scientists.

Taken at face value and assuming everyone is operating in good faith, the level of both regulation and certification should be primarily risk driven. There is no need to check every Coke bottle to confirm it displays a calorie count – but checking every cow for animal diseases may be prudent. The regional prevalence of a plant-borne disease or fungus may mean shipments from certain sources face greater scrutiny, while close regulatory cooperation and trust with a neighbour may mean their products can skip certain checks or certifications on the assumption of compliance.

As with everything else in trade policy, there is an inherent tension between competing objectives – not all of them strictly kosher. For regulators and enforcement agencies at the border, the central priority is generally protecting the public interest. If a bad batch of shrimp or some lead-covered toys end up on the shelves, it is regulators and border officials who will take the blame. While in principle regulators and those enforcing regulations should aim to make the process of compliance as painless and predictable as possible, the incentives do not generally push as strongly in this direction. For a regulator, an importer having a rough time at the border is simply nowhere near as big a problem as that same importer getting something forbidden into the country because the screening process was too lax.

There are two other reasons regulators and those testing against regulations may be stricter or more onerous. First, as a form of protectionism – in the absence of tariffs, a sufficiently stringent regulation may keep foreigners from competing in your market or limit competition to those firms who have already invested the resources to meet or navigate them. Second, out of either corruption or bureaucratic inertia. Lowering regulatory requirements or making them easier to navigate may save time in the long run, but in the short term it could require a lot of work by bureaucrats to establish, communicate and fine tune the new procedures. It also, if we're being frank, might reduce opportunities for corruption and bribery by rendering automatic what was previously discretionary.

Regulatory Reform Rant

I mention the above somewhat shady reasons for keeping regulations higher than they need to be because of what I'm about to say next: politicians love nothing more than declaring that they are going to cut through red tape and reduce regulations... but somehow it never quite seems to happen. In every system, regulations at the border could be better tuned and/or more logically enforced. Policy is a journey and there are always improvements to be made and inefficiencies to be excised. Yet just like tariffs, most regulations work the way they do for a reason, and have an often powerful constituency behind maintaining them. Governments will be gung-ho about reform until they are informed of the added risks, costs, implementation challenges and vocal opposition. Where reforms are made, 'cutting red tape' often becomes 'changing red tape' as the underlying risk still needs to be managed.

Inflated promises of regulatory reform are not confined to trade policy, of course. Politicians from Samoa to Chile and everywhere in between have vowed to unshackle business from the nanny state to unleash its potential. In most cases, these promises are made either with no specifics whatsoever or a single out of context example cherry-picked to strike the casual observer as ridiculous. Once in power however, they inevitably announce a regulatory reform 'review' or 'challenge' to find some regulations they can cut easily, cheaply and without offending any voters. When equally inevitably this review produces little actionable, they quietly shelve the whole thing until the next electoral cycle or op-ed invitation when they can begin the cycle of grand promise and tepid delivery afresh.

All of this means that for the most part, businesses trading across borders take the world as it is and not as what politicians promise it will be. They work to identify the relevant regulations for their products, and what the destination government will require as proof they meet them. They will price in delays at the border while waiting for relevant clearances, and gnash their teeth in frustration as paperwork and certification problems block deliveries... and they will largely have to accept the challenges as being frustrations born from (mostly) legitimate objectives.

The picture I have tried to paint here of what it's like to move goods across borders is simultaneously denser and more detailed than you probably strictly speaking need, and barely scratching the surface of the complexity of navigating the rules of international commerce. It is unfortunately not going to get significantly lighter going as we move into services trade or the joys of regulatory alignment. If the one thing you retain from all this is a general, back of the mind sense that moving things across borders is a lot more complex than it intuitively feels then that's a great start. If you know something is complicated you'll instinctively rebel against anyone claiming it's simple, and that's what this book is all about.

Chapter 6
Services Trade

Statistically speaking, you work in a services job, have retired from one, or are studying to work in one in the future. Once economies reach a level of development where the basic needs of a substantial proportion of the population for food and shelter are largely met, services begin to rise as a percentage of the economy until they dominate. This is in part because as the complexity of the goods we produce and consume grows, so too do the services in producing them, distributing them, marketing them, and supporting them after sale. Just consider the exponential rise in the workers involved as you move from buying a potato at the market and cooking it at home, to eating a potato stew at the local food hall, to buying a McDonald's hashbrown (and thus indirectly supporting the marketing, corporate, legal and administrative teams of the McDonald's corporation).

Advances in technology have recently made a whole range of services tradeable across borders for the first time. In the 2020s it is entirely possible to have your payroll department in Hungary, your graphic designers in the Philippines, and your therapist in New Zealand. Our ability to communicate instantaneously and cheaply with those on the other side of the world, and to do so in data-intensive ways that would have melted the dial-up modems of my childhood has created trading opportunities we never imagined.

Yet despite their growing prominence in our daily lives and their importance to our economies, services trade as both a concept and a subject for negotiations has generally been relegated to the fringes of the conversation. This isn't because of some grand conspiracy by 'big goods' or the dark influence of the freight shipping industry (themselves a service provider, by the way) but because services trade is hard to measure, hard to understand and governed by rules that are hard to change through international negotiations. Services workers, and services exporters are also not as sexy politically as their hard-hat or farm coverall-wearing counterparts in goods, which relegates their interests to second tier. Politicians just aren't as excited being photographed in front of a new co-working cafe filled with remote-working hipster social media managers as they are in front of a car factory – and their focus has reflected that.

This is gradually changing, but unfortunately for the policy debate and my blood pressure, the entry of services trade into the political discourse has been driven more by its expediency as a catch-all talking point than any profound insights by the political class into how it actually works. We'll get to that in a bit, but first ...

How It Works

Services trade is complicated. Unlike goods, which are fundamentally just things of different shapes, sizes and values, services can range from an insurance policy to a website design to a museum visit while traveling. Services are also never subject to tariffs, which at least provide a pretty cross-comparable reference point for how restrictive a market is, and are instead restricted through a hodgepodge of regulations which can make it hard to work out if selling a specific service to a specific destination is even legal. Indeed, unlike physical products, which WTO members are supposed to accept from anywhere provided they are safe and in line with local standards, many services can be restricted to only those provided by locals and chosen partners without any violation of WTO rules.

There is no simple way to explain services trade, so we have little choice but to wade through the different ways services can be sold across borders and hope some elucidation appears along the way. If you feel your eyes glazing over at any point during the next few pages rest assured you are in the finest company as everyone from economists to national leaders has at one point or another tried to avoid learning the intricacies of services trade.

Remote Selling

When classifying services, trade wonks tend to do their grouping according to the question 'Who or what travels?' In the case of this first category, no one does. This category refers to truly cross-border services – those in which whatever is being paid for is delivered to the client remotely. The buyer remains in their country, and the service provider remains in theirs – the only thing that crosses borders is the payment, the service itself, and whatever data, components or materials had to travel to deliver it.

Historically, the kind of services traded in this manner were fairly limited because the technology of the time made remote work, communication, and payment across borders onerous, unreliable, and slow. The 1995 multilateral trade agreement covering services, called the General Agreement on Trade in Services (or GATS) largely reflected this era. Governments were pretty relaxed about signing away many of their rights to interfere with this kind of trade because it was largely non-existent. You don't need the government to make international call centres illegal if the cost of a 30-second international phone call is so high no one would ever consider setting one up. There's no harm in a Swiss luxury watch brand offering repair services for a fee on the watches mailed to them because there is only ever likely to be a very limited clientele for such a thing, so the jobs implications are minor.

The lightning-fast pace and proliferation of technology have transformed this. Jobs few could have imagined being done online, like surgeon or yoga instructor, are now potentially remote offerings. The ability to move data around the world near instantly and in comparative security has allowed entire business processes to be outsourced. International payment providers and trusted marketplace platforms have significantly reduced the risk of hiring freelancers in distant countries, as well as making them easier to find and engage. Meanwhile we have all become hooked on subscription services and other digital products, the vast majority of which are firmly in this category. I'm writing this particular paragraph in Switzerland while listening to Bohren & der Club of Gore, a jazz band from Nordrhein-Westfalen, Germany, on Spotify, a Swedish-owned streaming service. The wonders of services trade.

It may feel instinctively implausible for governments to regulate such virtual offerings. After all, it's really hard to stop someone just going online and paying someone abroad to do something for them. Short of severely curtailing internet access through something like the Great Firewall of China, or demanding local banks and financial services providers refuse to process payments, intuition would suggest these types of service are government intervention-resistant. Intuition would be right to an extent, but not entirely.

Governments can and do restrict these kinds of services in three distinct ways you should know about. First, they can and do simply ban the sale of certain services to their citizens from abroad. Financial services are one area where you often see this. Many governments simply do not allow foreign insurance providers to sell policies to their citizens and may limit which international investment funds their citizens or banks can use, to name just two examples. Sure, if a foreign firm in another jurisdiction decided to sell you something called an insurance policy the government wouldn't physically stop them, but they'd be breaking the law and whatever they sold you would be unenforceable. Few legitimate businesses have any appetite for that and few consumers want an insurance policy the provider could disavow if it ever came to paying out.

Second, governments can make using a domestic service provider an explicit condition for legitimately undertaking certain activities. For example, planning permission for your new home may require architectural plans drawn or at least signed off by a local architect. You could go abroad and find an architect in another country to design your home and email you the blueprints, but you wouldn't receive the go-ahead to actually build anything unless a local architect was willing to put their stamp on it.

Third, governments can make it illegal to transfer certain kinds of data across borders. Consider for example a hospital in a wealthy, high-wage country. Every day the doctors and nurses do their rounds on the wards and scribble (probably semi-legible) notes on the charts of each patient. Digitising these notes and appending them to the electronic record of a patient would have all sorts of benefits, and having this done overnight in a foreign country with lower wages would be cheaper. Yet not every government would be comfortable with this, because in order to procure this kind of work the hospital would have to send gigabytes of patient data each day to a server or territory over which it has no jurisdiction or oversight. Governments can and do restrict where certain kinds of data can be stored, and how it can move across borders, effectively restricting certain types of services to firms operating locally.

Now granted, there are entire categories of services the above do not typically apply to. While your government can make it difficult for you to make a legitimate living selling explicit videos of yourself on OnlyFans, the level of intervention required to instead prevent you from paying for such content abroad is well beyond the appetite or capability of most states. Indeed most services which can be delivered digitally to the business or consumer, and do not interact with or rely on the government, can slip beneath the bureaucratic radar – which is incidentally why a lot of statistics on international services trade are best guesses.

Selling to 'Tourists'

The second category of services trade wonks think about are those where a customer from abroad travels to one's country to buy services from them. If as a tourist you pay to enter a museum, trade nerds would consider you to be an importer and that museum to be an exporter, even though at the time of the transaction you were both standing in exactly the same place.

Historically this category was almost exclusively reserved for transactions just like that, as part of recreational tourism by visiting foreigners – with education (especially higher education) later emerging as a significant category as well. As travel costs have fallen, more people have started travelling to consume services beyond what is traditionally thought of as tourist fare – like having medical procedures done abroad. It is now increasingly commonplace for those with resources to shop globally for the types of healthcare or cosmetic procedures they cannot or do not wish to receive in their own country. On a potentially darker note, some are traveling to partake in services which are illegal in their own country, but which are either legal or laxly policed abroad. This ranges from the relatively benign, like American college students travelling abroad to take advantage of lower drinking ages, to horrific practices like sex tourism with underage victims or cruel forms of entertainment featuring animals.

As with the fourth category below, the biggest government barriers to services trade in this category come through visa restrictions. Not all countries are open to tourists, and many of those that are strictly limit how long a tourist can stay in their country and how many times they can leave and re-enter on a single visa. I could not simply announce my intention to spend the next 12 years as a tourist in France, no matter how many wineries I promise to visit. Similarly, not all students who would like to study at a university abroad are guaranteed a visa to be able to do so, and not all governments consider wanting to receive healthcare or buy some other service from one of their citizens as sufficient grounds to grant an entry permit.

Branches, Franchises and Offices Abroad

Perhaps the most complex category of international services trade is this third one where what travels to deliver the service is neither the provider, nor the customer, but a corporate entity. If a major US law firm opens an office in Canada, to provide legal services to Canadians, then that is considered a form of services trade even if everyone working in that office is a Canadian citizen with no ties to the US. Any time you provide services to foreigners through an entity you own on their territory, trade nerds class that as a form of export.

In some ways, this is probably the type of services import governments like the most. A foreign investor or company has taken a bunch of their foreign capital, converted it into the local currency, bought or leased some property and likely hired a bunch of locals to start selling other locals a service those locals want to buy. Under most, though of course not all circumstances, that's a pretty good result – and one that seems to reverse the normal 'imports bad, exports good' thinking of many politicians because all the jobs remain local.

Despite mostly being supportive in principle of foreign investment, governments can still put up barriers. Rules and regulations can restrict the type of services business foreigners can own, place limits on their maximum ownership stake (say, foreign investors can only ever own at most 49 per cent of the business), require such investments be done as a partnership with a local or that a certain number of board seats be reserved for citizens. They can restrict whether a foreign business can open a branch office, or must create a subsidiary (the latter is a lot more onerous and expensive, equivalent to creating a new business instead of just extending a tentacle of your existing one). The motivations for this vary, from instinctive resistance to foreign ownership in some sectors to ensuring the majority owners of a business are within the reach and jurisdiction of one's legal system.

Temporary Entry – Come Fix My Thing and Get Out

Perhaps the most controversial form of international services trade is this last and fourth category of temporary entry. Right off the bat, it's critical to separate this from migration or getting a job abroad. If you move to another country and get a job there, you're not considered a services exporter but just a regular worker in the local economy of wherever you've settled. For you to be in the trade basket, your personal and professional homebase has to be abroad.

I appreciate that it feels like a strange distinction to make. If I'm an expert in maintaining industrial boilers working for an Indonesian company, then I'm considered an exporter if that company sends me to Malaysia for a year to maintain boilers, or if I go freelance and sign a year-long consultancy contract to do so. However, if instead your Malaysian company hires me as an employee on a year-long contract for which I move to Malaysia, then I am no longer considered to be exporting. A useful way to think about it is asking where the person doing the work is paying income taxes – if it's somewhere other than where the work is being done, they're probably 'exporters'.

This is by far the most restricted category of services trade. First and foremost, in most countries working visas are strictly limited in quantity, duration, and by sector. Some jobs may always be open to foreign workers, others may sometimes be open (either seasonaly or in line with government lists of 'shortage' vocations) and some may never be. Governments can and do also discriminate openly in their visa regimes between different sending states, allowing significantly greater pathways for temporary workers from some countries than from others. The notion of foreigners arriving and collecting payment for a job a local might have been willing to do is politically charged – often in ways completely disconnected from the market realities of whether qualified locals were ever remotely interested in doing the jobs in question.

Governments are also often pretty stingy about whose foreign qualifications they recognise – sometimes going so far as to outsource qualifications to industry bodies which can have very little interest in allowing foreigners to compete for jobs in their backyard. Naturally, this is not the publicly stated reason for these limitations. Governments and industry alike would argue their motivation is primarily consumer safety – and that they simply cannot risk letting those trained and accredited by systems over which the government has no control or visibility perform certain sensitive jobs.

Combined, the above four so-called 'modes' of services trade provide governments with a shared language for categorising the restrictions they can or do place on various forms of services trade, and thus any treaty commitments on ways they will not do so in the future.

Where Trade Deals Come In

Historically, trade officials and ministers have either largely ignored services trade when negotiating trade agreements, or made very few commitments. There are several reasons for this. First, services as they're expressed in trade agreements are hideously complicated to wrap your brain around. Unlike goods, where there tends to be a number to focus on (the level of the tariff), services are governed by regulations, approvals, licensing requirements, data limitations and visa rules – often unique to each sector or type of service. The more complex an issue is, the harder it is to agree binding rules on, the more people will want to sign off on any commitment, and the more difficult it will be to sell as a huge triumph publicly (unless you lie, but more on that later).

Second, because services trade is a comparatively new (though proliferating) area, participants aren't as experienced in talking to governments about what they want out of free trade agreements.

This is especially true of smaller firms in the exploding field of digital services. The team behind FlexiTroth(c), the remote pig feed monitoring company which uses blockchain technology and AI to streamline hog diets in the cloud, have probably never before had to consider how to get the government to champion them against restrictive pork data privacy rules abroad. They may not even know that's a possibility and they certainly haven't been lunching with their trade minister once every month since 1894 as might be the case for their more established and connected counterparts in traditional manufacturing.

Third and probably most significant, many of the changes you might make to liberalise services through a trade agreement would require adjustments to some highly sensitive areas of governance. There are very few countries in which the debate around visas and foreign workers isn't at least potentially fraught. Also often contentious is the question of foreign ownership, and the acceptance of professional qualifications earned overseas. Faced with the prospect of negotiating something they barely understand which is also hideously complex and politically sensitive, without a vocal and influential lobby pushing for it, governments have tended to focus on goods instead.

Trade ministries too have been hesitant, as services trade regulation is generally the purview of other ministries who are often less than thrilled at the prospect of locking in legally binding commitments about how they do their jobs in order to help the trade folks land a deal. In emerging areas like digital and e-commerce, regulators and legislators are understandably cautious about limiting their options in the future given that the field is changing so fast.

This isn't to say nothing has ever been achieved in a trade agreement on services, only that the achievements have tended (with some exceptions, like the telecommunications or air transport services agreements) to be modest. Governments have tended to be most generous in improving conditions for foreign investors, because foreign capital is desirable and creates jobs. They have also at times created strictly limited and heavily qualified opportunities for foreign workers in select fields. Remote work and tourism have generally been left untouched, or with provisions that legally lock the way the system already works.

The services section of a trade agreement might commit to:

- Not place numerical limits on how many foreign firms selling a service can establish in your market;
- Not to charge unreasonable fees on foreigners applying for a licence to perform a service;
- Create a visa class for foreign workers with specific skills who have a contract to deliver a service;
- Not to place restrictions on the movement of data across borders beyond those necessary to provide reasonable privacy protection;
- Not to require technology firms selling from or incorporating from abroad to reveal their source code or algorithms to the government;
- Not to require foreign firms have a local partner or a certain number of local board members in order to operate;
- Ensure that rules about who can open a branch office or provide a service are fully and transparently posted online.

Lying About Services

The comparatively obscure status of services in the trade policy conversation has somewhat limited the number of lies politicians have told about it – in the same way that not being famous significantly decreases the likelihood of a tabloid hit piece being written about you. As services trade grows however, and trade agreement achievements in already pretty liberalised goods become harder to come by, this is beginning to change.

Will This Services Deal Change Your Life?

Near the start of this book I suggested a simple question to ask those claiming a trade agreement is about to transform the business landscape or rain opportunities: 'What precisely will change for someone selling across borders as a result of this deal?' Please keep this principle in mind when considering deals on services, because governments have fallen into the habit of labelling every new deal as 'the most ambitious ever' or 'cutting edge', especially where one involves technology.

The truth is almost always more modest. We've already discussed why services provisions in trade agreements tend to be somewhat underwhelming. In addition, governments don't know what kind of regulatory tools they may want to deploy in the future because they barely understand the technological offerings on the market today, let alone tomorrow. Faced with this uncertainty, they make commitments only in areas they know they're not going to want to legislate or regulate in the future, and then throw in caveats and exceptions just in case they're wrong.

For day-to-day life, temporary entry provisions have the most potential. In theory, if you can suddenly access a new visa type and deliver work overseas, that could be really important. Similarly, if your fellow citizens can now source specialists or temporary workers from abroad, that might make certain services more accessible – but it could also mean more competition. Yet, as we've already discussed, liberalisation in this area is always a political struggle. Except in exceptional cases like the EU's Freedom of Movement as part of the Single Market, new visa openness as part of a trade agreement tends to be limited and narrowly targeted. This is important to remember, because we so frequently hear . . ..

Does Distance Matter?

Tell me if this sounds familiar. A government announces a new trade agreement with some country halfway around the world. A bunch of economists are interviewed on the news to say that their analysis suggests the agreement won't change much. A government spokesperson fires back by saying these economists are cretinous has-beens utilising an outmoded 'gravity theory' of trade and ignoring services, which are unaffected by distance.

This lie drives me up the wall because if delivered with enough confidence, it sounds like common sense. Certainly if I'm shopping online for a one-off service like touching up an old photo, I'm not particularly fussed if the seller is in Brussels, Bogota, or Brisbane. It's not unreasonable to extrapolate from this that services are therefore less subject to the tyranny of distance than physical products are. But are they?

The answer is 'maybe theoretically but not always and frequently not.' Services that require an expert from one country to get on another plane to another are an obvious place to begin the scepticism. Flying in a team of Bain Consultants to do . . . whatever it is they do, is a lot cheaper if they're coming from a neighbouring country than from halfway across the world. Any company bidding for a contract that involves flying in staff often is going to be at a marked disadvantage if every flight is going to take hours longer and cost five times more. If you're in Paris it is possible to fly in someone from London, have them spend the day working and get them home in time for an aperitif. Less so if you're in Bogota. The responsiveness and cost advantages of a local provider are considerable, even in the age of frequent and reliable air transportation.

Tourism also has a similar proximity bias. Of the 50.9 million international visitors to the US in 2022, more than half were from Canada and Mexico. Meanwhile, despite having over 4,000 universities to Australia's 43, the United States only attracts between 33% and 100% more Chinese students than Australia does every year (and yes, those statistics predate the current tensions).

In investment, things are a little bit murkier but there are still clear regional patterns. The largest source of foreign direct investment in

Latin America is the United States. European capital is the largest foreign investor source in Africa (though China is catching up). In Asia, China is by far the largest investor followed by Japan and the US. For a range of convenience, cultural and regulatory reasons investors tend to prefer to put money into ventures in their region.

Even in remotely delivered services, there are advantages to being closer. As anyone who has ever managed remote workers or contractors will tell you, having service providers that are in or near your time zone often helps. This is especially true when the type of service you're procuring requires an emergency response or detailed engagement on details difficult to convey by email. As an Australian official in Switzerland I often envied my European colleagues who didn't have to wait 14 hours to 'quickly check something with capital and get back to you'. There can also be linguistic and cultural differences to consider, though of course, the expanse of European colonialism has meant a significant portion of the world now has many people capable of working in English, French and Spanish.

To be absolutely clear, none of the above are universal obstacles or impossible to overcome. People and companies routinely buy online services, travel to, study in, secure investment, and fly in contractors from the other side of the globe. In some cases geographic distance and disparate time zones might even be an advantage. Yet equally unquestionably, distance and geography do matter to a wide range of services. Thankfully for those of you who may not want to spend the next five months delving into the academic literature and economic modelling of precisely how much distance impacts services exports, this debate is something of a sideshow. Even if distance had absolutely no impact on services exports whatsoever, a services deal with a distant land would probably not be transformational for the country because most free trade agreements have limited provision for services and remain mostly about goods – and despite recent fanfare about digital provisions, that's not likely to change.

What About Our Public Services?

A frequent concern raised by voters about trade deals is whether they'll negatively impact the quality and affordability of the services they currently receive from the state, such as electricity, water, public transportation and health care. This is especially true in countries where services are still partly or predominantly in public hands – with the spectre of greedy foreign corporations evoked as the menace *du jour*.

For obvious political reasons, opposition politicians and activists lean heavily into this trope. A trade agreement, especially one that hasn't yet been concluded, can be painted as *potentially* imperilling just about anything – and public services are simultaneously something people feel passionately about and have no trouble believing politicians might sell out. Claiming that the government's latest trade deal plans to let evil foreign corporations strip-mine your national health service for parts, massively drive up electricity costs, or allow effluent to be dumped in the rivers is good politics, even if it's usually nonsense.

In truth, there is little reason to suspect that a free trade agreement itself will threaten public services. A trade agreement might include clauses that, for example, open up procurement processes for elements of healthcare delivery to the other nation's firms – but the decision to privatise the service would be one the government has already made or was planning to make anyway.

This is not to say that trade agreements can't have any impact on public services. The intellectual property protection clauses of a trade agreement can impact anything from the price of textbooks to which drugs are sold at a subsidised price. The investment protection clauses could be a hurdle to nationalisation or de-privatisation, especially if it is being contemplated without adequate compensation or remuneration. Expanded visa access could mean public services are cheaper and more diversely delivered. Provisions around data flows could mean some information is sent abroad with all the resultant implications around price, efficiency and privacy.

To be fair to those raising these concerns, it's not that there's anything inherent in trade agreements that prevents them from imperilling public services. A trade agreement is a deal between two countries, and as such can consist of almost anything imaginable. Trade agreements do not typically harm public services for the same reason that most governments don't typically harm them through other instruments – because doing so would be deeply unpopular. In other words, if you have concerns about your government undermining public services then there are probably better places to draw the battlelines than on trade agreements.

Chapter 7
Free Trade Agreements

The most publicly visible manifestation of trade policy being made is the negotiation and (occasionally) conclusion of free trade agreements. These are deals between two or more countries aimed at facilitating trade and investment.

Such agreements have historically had three primary purposes. First, they lower tariffs. This not only makes it easier to sell goods into another territory on a more equal footing with that territory's own producers, but also advantages the parties to a free trade agreement over those without one. A free trade agreement is one of the few exceptions to the WTO rules that otherwise oblige you to maintain the same tariffs on goods regardless of their origin. If South Africa has a 15 per cent tariff on cars from any WTO member and Kenya signs an agreement with South Africa reducing that tariff to zero then Kenyan made cars will not only be on a level playing field with South African ones, but will also have a 15 per cent advantage over cars from any country without such an agreement.

Governments enter into these side deals because there are some countries they are open to having freer trade with than the rest of the world. In the example above, South Africa has the option of simply reducing its car tariff to 0 per cent for all WTO members, but may not be comfortable doing so – either because there are car-producing countries it does not wish to compete with or because maintaining the tariff gives it something to trade away in deals like the one with Kenya. In purist economic theory, negotiating a grand bargain at the World Trade Organization where everyone reduces their tariffs for everyone else would be preferable. However, this has proven impossible in practice, which only increases the appeal of separate free trade deals.

Second, free trade agreements have symbolic and geopolitical performative value. Launching a trade negotiation can demonstrate how close you are with an ally, or (if your market is significantly larger and more lucrative) serve as a way to reward them for their loyalty. Some see a trade agreement as an indication of geopolitical 'direction of travel', which can be especially significant for countries caught between two powerful blocs like the EU and Russia or the West and China. They also serve as visible proof that a dynamic trade ministry and government are working toward furthering national prosperity. If the communications are managed properly a free trade agreement will net positive headlines when it's first publicly contemplated, when it's announced, around many of the negotiating rounds, at the conclusion of negotiations, at signature, when ratified by the legislature, and upon entry into force.

Third, some wealthier countries enter into trade agreements with poorer ones as a way of encouraging their development. These agreements tend to be uneven, with the richer country lowering its tariffs considerably more. This greater access to the richer country's consumers is supposed to encourage business development and investment. By giving a country better access to your wealthy consumers, you're encouraging factories to relocate there to take advantage of the lower tariffs. This is something developed countries will generally provide unilaterally to least developed countries and smaller economies, but package into a trade agreement with emerging economies or slightly larger partners.

Traditionally free trade agreements have primarily contained tariff reductions plus a set of additional provisions mostly intended to prevent those tariff reductions from being nullified through other government policies or procedures, such as using regulations or border procedures to unfairly keep out or hamper imports.

Over time more and more issues have been included in free trade agreements, significantly broadening them beyond an exclusive focus on tariff reduction. This can be partially attributed to the rise of other forms of trade, such as services, as well as trade itself becoming more complicated. The end result is that many modern agreements include chapters on areas like investment, digital and electronic commerce that weren't present in previous deals.

During the last decade awareness has also grown of how trade intersects with other areas of public policy, leading to the insertion and expansion of chapters covering sustainable development, gender, labour, and the environment. Some of these may have already been present in past agreements, but were primarily focused on ensuring that environmental or labour rules weren't used to subvert or nullify the agreement's tariff reductions. These days such chapters often have more 'positive' agendas focused on how the trading partners can cooperate and make commitments that advance shared objectives in these areas.

Another reason free trade agreements have grown in scope recently is their attractiveness as a vehicle for international commitments. Trade agreements are fundamentally a series of promises between governments and can contain just about anything both sides agree. The only real limitations the World Trade Organization imposes are that trade agreements be a reciprocal exchange of commitments, that they cover substantially all trade, and that nothing in them can make trading conditions worse for non-parties.

The first two rules, on reciprocity and substantial coverage, are designed to prevent countries from getting around their obligations to treat all WTO members similarly by rapidly firing off small bespoke 'agreements' whenever they want to give someone slightly improved market access. By making sure trade agreements are big and reciprocal, the WTO slows down the pace of changes to global tariffs, making the whole system more predictable and easier to navigate for businesses and investors.

The last rule, which prohibits twisting a trade agreement to make trading harder for non-parties, is about limiting loopholes from WTO rules. You are allowed to indirectly hurt a non-party to a trade agreement by charging the other signatories lower tariffs, but you are not allowed to include something in a deal which directly harms a non-party. A trade agreement should be making trade easier for those in it, not harder for everyone else. You can all agree to lower your cheese tariffs for one another, which would give your cheesemongers an advantage over a non-party like France, but what you can't do is sign a deal requiring all parties to raise their cheese tariffs on the French.

Having so few limitations means trade agreements can be an attractive opportunity to nail down shared commitments in many areas. While governments can theoretically talk to one another at any time and agree to a treaty on anything they want, most don't have teams of treaty negotiators sitting around waiting to be deployed. A trade agreement negotiation where everyone involved has negotiating teams that will be spending years locked in a room together is a good opportunity.

Trade agreements also potentially provide a more binding mechanism than other treaties. The dispute settlement mechanisms in trade agreements tend to be some of the more robust in international law, with well-established procedures and real consequences for those found in breach. Moreover, because trade agreements are a single large treaty covering lots of areas, each area becomes effectively linked to all others. Pulling out of the gender chapter, for example, would mean voiding the entire treaty, with potentially significant commercial consequences – which might make a government think twice.

In this chapter I want to walk you through how a trade agreement is negotiated and what the people involved are doing during the various stages. In reading further please note, I will be painting with a very broad brush and drawing on my own experiences which aren't fully representative of all systems worldwide.

Negotiating Trade Agreements

Stage 1: Choosing a Dance Partner

The decision of who to negotiate a free trade agreement with is almost always a combination of politics, and the paucity of realistic options. Governments will generally want to start by doing deals with countries in their immediate region, countries that have a similar ideological approach to trade policy, countries that they already trade with extensively, and perhaps most importantly the countries that are willing to enter into trade negotiations with them and with whom there is a chance of a successful conclusion.

Governments commence negotiations for a variety of reasons. It could be because they genuinely sense an opportunity to improve prosperity meaningfully. They may wish to strengthen diplomatic relations, as a way of rewarding a trusted ally, or simply because they have spare negotiating capacity available. They may be looking to get ahead of, or catch up with, trade agreements signed by others, so their exporters aren't disadvantaged in lucrative markets. Finally, especially when it comes to large agreements with multiple partners, there may be a geostrategic logic – trade agreements used to create blocs with incentives to trade amongst themselves and regulate in mutually interoperable ways.

Perhaps counterintuitively, while economics certainly plays a role in how a government chooses a negotiating partner, it's often just one variable in a much larger political equation.

Stage 2: Assembling the Team

Having agreed in principle that a trade negotiation will happen, a government's next step will be to instruct whichever ministry runs trade policy to begin putting together a team to handle the talks. A free trade agreement negotiation is a huge undertaking that takes years and involves a vast amount of work. It's simultaneously an exercise in diplomacy, public relations, domestic stakeholder management, creative legal drafting and the balancing of competing priorities. Putting the right team in place is critical to ensuring your side can navigate the process so as to minimise the risks and maximise the upsides.

Typically the negotiation team will resemble a pyramid. At the apex will be the chief negotiator who has overall responsibility for steering the negotiation to a successful conclusion and reports directly to the trade minister, Cabinet, and the national leader. Below the chief might sit a row of senior officials with responsibility for broad issue areas within the negotiation such as goods or services. Answering to them are the chapter leads, who look after all negotiations in a given section of the treaty, like tariffs or digital trade. Finally the chapter leads may have negotiators working beneath them on even more granular questions like agricultural tariffs or online consumer protection.

Those at the bottom of the pyramid will generally be in the best position to get into the fine detail of their patch, but will lack the authority or visibility to make trade-offs or compromises across different areas in the negotiation. Those higher up the pyramid will typically be less granular in their perception but better able to identify and offer trades between progressively larger sections of the text, with the chief negotiator having the broadest vision and authority to make trades across the whole deal. A well functioning trade negotiation team will ensure that the information flowing up the pyramid highlights the key issues without drowning more senior team members in unnecessary detail.

The closer you are to the top of the hierarchy as a negotiator, the more empowered you are to make concessions in areas your government finds a little painful. Ultimately though, it is up to the chief negotiator to choreograph your side's negotiating strategy, determining where and on which issues you'll fight hardest and allowing you to make trades or concessions when the moment is right.

Countries source their trade negotiators in different ways but it is common for the majority of the team to come from the trade ministry or its equivalent. Other departments may also be asked to second someone with valuable expertise, especially when there is an expectation the deal is going to dive into highly specialised areas with which a trade policy generalist may not be familiar. Sometimes such departments even insist on it, though generally still under the understanding that any seconded expert from agriculture, treasury or wherever will still follow orders from the chief negotiator on strategy and tactics. It is virtually unheard of for the private sector or civil society to be represented in the negotiating room as part of the team. It's a government-to-government affair.

Stage 3: Initial Consultations

When embarking on a trade negotiation the team and the ministry will probably have a general idea of the kind of concessions it wants out of the other side, and the requests it may want to push back on. However not even the most engaged trade ministry can possibly hope to be across every potential trade barrier, sensitivity and collaboration opportunity. It is therefore standard practice to begin negotiations by soliciting ideas and opinions through a formal process of engagement with domestic stakeholders like the business community, civil society groups, other government departments, think tanks and academics.

If done properly these consultations can simultaneously achieve a number of objectives. First, they can identify elements of the other side's trade regime that are impeding exports. This generates ideas for asks, which negotiators call 'offensive interests'. This is especially important because not all trade barriers are obvious. While it's easy to see how a high tariff may be hurting exports, it's much less readily apparent when the blame lies with some quirk of the other side's regulatory framework or procedures. Even if the other government ultimately refuses to move on a request, just having something specific to ask for is an asset for negotiators.

Second, consultations indicate where the most commercial and politically sensitive areas, sometimes called 'defensive interests', are for your own side. If a business organisation or civil society group is able to get mobilised and send a robust message on an issue during consultations, that's a pretty strong indicator that they will make their voices heard throughout the process and cause major problems if the final deal doesn't meet their expectations. This is vital to properly 'pricing' these issues once the negotiation gets underway.

Third, the contacts made during a properly executed consultation can serve as a brain trust for negotiators down the line. Having a phonebook full of the most informed, passionate or engaged people in the country on a given issue can be invaluable when a negotiator wants to sense-check an idea, brainstorm creative ways round an impasse, or run a potential outcome past a directly affected business. Within the government, these consultations can also help to identify and build relationships with decision makers in other ministries whose input and sign off the team will need later.

Fourth, a consultation process can serve as a roadshow for the upcoming trade agreement and a public relations exercise on its behalf. It's a chance for the trade ministry to send some positive messages about what it's hoping to achieve and the potential benefits for the country. In practice, this sometimes means sitting in a rural community hall getting screamed at by a passionate senior citizen convinced you're planning to exchange their pension for a handful of magic beans, but at least that person gets to have a good shout.

Fifth, if the other negotiating team knows what they're doing they will probably attempt to quietly reach out to the stakeholders a consultation might engage with during the negotiation to try to assuage their concerns or lobby them onside. Good consultations lets you get ahead of that, potentially even positioning your stakeholders to send the right messages. Being able to say, 'my stakeholders are freaking out about this' is an asset in the negotiating room, and even more so when you know they'll confirm it if called!

Unfortunately, many ministries responsible for trade struggle to run effective consultations. Most people in society have only a very general understanding of what a trade negotiation consists of and what it might deliver. Only the largest businesses trading across borders can afford to have government relations professionals on staff with a specialised understanding of international trade policy. The smaller businesses that may actually be most affected by the onerousness of an existing trade policy and have the fewest tools to get around barriers abroad, are also the least likely to have sufficient capacity to engage with a government consultation. Sending out a general questionnaire which asks what the general public are hoping to see out of an upcoming negotiation tends to produce a very mixed bag of inputs – as does the other frequent government go-to: a 67-page form with 284 questions.

In an ideal world those working at trade ministries would be in constant dialogue with local businesses, think tanks and interest groups even when not negotiating. They would then draw on that extensive network as well as the deep understanding their engagement has given them of trading realities to drive specific and focused consultations. For a range of reasons including resource constraints, government risk aversion limiting the number of civil servants allowed to deal with the general public, and both civil servants and the people they would need to talk to having competing demands on their time, this rarely happens.

Unfortunately, this means that formal consultation processes can at times be perfunctory, box-ticking exercises that produce few usable inputs and are quickly forgotten by the government. That said, if you're passionate about an issue being included or excluded from an upcoming trade agreement, even a somewhat disingenuous public consultation may be useful for eliciting media attention, finding like-minded stakeholders you can work with on the issue, and putting your concerns on record so that the government cannot later claim that they weren't aware of them.

Stage 4: The Formal Mandate

In many systems, the civil servants in the trade ministry will at this point prepare a document for the consideration of their minister or Cabinet. If signed off on, this document or 'mandate' gives the ministry the authority to open negotiations, sets the high level objectives, provides a general flavour of what the negotiators should aim to achieve in each subject area, and includes a list of items that absolutely must be, or absolutely cannot be, in the deal for it to be acceptable.

For example the negotiating mandate of Canada with Peru might say that the overall objective is a modern and liberalising trade deal, that the negotiators will seek to eliminate as many of Peru's tariffs as they can, but, specifically, they will under no circumstances conclude the deal if it includes Canada reducing its cheese tariff below 10 per cent. As you can immediately tell, the first two of those are fairly subjective metrics whereas the third is more or less a 'yes' or 'no' that leaves very little room for interpretation.

The specific provisions in a formal mandate are especially important because typically even the chief negotiator will not have the authority to conclude a deal that runs contrary to them. If, having tried absolutely everything, the Canadian chief negotiator concludes that Peru simply cannot be convinced to accept a deal that doesn't include reducing Canadian cheese tariffs to 5 per cent or less, they will need to put that to their minister, national leader, or Cabinet for a decision on how to proceed – either dropping the demand or accepting a deal may not be possible until either Canada or Peru change their minds.

The formal mandate with its mix of general and specific commandments becomes a foundational holy text for negotiators crafting a deal. The specific instructions become the points both sides push hardest on because they know they are simply not permitted to conclude a deal that runs contrary to them. Where during the course of negotiations it becomes clear that the two sides have specific mandated directives that run contrary to one another and cannot be creatively reconciled, negotiators will typically park such issues until the very final rounds, which benefit from the presence of ministers or national leaders with the authority to derogate from the mandate.

A key reason to get involved in the trade negotiation process as early as possible is to maximise the chance of having an issue you care about being included in the formal mandate – and thus placed at the top of the negotiators' priority list. As a general rule, negotiators will sacrifice something not in their formal mandate or only mentioned in general terms if it allows them to make progress on something they have been specifically mandated to deliver.

Stage 5: Pre-negotiations

Typically, negotiation teams will start talking to one another at various levels well before the start of the first official negotiating round. Not only does this let both sides get to know each other but it's also a chance to negotiate about the negotiations. This could mean agreeing logistical questions like how often rounds will run, where they'll take place, and how issues like visas and accommodation will be handled. It could also mean negotiations on the so-called scope of the agreement.

'Scope' is a word the trade policy community is mildly obsessed with because it demarcates the outer edges of what can be in a deal, and what kind of policies will be affected. If there is something your government is particularly sensitive about, the best way you can ensure you'll never even be asked to make a commitment on it is to get the other side to agree in pre-negotiations that it will be excluded from the scope of talks.

For example, permanent immigration is one of the most sensitive areas of policy for many governments and something they are completely unprepared to talk about in the context of a trade agreement. Agreeing before the talks formally start that immigration is off the table gives both sides peace of mind and allows them to confidently rebut any accusation from the media or their political opponents that a prospective deal may have implications for immigration.

On the other hand, this could also be the opportunity to agree to discuss areas not always included in trade agreements, such as women's economic empowerment or fishing rights.

Stage 6: Initial Offers and Requests

Any negotiation needs a starting point and trade talks tend to start with an exchange of initial offers and initial requests. You can think of these as wishlists. In giving you my initial offer and request I am showing you what the deal would look like if I were allowed to write the thing myself and have you sign on the dotted line.

A good example of this are the initial offers and requests on tariffs. Picture two very long spreadsheets. The first is my initial goods offer. It consists of a long list of all of the tariffs I currently have in place, alongside a column of reductions that I am prepared to offer you right from the start of our negotiations. The second is my initial goods request. This is exactly the same thing, except instead of listing my tariffs I list all of yours, alongside the reductions I'm hoping you'll give me through this negotiation.

There's a lot to consider in drafting these opening gambits. The operating assumption on both sides will be that counterparts will give more than what was in their opening offer and accept less than what was in their initial request. Too stingy an initial offer will start the negotiation off on the wrong foot and sour your relationship with your counterparts, but too generous an offer may leave you without any room to make further concessions. Similarly an initial request that is too ambitious and completely out of touch with reality will not only annoy the other side but give them very little idea of what you actually want out of the negotiation.

In areas that aren't, like tariffs, just lists of numbers, initial offers and requests might consist of an exchange of draft text for a chapter between the two sides. So for example the European Union might hand over to Japan its ideal version of a rules of origin chapter, and Japan might reciprocate by either handing back its own version, or marking up the EU's in the places where it would prefer to re-word the text. The rest of the negotiation would then be spent trying to arrive at a version of the chapter both sides can live with.

Sometimes, there will be a bit of a fight as to who 'holds the pen' – which is negotiator parlance for writing the first draft that the other parties mark up where they have issues with it. In theory, holding the pen shouldn't provide any advantage because the other negotiators could object to every single letter or submit alternate language for every paragraph. In practice however, the party submitting the draft exercise some control over the format and structure of the final outcome, making it more closely resemble what they have done in the past and what their stakeholders are comfortable with. Who ends up 'holding the pen' on each chapter is something discussed in the pre-negotiations, and can come down to which side cares more, which side has more market power, or some attempt at dividing up the chapters between the parties to keep things equitable.

Combined with the pre-negotiated scope these initial exchanges of offers and requests set the outer edges of the talks, with the rest of the negotiations being an attempt to find a compromise within those parameters. It's critical to ensure that absolutely everything you want is included in your initial request, and nothing that you can't live with makes its way into your initial offer.

No negotiator wants to turn up late in the day with a new demand which did not feature in their initial request. Even more so, no one wants to suddenly withdraw a concession that was previously seen as so trivially easy to make that it made its way into the initial offer. While sometimes circumstances such as new information or a newly elected government amending the negotiating instructions will necessitate this kind of change, it looks bad and can ruin working relationships with one's counterparts. As an outside stakeholder therefore, making sure your desires and concerns are on the trade team's radar early enough to be considered for inclusion in the initial offers and requests is vital.

Stage 7: Negotiating Rounds

Once a negotiation formally commences, the majority of the progress will be made during negotiating rounds. The negotiating teams will meet in a common destination (or online), break into smaller groups, and begin working in parallel on all of the many issues that make up a complete trade agreement. In between multi-hour sessions working with their counterparts they'll gather to update the chief negotiator on their progress and seek instructions and guidance.

People have a lot of funny ideas about what a trade negotiation looks like. Hollywood has done the profession few favours by cementing in the public imagination the image of the negotiator as a table-thumping bully rolling over the other side with threats and intimidation, or a hyperarticulate debate prodigy trapping counterparts in a clever web of words and dazzling them with soaring *West Wing*-style oratory. While I have personally seen people try both, they've rarely been successful and were mercifully the exception and not the rule. The vast majority of negotiators aim for a professional, amiable and personable tone that is firm where it needs to be, but strives to demonstrate empathy for the other side's position and a constructive spirit.

There are reasons for this beyond just how exhausting it would be to spend weeks at a time locked with a blustering blowhard or a wannabe Cicero. Rather than making speeches or demands, good negotiators spend the majority of their time asking the other side questions. They do this to try to ascertain why the other side is taking a particular stance, what their underlying concern is, and how strongly their system and decision-makers feel about it.

Imagine you're in a negotiation with Switzerland and your Swiss counterpart has just told you they can't consider lowering any industrial tariffs. This should immediately trigger a few obvious questions. Is it really possible that not a single existing Swiss tariff on industrial goods can be touched? At all? If elimination is too much, could any of them be reduced? What is Switzerland concerned will happen if the tariffs are reduced or eliminated? Are tariffs really the only thing keeping all of these Swiss industries competitive? Who are the actors in the Swiss system for whom this kind of reduction is unacceptable? How influential are they and is there anything else they might want?

These questions allow you to begin better understanding the nature of the Swiss objection. They may also reveal that the real Swiss concern is actually narrower than they have suggested. For example, the two industries kicking up a fuss might be automotive parts and industrial boilers, which might mean there's a deal to be had on eliminating tariffs except on those products. You may also be able to arrive at a creative solution that achieves what you want while still respecting the Swiss sensitivity. For example, if the Swiss are primarily concerned about very expensive high-grade imports, whereas your focus is on access for your lower-cost producers, you might propose eliminating the tariff only for goods below a certain value.

Questions also help you to 'price' any potential Swiss concession. At some point in a future round your counterpart may turn to you and suggest that they are, in fact, willing to move on industrial tariffs if you're willing to move on something of equal value. It is in the interest of the Swiss that you think this concession is incredibly painful for them to make, because they can then reasonably demand an equally painful offering from your side. By asking the right questions and perhaps working with your country's diplomatic network to verify and further research the answers you hear, you can prevent this kind of upselling.

'Pricing' can also help those closer to the top of a trade negotiation's hierarchy identify where potential trades might be possible. You can group the other side's positions into three broad categories: the things they can easily concede on, the painful concessions they might be able to make in exchange for something juicy from your side, and the absolute red lines they're not even allowed to consider regardless of what's on offer. Working out which of the issues the other side is claiming to be a red line they might actually be willing to do business on is amongst your most important skills as a negotiator.

Central to all this, and another reason why neither bullying nor speechmaking tends to be a particularly effective approach, is that the person you're talking to is almost certainly not the one with authority over whatever it is you're discussing. If you want Singapore to commit to allowing your telecommunications firms to operate in their market, then both the final decision and any opposition to that request is likely to come from Singapore's communications ministry, not the trade ministry official across the table from you. In fact, the negotiator in the room with you is both your best chance of finding out what the communication ministry's actual concerns are. They are also your only reliable way of sending messages to the Singaporian system, either to signal that this issue is not one you'll be able to conclude the deal without or to share any arguments or evidence that you hope will allay their concerns.

This is an important point. The other side's negotiators are the link between you and their system. If you spend your time in the negotiating room yelling at your counterparts, trying to deceive them or boring them to tears, that will colour how they frame your messages, and how forthcoming they are about what they're hearing back in their capital (or just 'capital' as negotiators like to say). The more they like and trust you the more likely they are to faithfully and positively convey your thoughts to the decision makers in their system – as well as being forthright with you about what they're really hearing back home. The optics of a negotiating room, with the sides sitting across the table from one another, appear adversarial, but in practice the negotiating teams are the only ones on planet Earth with the shared primary professional objective of reaching a mutually acceptable conclusion. It's easy to forget that. Bad negotiators do.

When confronted with a negotiator who is rude, needlessly adversarial or unconstructive, a team always has the option of elevating the issue and asking their chief negotiator to bring it up with his or her counterpart. Regardless of how that conversation goes that's a negative outcome for everyone involved. It requires the chief negotiators to put aside the substantive issues and essentially debate personalities, brings any friction out onto the surface and forces the chief negotiator who receives the complaint to make tough decisions about who to believe, and what to do about it.

A final reason you want to be polite and friendly with your counterparts is the eternity you will spend playing legal word games with the draft text. Apart from the tariff schedule, which is a long list of numbers, the rest of a trade agreement consists mostly of legal prose in numbered paragraphs. At the start of a negotiation all the draft text will be in square brackets to indicate that it has not yet been agreed.

Over the course of many many negotiating rounds officials will work through the text paragraph by paragraph, line by line, and sometimes literally punctuation mark by punctuation mark, to try to remove those square brackets. In many cases, the square brackets will be around language the intent of which all sides agree on in theory, but whose legal phrasing has raised concerns in practice. Negotiators work to understand those concerns and where possible address them through alternative phrasing, clarifying footnotes or the inclusion of illustrative examples. What this means is that many times a paragraph will be projected onto a big screen, and the parties will stare at it with furrowed brows, waiting for someone to say, 'What if we....'

Because a trade agreement is legally binding, every syllable is carefully considered for how it could be interpreted by a future dispute settlement panel. Negotiators also have to think about the implications of any draft language for their other treaties, any precedents it could create, and how well it aligns with the country's existing laws and regulatory practice. The last thing a trade ministry wants to discover six months after ratification is that a poorly placed comma means Pokemon cards are now the only treaty compliant form of legal tender.

Over the course of multiple rounds, negotiators will look to trade off or creatively solve as many of the outstanding issues as possible and arrive at legal language everyone can live with. Inevitably, it will quickly become apparent that there are some issues on which neither side can give ground and on which no neat 'third way' compromise is possible. These then are almost certainly the issues that will need to be elevated to ministers in the final rounds. However, before grappling with them, ministers will want to be absolutely sure there is no chance of some miracle emerging from within the negotiating room that saves them from having to make a difficult decision. If handed a text that still looks like it has dozens of unresolved questions, ministers will avoid making a decision on the hard stuff by sending negotiators back into the room to do more work. To avoid this, negotiators on all sides will therefore aim to get the agreement to the point where it is only a small handful of the most contentious issues away from being finalised before calling in the politicians.

Stage 7.5: Between Rounds

Almost as important as what happens when the teams meet for formal negotiating rounds is what they do back in capital between rounds. While by the end of a negotiation a trade official will have become an expert on a given chapter, they are unlikely to be a practitioner nor the one within the government with day-to-day responsibility for it. Moreover, anything they want to lock in as an agreed bit of text probably needs to be signed off on by someone else within their government. The time in between negotiating rounds is supposed to be spent updating and consulting with key stakeholders on how the deal is evolving and any potential new text.

Negotiators understand that sometimes the language they all seemed happy with during a round will raise concerns they hadn't considered once it is mulled over by colleagues in capital. However once a negotiator has said their system has signed off on some language and that the square brackets can be removed, it is considered both highly demoralising and an act of bad faith to return and ask that they be put back because someone they neglected to talk to flagged an issue.

It is therefore imperative for anyone with a strong interest in the specifics of a negotiated outcome to try and make sure they are among those consulted by negotiators in between rounds. This is especially true for those with practical first hand experience of the issues being discussed or specific subject matter expertise that may not be readily available to the negotiators or their colleagues.

For the negotiators, these between-round consultations are also a way of slowly building up the comfort level of their own system with what a final deal may look like. Signature, ratification and effective implementation will require the active collaboration of many actors who will never get anywhere near the negotiating room. The more negotiators can get them across what the deal is going to look like, make their concerns feel heard and incorporate their input, the fewer surprise hurdles are likely to emerge down the line. Partly because of this, negotiators tend to be precedent focused and prone to wanting to reuse language from previous trade agreements – language their stakeholders will have already seen and approved of in the past.

Stage 8: Final Round and (Maybe) Agreement in Principle

As the negotiation narrows down to the last few most contentious issues, the sides will generally try to shape the battlespace a little bit to encourage a deal to be reached on as close to their terms as possible. Ultimately, whether a deal gets done will depend on whether ministers are prepared to spend political capital on the painful concessions required to get it over the line. It's a question of cost, benefit and risk. How politically painful are the compromises required, how much political upside would a successful conclusion bring, and how bad would it look if talks stalled or combusted. The more both sides hype up a round as the one in which they hope to conclude talks, the more it then costs ministers to part ways without a deal.

There are two power dynamics at work here. First, the minister with the stronger hand in this final negotiation is almost invariably the one more comfortable with there being no outcome. A thought experiment I have used to horrify government negotiators I'm training is asking them to imagine a meeting between their minister and a counterpart. The deal they're working on is almost concluded, but the other minister is insisting on a demand that's simply unthinkable. When told it's not happening, they smile, say they completely understand and suggest the two of them walk out to the press corps outside and announce talks are to be suspended indefinitely due to irreconcilable differences. The officials I was training, whose minister and national leader had talked up at least one potential free trade agreement as an inevitable triumph and a cornerstone of their policy, went very pale indeed.

The second dynamic to think about is an internal one. Making the final compromises required to get a deal across the line is almost inevitably a robust debate (aka a fight) within Cabinet between the trade minister and whichever minister's portfolio concessions would be coming from. A common example might see a showdown between the trade minister who says a deal simply can't be done without more tariff cuts in agriculture, and an agriculture minister who strongly opposes making them.

As a trade negotiator for the other side, part of your job is thinking ahead to that fight and doing everything in your power to make sure that the trade minister, who will effectively be fighting your corner, comes out on top. That means passing along to them, through their negotiators, the strongest arguments possible for why the agriculture minister's concerns may be overblown, why there's no chance you'll agree a deal without what you're seeking, and why the benefits of the rest of the deal exceed any costs that might vex the agriculture minister.

If the respective trade ministers win these fights in Cabinet, a final deal can be struck. Sometimes, to save time, negotiators will even pre-agree different versions of the final text so that when ministers reach convergence in principle on the outstanding issues there is stabilised text ready to go and a smiling handshake can conclude the substantive portion of negotiations there and then.

Stage 9: Legal Scrub and Signature

With the text agreed by the negotiators, it must then be made ready for signature. For this to take place a process called 'the legal scrub' must occur. It is utterly horrific. Teams of lawyers from all parties lock themselves in a windowless hotel conference room somewhere and pore over the text word by word and line by line. In doing so they are not only fixing the formatting, paragraph numbering and so on but also looking to standardise some of the terms used and mutually agree that the text as written fully reflects the shared understanding of everyone involved on what was actually agreed. Participating in this is not something I would wish on my worst enemy, as spending weeks in a small room full of government lawyers retroactively litigating comma placement choices would for most people be a sub-basement of Dante's *Inferno* . . . and that's before you do it in multiple languages for the treaties that have legal force in several.

When the legal scrub is complete the text may or may not be released to the general public ahead of its formal signature by trade ministers or national leaders. It's important to understand that changing literally anything about the deal at this late stage is virtually impossible. Modifying so much as a single word in any substantive way would amount to reopening the text, with the other parties having every right to seek balancing concessions in exchange for whatever change you want. This effectively kicks the trade agreement back to somewhere around Stage 7 and is therefore almost unthinkable, except in the most extreme circumstance.

Once an agreement is signed, the parties may begin to apply it to one another provisionally even before it has been formally ratified through whatever domestic processes they have for such things. This means that, for example. traders may be able to begin taking advantage of the lower tariff rates the trade agreement delivers very soon after signature. It could also mean, as it did with CETA, the Canada-European Union Comprehensive Economic and Trade Agreement, that a deal is effectively in force for years despite ratification having been blocked or denied.

Stage 10: Ratification and More Implementation

The procedures under which a trade agreement negotiated by the government must be scrutinised, and whether it must be voted on by the legislature vary wildly. In most cases the operating assumption is that a trade agreement will have been negotiated with sufficient mind paid to the views of those who might have to ratify it to ensure there are no surprises at this late stage. Furthermore, rules that require the legislature to actually vote on ratifying a free trade agreement aren't ubiquitous. In some systems the role of the legislature is to scrutinise and debate a deal, but approval is automatic and no vote is required.

As an activist or other concerned stakeholder, ratification may offer an opportunity to block a trade agreement which contains provisions you find unacceptable. It can be an uphill battle, however. Even if your system does allow legislatures to reject a deal negotiated by the executive, this is quite hard to achieve. Members of whichever political party the leader is from will be reluctant to embarrass them by shooting down their trade deals and opposition legislators will want to avoid creating a precedent under which their own future deals could be blocked.

Even where an agreement isn't already provisionally enforced anyway, the denial of ratification is sometimes short-lived. A government whose trade deal is blocked by the opposition is far more likely to publicly sulk and bide their time for more favourable legislative math then they are to go back to the negotiating table to reopen a deal that's already been agreed, scrubbed, and signed.

That said, the ratification process, with its resultant media attention, does offer an opportunity to put your concerns about the deal to a wide audience and shape the narrative heading into future negotiations and even future governments. Media obsession and public attention is often a far more accurate determinant of red lines in a negotiation than any economic analysis.

Free Trade Agreements – Final Thoughts

Hopefully the above gives you a little insight into how free trade agreements are negotiated and some of the key points at which someone outside the negotiating team might look to influence their outcomes. I also hope it gave you some appreciation for the difficult work undertaken on your behalf by civil servants. Hidden behind the somewhat glib paragraphs above are weeks of 20-hour days, immense pressure from every side, and at times utterly impossible expectations.

Though I focused on free trade agreements, most of the above would apply equally to just about any negotiation between states. Bilateral Investment Treaties, for example, would be negotiated in almost the same way.

The best recommendations I can give to anyone who believes an upcoming trade negotiation will touch significantly on their interests are:

- To engage as early as possible, making your demands specific and putting on record the damage you feel the government would do if it ignored you;
- Build a constructive relationship with the negotiators themselves to incentivise them to view you as a resource and as someone who can help them at least minimise any downsides and, hopefully, accommodate your desires;
- Think about how to frame your concerns in the most concise and accessible format possible so that it resonates with political journalists and the general public;
- Treat with extreme scepticism anyone telling you that significantly improved outcomes could be achieved and seemingly intractable impasses overcome if only your negotiators were 'tougher'; and
- Remember that the people negotiating on your behalf are human beings and civil servants who believe they are serving their country to the best of their ability, not cartoonish villains wallowing in national sabotage at the behest of shadowy corporate overlords. So be nice.

Chapter 8
Trade Negotiation Secrecy

Boring Things We Do in the Shadows

Does the public deserve to watch us argue about comma placement? Politicians lie about trade all the time. Trade negotiations are secret. It would therefore be entirely reasonable to infer that trade negotiations are secret to help politicians lie about them. After all, if talks are secret then you can say just about anything about them and, unless there's a leak, no one will be able to prove you're lying until the deal is signed and published. In fact, even if a leak does occur you can simply question its veracity or refuse to engage with its contents citing a policy of never commenting on leaks. All of this would make a lot of sense, and it may be a minor factor behind trade negotiation secrecy, but it's not the primary one.

The Real Arguments for Secrecy

Three elements of a trade negotiation are generally kept secret:

1. The initial offers and requests the two (for the rest of this section I'm going to pretend trade negotiations are strictly bilateral purely to avoid adding 'or more' after every sentence) sides exchange. These are the starting points for the talks, a combination of 'opening bid' and 'wishlist' exchanged with the expectation that getting to a final deal will require both sides giving up more than they offered in their opening bid and receiving less than what was in their wishlist.
2. The 'working version' of the agreement text during negotiations.
3. The meetings and conversations that happen between the negotiating teams.

The logic behind keeping all three of these secret is the same: to provide the negotiators room to manoeuvre and experiment, and to stop the public from freaking out based on an incomplete picture.

Trade agreements require making choices between competing priorities and interests. Politicians and officials work to craft an agreement with their counterparts that is, overall (hopefully) good, and that they believe they can sell to the public as a 'win'. Inevitably though, any deal will include elements that make specific constituencies unhappy – even if the deal as a whole is a net vote winner. So for example, if Canada is negotiating a deal with Morocco, it may open up its textiles market (thus annoying Canadian textile manufacturers) but receive lower tariffs for Canadian dairy in exchange. The Canadian government's concern is that someone looking at the negotiation halfway through, or only examining the 'offer' side, could depict them as abandoning the interests of textile producers without putting that into the context of the 'win' on dairy. Governments want the ability to present an entire deal to the public at once, rather than having individual elements emerge bit by bit.

Chief negotiators also live in perpetual terror of having a microphone thrust in front of their minister for the question, 'Can you guarantee this deal won't...' – with the ellipses replaced by a defensive interest like weakening protection for the car industry or allowing in more foreign workers. In most cases the answer negotiators would prefer to hear from their minister is, 'We understand how sensitive that issue is and are treating it with every possible caution, but we will of course have to see what the other side is willing to put on the table.' This line signals to the other side that you're reluctant to give anything away on this issue, makes it clear that any movement will come at a high price, but it still leaves the door open if a juicy offer emerges. Ministers unfortunately are not always the most courageous beasts and have a tendency to blurt out vows of immobility so as to look decisive and avoid hard questioning. This robs negotiators of space within which to find a mutually acceptable deal, creating a bias for at least enough secrecy as to prevent reporters from being able to point to specific, textual requests by the other side in posing such questions.

Another concern for negotiators is that in many cases, both the initial requests and the working documents of an agreement under negotiation contain elements neither side considers remotely realistic. The general convention in a trade negotiation is that any side can add draft language to the working document in square brackets – which denote text that has yet to be agreed by all parties – and such square bracketed text can only be removed from the document by consensus. An agreement the UK was negotiating could include, until the final minutes of the final round, a paragraph of square bracketed text that would hand over Essex. Of course, the UK would never sign anything that included such a line, but that wouldn't be immediately obvious from the text. Someone looking at the draft agreement mid-way through would find a square bracketed paragraph handing Essex to Iceland – a paragraph visually indistinguishable from any other square bracketed text in the draft deal where the two sides are simply haggling over phrasing or yet to reach a deal on substance. Meanwhile, on the other side, the Icelanders would find themselves having to explain to a vocal 'give us Essex' constitutency why they folded on this issue, making it harder for them to drop the demand.

Now consider how this hyperbolic example would play out in the press if a copy of the negotiating text with '[Essex will now be ruled from Reykjavík]' were made public. First, the UK government faces a barrage of accusations that the trade deal is a secret plan to hand over Essex, which it will struggle to deny because it's in the text. Next the Icelandic ministers get microphones shoved in their faces, with demands they vow not to yield on the Essex question. Fearful of looking weak or inadequately championing Icelandic interests they double down. Suddenly a fringe demand included to appease a small domestic constituency or create some negotiating capital but which was never expected to make the final agreement becomes a major impasse neither side can give ground on without publicly breaking their word.

Even where the demands and requests are not outrageous, much of what is in a trade agreement is written in barely comprehensible legalese, dense tariff schedule attachments, and other impenetrable arcana. As a result, there is ample room for misunderstanding and misconception, and a sensationalised story can gain traction even in the face of a fact check or clarification from government officials (who may not be able to comment or dive into the details of a leaked text anyway).

Generally speaking, it's also the case that the larger, more formal and more public a meeting the less conducive it is to constructive negotiations. The willingness of a government representative to be creative, speak candidly, or take risks decreases exponentially with every additional set of eyeballs or the presence of a formal record. Smart, engaged and imaginative diplomats will, when sat behind a national flag at the United Nations with 191 other representatives, a formal record and a camera trained on them, suddenly lose all higher brain function and revert to reading verbatim the carefully vetted and committee-drafted statements their capital sent them. Then if there are questions, they'll read them again.

A lot of what negotiators actually do during negotiating rounds is experimentation. When faced with an impasse they package together different options, try different formulations of how a paragraph is written, and propose alternatives to what's on the table:

- 'What if instead of lowering your tariff on cars, you only did so on light trucks?'
- 'What if we phased in this provision over five years?'
- 'We can't legally commit to doing what you're asking for, but what if we committed to "trying"?'
- 'Would you be open to extending patent protection on music to 30 years if we agreed to drop our demand on literature protections to 15?'
- 'How about if instead of the language you're asking for, we used the text you agreed to in your recent agreement with Mexico?'

The assumption built into negotiations is that not everything a negotiator says at the table has been fully cleared and vetted with their own side, because that would completely gridlock discussions. Instead, negotiators might say, 'I have an idea that I think my side might go for, and if you think your side might be open to it, I'll go ask them and make sure.'

Inevitably, some of the things proposed in this manner are going to turn out to be non-starters even for the country of the negotiator who proposed them. If negotiations were conducted with an audience, these ideas would risk becoming national news scandals rather than what they are – thought balloons that, when scrutinised, popped harmlessly. The secrecy allows negotiators to throw things at the wall to see if they stick without fear of being dragged in front of the media to defend each and every experiment.

Somewhat relatedly, negotiators do at times have to be able to say things to one another that are candid in ways not conducive to an audience or a formal record. 'No matter how hard you push on flour tariffs, our minister isn't going to budge because she is from a marginal electorate with a big bread factory,' is the kind of statement that's really helpful to share with the other side (but no one else). So is one chief negotiator telling another that their services lead has gone off the rails and is causing problems, or not to stress too much about the current impasse over financial services because when push comes to shove the trade minister will win the argument in Cabinet and concede. Whether personal, political or strategic, these nuggets are not only intensely useful in clarifying sensitive matters, but in building the rapport and trust negotiators need in order to forge consensus. Now granted if the talks were televised, for example, negotiators could still find more private ways to share this kind of candid information, but that just brings us back to where we started.

The Counterargument

The problem with all the arguments laid out above is that they're predicated on a fairly dim view of the general public. The assumption they make is that people are too unsophisticated to recognise when something is merely the opening gambit of a negotiation, too blinkered to consider a concession in the wider context of a full deal or to recognise that just because something was floated as a possibility doesn't mean it's inevitable, likely, or even desirable. It assumes that the risks of bad faith actors taking limited or out-of-context information and presenting it misleadingly justify secrecy. It is without a doubt paternalistic and condescending regarding the collective intelligence of the general public.

It's also more than a little convenient. If a government follows the traditional negotiating secrecy model of only releasing the full text to the public once the deal has been signed, any negotiator will tell you it is generally too late to actually change anything in the deal. The negotiations are effectively concluded. The teams may have even been disbanded. The press has been briefed that a deal is done. To go back and request changes is virtually unthinkable, and would mean re-opening a precariously balanced agreement. It's rarely done. The government is therefore taking a complex package of hundreds of provisions, tariff lines and mini-deals and opening it up to public scrutiny at the point when (at most and not always) the legislature can vote to take it or leave it.

There is also a great and growing body of evidence that secrecy doesn't prevent many of the above problems, at least in the internet age. Negotiations like the Trade in Services Agreement were plagued by selective leaks of old negotiating texts to reporters utterly hostile to the deal who framed every paragraph in apocalyptic terms. Ironically in that instance, the secrecy surrounding negotiating texts not only failed to prevent these one-sided attacks but left the governments and negotiators unable to quell them. 'That's not what the deal does!' 'Oh yeah, what does it do?' 'We... can't tell you, but not that!' is not a winning formula for public engagement.

The European Union, having been scarred by endless accusations during the negotiations over the (failed) Transatlantic Trade and Investment Partnership with the United States became increasingly open and transparent in at least some of its trade negotiations. In negotiations with the United Kingdom over the Trade Continuity Agreement, for example, the EU released its negotiating mandate, draft versions of its ideal agreement, and at times the text as it stood at that point in the talks – with the UK doing the same. While this wasn't full transparency, and the actual negotiations remained strictly secret, it was significantly more openness than was common in the past. Whether this becomes a model for others to follow in the future remains an open question, but it is worth noting that a deal was reached despite the transparency and in the face of intense, hyper-partisan and not always good-faith or well-informed media attention on both sides of the English Channel.

Secrecy: Good or Bad?

As with a lot of questions in trade, and public policy, there's probably a balance to strike around the secrecy in trade negotiations. My experience in the room tells me that we simply wouldn't make any progress if every discussion was televised or took place in front of a large audience. We would either achieve nothing or find ways to move our talks to informal and private channels. I'm also inclined to think that more transparency around negotiating texts would not be fatal, which in democratic societies at least should be an argument for greater openness.

Those operating in bad faith or from a deeply ideological position will not be thwarted in attacks on a government's negotiating agenda by secrecy. Even in the absence of leaks they can speculate, infer from public statements, or quote 'concerns' about what a trade deal might do. Not giving the negotiating team and the media office the ability to pull out the actual draft text and say, 'That's not true, here's the language on it and what we're currently arguing about' is hindering the pushback, not preventing the attacks.

Negotiators and government officials more generally can grow to be pretty cynical about transparency and the public discourse. Being in government breeds a bunker mentality – a perception that you and your colleagues are beset on all sides by bad faith actors waiting to attack you, and sensationalist journalists looking to exploit or distort your every utterance. It is easy to grow scathing about the general public's appetite for nuance, or attention span for complexity. My personal horrifically naive view is that transparency and good communication may be harder than secrecy and manoeuvring, but are still worth trying. If we lose the argument anyway, that's on us.

Chapter 9
The World Trade Organization

Sorry But It's a Trade Book - It Was Going to Come Up

The World Trade Organization or WTO is both a set of international treaties between (at the time of writing) 164 economies and the international organisation where their representatives negotiate changes to treaties, discuss how to implement them and settle disagreements about what they mean.

With all love and respect, the WTO is not something the average person should be thinking about daily, weekly or even monthly. It is important in the manner of the Universal Postal Union: what it does is vital and many smart and dedicated people work very hard at and around its Swiss headquarters, but you're probably safe ignoring it most of the time.

Unfortunately, the WTO does get semi-frequently invoked, attacked or lavishly over-praised by politicians and other vociferous actors in the melodrama of our political discourse. Cast alternatively as villain or saviour, it is almost always semi-submerged in a soup of exaggeration, hyperbole or deception. Since this book aims to help you swerve past this kind of trade-related nonsense, indulge me as I provide the basics.

What is the WTO?

The WTO is a 'member-driven' intergovernmental organisation. Each of those signifiers is important, but easiest understood if you take them individually, backwards.

- It's an *organisation* because it is a permanent, standing entity with a staff called a secretariat, a headquarters, and a budget.
- It is *intergovernmental* because it exists almost exclusively to resolve issues between governmental actors – membership is only open to governments (though not all members are 'countries' as the UN defines them. The European Union, Hong Kong, Macau and Taiwan are represented because each is considered to control their own customs territory), and participation is reserved for government representatives with delegations lead by 'Permanent Representatives' that are functionally ambassadors, and comprising 'delegates' that are functionally diplomats. Neither the private sector nor civil society has any meaningful standing within the World Trade Organization and can't even attend its meetings.
- It is *member-driven* because all major decisions have to be made and initiated by its member governments. The staff of the organisation, from the Director-General down, have limited authority and serve at the pleasure of the membership.

The WTO exists because by 1994, the volume and complexity of international trade agreements had outgrown the more modest secretariat which previously supported the General Agreement on

Tariffs and Trade (the GATT). The GATT, which was already a complex agreement, was expanded with additional treaties and commitments in areas such as agriculture, intellectual property and investment, as well as a permanent dispute settlement system with a standing body of adjudicators to hear and issue final rulings on appeals. Moreover, this was all seen as just the beginning. Governments envisioned an ambitious forward agenda to keep evolving these rules, standing committees to discuss how they were being implemented and high level ministerial meetings to provide political guidance and calendar milestones for which negotiators could aim to deliver key outcomes. All of this would require a large, capable and permanent staff.

What is it Actually for?

In earlier chapters, we discussed at some length why governments felt the need to negotiate and sign on to the rules that comprise the WTO, but what is the organisation itself there for? It has three core objectives of which some get a lot more press attention than others, and while reasonable people can disagree about their comparative importance, all three are integral to the WTO's work.

Function 1: 'Negotiating'

As I mentioned above, while the treaties that collectively make up the World Trade Organization legal canon are extensive, they were always intended to be a starting point for further talks. The idea was that government representatives would continue talking and negotiate changes to either the scope of individual agreements (how much they cover), or their depth (how meaningful they are) – or negotiate entirely new agreements.

Critically, because the World Trade Organization's rules are legally binding on its members, decisions were expected to be arrived at by consensus – that way no WTO member could ever find itself being held to a rule it hated. While technically the WTO rules do allow for the possibility of a vote, members avoid this like the plague. Few believe that larger members especially would remain in an organisation which could impose legally binding rules changes upon them against their wishes. While individual voices do at times raise the possibility of voting, especially when one or a small group of members block what is seen as a pressing and important outcome, the organisation has thus far avoided direct democracy and is likely to continue doing so, no matter the costs in paralysis.

Because any change or addition to the WTO rules is legally enforceable, every syllable and comma could have significant implications when picked apart by top legal minds in a trade dispute. This makes the 'stakes' of a negotiation in the WTO very high, both in terms of the substance and how that substance is captured in the legal text. Many governments are naturally conservative when it comes to proposals to change the foundational rules of global trade, and paranoid about missing some legalistic nuance in the text which creates a loophole for their trading partners or an unforseen obligation upon themselves. It is therefore devilishly difficult, and vanishingly rare for the WTO's membership, to find an idea on which they can all agree in principle, and to then arrive at a legal text capturing it which all parties can live with.

Advancing even the most modest, innocuous, non-binding feel-good proposal can take months, or years. Delegates will begin cautiously and informally, meeting over coffee with counterparts to float an idea and begin sensitising counterparts to it. They'll circulate non-papers, an absurd WTO invention consisting of a document that lays out some thought or idea but which its proponents want to make very clear is not a formal proposal worth getting worked up over. Eventually, if they are bold, they may circulate a paper [*horror movie music*] that formally tables their intention to *do something* and may even suggest what that would be - all before formally tabling a proposal with the proposed legal language.

Just getting to the proposal stage can take months of painstaking engagement, drafting, redrafting and negotiating as the advocates of an idea work to accommodate the concerns and feedback they hear from the membership. It's a slow, laborious process often conducted in the face of scepticism, criticism and alarmist warnings from at least a few delegations who either hate the idea itself, hate all ideas they aren't themselves championing, or just hate you personally. Once a legal text is actually on the table, the difficulty level goes up another notch. Now not only must you overcome principle objections but legal ones, with any modification to the text potentially creating fresh problems for those you thought were already backing you.

The sheer nightmare of the process demands that negotiators have a place to meet, a secretariat to help them manage their meetings, and, when required, the input of neutral experts. The WTO and its secretariat of international civil servants exist to provide all three. Moreover, the WTO Director-General themselves can help bring people together and engage politically, remaining neutral on what an outcome should be but nudging everyone toward consensus. Finally, given that most of the delegates to the World Trade Organization are diplomats on comparatively short three to five year postings, the WTO secretariat can provide an invaluable source of institutional memory and negotiating history, able to explain why a rule looks the way it does.

In practice, the WTO channels much of this function through negotiating committees – formal and regularly scheduled meetings of the membership on thematic issues or individual negotiating topics whose job it is to iron out the disagreements and eventually present ministers or their proxies with a consensus proposal the entire membership can get behind. These committees are served by their own dedicated staff within the secretariat, many of whom have been working on the underlying issues for decades.

Negotiations are probably the most visible and commonly discussed aspects of the WTO's work – but the WTO's record on reaching consensus outcomes is lacklustre. For decades, members have largely disagreed on some fundamental questions like whether trade rules are good for economic growth or the equity of the existing agreements – and growing complexities around climate change and geostrategic competition are complicating things further. Moreover the driving force behind the creation of much of the GATT and WTO agreements had been wealthy countries trading improved access to their markets for getting to write the rules of the game, and occasionally bullying other states into falling in line. That era appears over, with the US and EU in particular neither having much market access left to give nor being willing to unilaterally offer what remains to strengthen the global system. At the same time, large emerging economies like China, India, South Korea, Indonesia, Brazil, Argentina and South Africa became far larger and more assertive players in the international trade conversation, further complicating the path toward consensus. Still, the WTO continues to provide the space for proposals new and old to be tested, discussed and negotiated, and the support required to give them a fighting chance.

Accessions

Historically, the most important negotiations at the WTO houses have been about who joins, and under what terms. By the end of 1995, the year the WTO came into being, the organisation had 112 members and since then more than 50, including giants like China and the Russian Federation, have joined through a negotiating process known as 'accession'.

This effort, which takes years, sees a prospective WTO member negotiating with the entire existing membership, effectively bidding for a spot in the organisation by offering access to its market and making commitments on its trade regime. A single WTO member can block an accession indefinitely, so each one has to be fully satisfied it has received its pound of flesh. The end result of these negotiations, if successful, sees a new state joining the WTO under the terms agreed, including adopting all the existing WTO rules they didn't negotiate an exemption from and combining all the best market access offers it made in all of those individual negotiations into one offer everyone gets access to. In other words, if in order to join you promised the Bolivians that you would lower your tariff on yachts to 5 per cent and the Norwegians you would lower your tariff on jeans to 10 per cent, you would have to cap your yacht and jeans tariffs at 5 and 10 per cent respectively for all WTO members upon joining.

While making of new rules at the WTO has largely dried up, accession negotiations have brought hundreds of millions of citizens into the system, generating rare outbreaks of good news.

Function 2: 'Monitoring'

The rather ominous sounding second function of the World Trade Organization is the least well known, but potentially the most important. As the custodian organisation for the treaties that make up the international rules-based trading system, the WTO effectively overseas hundreds of pages of legal commitments on everything from how a customs official can go about pricing goods for levying tariffs to what kind of subsidy a government can give to its industries.

To make matters more difficult, the level of ambiguity in these rules varies wildly. Some are comparatively straightforward and clear, such as, 'your cheese tariff will not exceed 10 per cent' and some leave a vast amount of room for interpretation and debate, like 'Your regulation must have a legitimate purpose and not be a disguised restriction on trade.' Add on top of this the potential for problematic issues to arise from the policies or behaviour of actors at the sub-national level, like specific port authorities, state or local officials, and there emerges vast scope for rule-breaking as a result of ignorance, miscommunication or honest disagreement about what implementing the rules means in practice.

The dispute settlement system, which we'll get to in a moment, exists to resolve disagreements if they prove intractable and the aggrieved party is sufficiently motivated to take on the effort and cost of seeing a legal case through. However, dispute settlement was never intended as the first, second or even third resort. Ideally, WTO members are supposed to resolve their disagreements about what proper implementation of the rules looks like through transparency, discussion and engagement, not litigation. The monitoring function of the WTO exists to provide structure and support for this effort and it does so in a few different ways.

By far the least sexy are the transparency and notification requirements. Basically, if you as a government change your trade regime by say, introducing a new measure to protect animal health or a new technical regulation about the number of wheels allowed on a truck, the WTO rules oblige you to promptly inform the rest of the membership about it by submitting a 'notification'. This is tedious to prepare and tedious to go through, but is also the sort of thing that's integral to transparency and a vaguely predictable international system. The WTO mandates and encourages this practice, provides a forum for discussing the content of notifications, and through the secretariat does its best to disseminate what members submit in slightly more readable formats.

A more interesting manifestation of the monitoring function is a Trade Policy Review. Put very simply, once every few years the WTO Secretariat does a tonne of research and writes a comprehensive report on absolutely everything about how your trade regime works. That report feeds into a meeting where any WTO member is allowed to ask you anything about your trade regime, including just criticising you archly, and you are obliged (albeit largely unenforceably except by norms and public shaming) by the WTO rules to provide accurate responses. Governments going through this process tend to take it seriously, sending high level officials to the meeting itself and devoting considerable resources to coming up with answers (and sometimes, non-answers) to the hundreds or even thousands of questions they receive from the membership. It is perhaps an underutilised tool, but a strangely egalitarian one, allowing Samoa or Lesotho to demand answers of giants like the United States, EU or China.

Finally in monitoring, the so-called 'regular committees' of the WTO are dedicated meetings on thematic areas like goods, services, technical barriers to trade, development, customs valuation and agriculture. They offer an opportunity to discuss issues, to engage other members and to raise questions about their trading regimes. They offer a stress release valve, letting members air their grievances with one another in a formalised setting and with an understanding that disagreements can be intense but not confrontational. At their best, these regular committees give members the opportunity to hear feedback on their policies, better understand how they impact others and make adjustments where feasible – avoiding acrimony or lengthy dispute settlement.

Function 3: 'Dispute Settlement'

If a member believes that another's trade regime is operating in ways forbidden by their WTO obligations, it can make use of the WTO's formalised system of dispute settlement. This entails a sequence of steps, beginning with a period of consultations and proceeding into increasingly legalistic procedures and potentially ultimately ending with a ruling from the Appellate Body which both sides are obligated by the WTO treaties to treat as binding and final.

For those not familiar with international law, it's worth stressing how remarkable that last part is. As a rule, governments are not fans of signing treaties that open the door to a future panel of law nerds ruling their policies illegal, and that oblige them to treat that ruling as binding. The GATT had dispute settlement procedures too, including panels that could issue opinions on the legality of the measure in question, though these were purely optional. Even the GATT member whose measure was being challenged was well within its rights to oppose a panel being convened, or even to allow it to deliberate and then block the adoption and circulation of its findings. Effectively, dispute settlement under the GATT was kind of optional.

Despite this fairly obvious loophole, the GATT's dispute settlement system was for decades actually quite well utilised. Even having a panel rule against you wasn't seen as the end of the world, as it provided a face-saving way for governments to withdraw a policy while blaming something beyond their control. As the decades rolled on however, the substance of trade disputes became more politicised and members began increasingly either blocking the formation of panels, or refusing to accept their conclusions when those proved unfavourable, because the rules gave them that option.

The creation of the WTO and its Appellate Body in 1995 changed all that. By signing on, WTO members gave away their rights to prevent a panel being formed, and if they lost a case, agreed to either implement panel findings or appeal them to the newly created Appellate Body for legal review – the results of which they would be obliged to consider binding. This is a big deal, especially when you consider the potential sums involved. The long-running disputes between the US and EU over the legality of their subsidies for (respectively) Boeing and Airbus cost around $100 million each in legal costs to fight and saw the Appellate Body ultimately authorise the US to impose punishing tariffs on $7.5 billion worth of EU products every year (the EU were also allowed to retaliate, albeit at a lower rate).

It cannot be stated often enough that the WTO does not actually want to see litigation and punishments. The dispute settlement system is designed to try to avoid disagreements rising to the level of requiring legal review, with that legal review offering an alternative to more traditional power politics as a way of determining whose interpretation of the rules is correct. If at any time the parties to a dispute can resolve it amicably or come to some sort of arrangement, the WTO is happy.

The Appellate Body – We Hardly Knew Ye
At the time of writing, the WTO Appellate Body is functionally dead. Appellate Body arbitrators serve fixed four-year terms, and

are approved by consensus, with even a single member able to block any appointment. Under the Trump Administration the US, which had long had gripes with the Appellate Body, started blocking all appointments. By the end of 2019 the WTO Appellate Body simply lacked the necessary three arbitrator quorum to take up cases. The Biden Administration did not reverse this policy on taking office in 2021 and while the WTO membership agreed to begin a reform process of the organisation in 2022, including dispute settlement, i an outcome that reinstates the Appellate Body is far from certain.

The reasons for the US blockade are still contested. Formally, the US has laid out a range of complaints ranging from the time taken to resolve disputes to what it sees as 'activism' by the Appellate Body – which it accuses of inventing new trade law never envisioned by members when they signed the treaties and of relying excessively on its own precedent rather than treating every case with fresh eyes. Informally, many suspect the US may just find the concept of binding judicial review of its trade policies unpalatable, especially as it gears up for a century defined by geostrategic competition with China. Competition in which trade is not always wielded in strict accordance with treaty obligations.

Whatever US motivations were, the end result is a gaping loophole in the system. Any member who finds a panel ruling against them can claim they have legal issues with its ruling and appeal it to an Appellate Body that does not exist and thus cannot hear the case – thus consigning it to a legal void. This has not thus far led to the complete collapse of human civilisation, but it is considered a big blow to the system.

Members have responded in different ways. A sub-group including big players like the EU and China (but not the US) have signed up to an alternative appellate system for deciding cases among themselves, with its own pool of mutually agreed arbitrators not subject to a US veto. Others have tried to resolve disputes either at or before the panel stage, or vowed to treat panel reports as binding even if they are appealed (though one suspects their enthusiasm for this approach will vary on whether the panel sides with them). A handful of cases have already been appealed into the void, remaining unresolved.

The WTO membership continues to make use of the dispute settlement system even without its crowning jewel of an Appellate Body. Still, the WTO enters into the third decade of the 21st Century bereft of a way to issue binding rulings on its own laws, just as political tides are turning against them. This combined with the disappointing performance of the negotiating function, questionable compliance by major players, and the open hostility of populists, has been the cause of many a sleepless night in lakeside Geneva.

Everything Else WTO

Negotiation, monitoring and dispute settlement are the three traditional pillars of the WTO, but the organisation has evolved into a larger beast that makes contributions in other ways, too. The WTO secretariat is home to some of the world's foremost economists and analysts, producing a wealth of public data and reports on all aspects of trade policy. It is a significant training provider, upskilling government officials in developing economies on trade policy, the WTO rules, and how to better participate in the system.

The WTO is a major player in the Aid for Trade Initiative, which seeks to use overseas development assistance to support the gainful participation of poorer countries, disadvantaged groups and others in international trade – and hosts several development initiatives itself. The WTO Director-General is a major public figure who participates at major events held by institutions like the G20, the OECD and the WEF, and the WTO itself offers considerable convening power for high-level meetings on issues like unclogging supply chains during the Covid-19 pandemic.

None of the above are mission critical and the globe would keep spinning if the WTO were to abandon any or all of them, but they are tasks being done by smart and hardworking people, so I list them here as a kind of palate cleanser before diving into the sewers of political deception around the WTO.

Actually being a WTO member entails participation in all of the above, though the level of engagement varies wildly between delegations. Some very well resourced or engaged missions will send someone to every meeting, join as a third-party in every dispute settlement proceeding and frequently raise issues, make proposals or otherwise engage. On the other side of the spectrum some don't even have any formal representation in Geneva, 'covering' the WTO from a regional embassy like Brussels, London, Berlin, Paris or Bern.

Lies by the Lake – Wrong About the WTO

People don't talk about the WTO a lot, but when they do they often say some things that are either false, misleading or incomplete. A non-exhaustive list is below.

'The WTO is undemocratic. No one elects the Director-General!'

This is silly for two reasons. First, the Director-General of the WTO is appointed to the role by consensus. When there is a vacancy (Directors-General can serve a maximum of two four-year terms) any member can nominate a candidate, but no one can become Director-General if even a single WTO member objects. If someone is Director-General that means that at some point in the last four years every democratic (and undemocratic, for that matter) government represented at the WTO approved their application. That's about as democratic as it gets short of sending a ballot to six billion people.

Second, the Director-General exercises virtually no formal authority over trade or trade policy. They are the head of a secretariat that serves the membership, and carry some moral authority, but they are not empowered to make any decisions about what the rules of international trade are, what they should be, or how anyone implements them.

'The WTO is biased against our country'

This could mean a lot of things. It could be an argument that the WTO as an institution is biased against your national interest. This is a complex claim. Certainly the people working within the WTO secretariat have their own prejudices and ideologies, as do the different Director-Generals and Appellate Body members. Moreover the institution itself has a culture, and a definite internal bias toward the fundemental premise of the organisation (that multilateral trade rules are good, and that governments should abide by them and seek to agree more). Yet even by the standards of other intergovernmental organisations, the WTO secretariat has very little actual authority, and is fastidious about maintaining both its neutrality and perception of neutrality.

It could also be an argument that the WTO membership continually gangs up on you whether by criticising your policies in committees, shooting down your proposals, or tabling proposals designed to target you. This is entirely possible, but it's hardly the WTO's fault. Any international organisation run by government representatives is going to see blocs emerge and temporary and permanent alliances form. Sometimes that will mean you're left standing almost alone against the world. Sometimes you'll deserve it.

It could be an argument that the WTO rules themselves are written in a way that disavantages you. WTO rules, like any instrument, will inevitably benefit some WTO members more than others (though not always the same ones). This may well be a legitimate gripe, but is probably far more accurately explained by power dynamics or error than by any systemic bias. At some point, your government signed up to each and every WTO rule – either because it thought the rule was fine at the time, because it felt the sacrifice was worth the gain, or because it didn't read the small print. The end result may be unjust, but bias is unlikely to be the cause and the WTO unlikely to be the culprit.

Finally it could be an argument about the dispute settlement system, effectively asserting that either panels or the Appellate Body are unfair in how they judge cases where your country is concerned. This is a difficult charge to answer, as legal rulings are inherently at least somewhat subjective and there is no expectation that a WTO member should win 50 per cent of cases it's involved in. Moreover, the costs and headaches involved in bringing a dispute tend to make cases somewhat self-selecting because claimants tend to avoid bringing a dispute unless they have strong confidence they'll win.

'That's illegal and the WTO won't allow it'

This is the sort of thing people shout about policies they don't like, relying on the listener's automatic association of 'illegal' with the domestic justice system and all that entails.

First, the WTO itself is in no way empowered to rule anything legal or illegal. A secretariat staffer may, if asked, give you their personal opinion about the likely compliance of a policy with the rules, but that's just like [their] opinion . . . man. Even the most blatant violation of the WTO rules is not considered as such until a member has taken issue with it, consultations have been held, a panel has been convened and potentially an appeal held on its ruling.

Second, even if a member does raise the issue and the legal proceedings rule in its favour, the WTO can't actually make anyone do anything. Even when the Appellate Body still functioned, the most it could do was issue a ruling telling you that you were in breach of your commitments and, if you failed to bring your policies into compliance, that the member who launched the dispute could levy tariffs on your products up to the value of the harm your breach of the rules did to their exports. At that point, you can just choose to accept those tariffs and keep your 'illegal' policy. No one can make you. The WTO rules do not allow for fines, arrests or even expulsion from the organisation.

'The WTO rules are preventing us from...'

One of the key advantages for governments of being a member of the WTO is having a vast and incomprehensible-to-most rulebook they can point to as the villain thwarting popular policy requests they themselves don't want to implement. WTO treaties do indeed include commitments not to craft policies in certain ways, but the temptation for governments is to pretend such commitments extend to whatever they don't feel like doing that day.

The fact is, the WTO rules are actually fairly flexible – and in most cases even if a specific policy might run contrary to them, it could be adjusted or reinvented to achieve largely the same results without much amendment. Government lawyers can and do frequently find ways around even what might be considered fairly clear rules, and their refusal to do so for you probably speaks more to the government's appetite for your cause than the intractability of the WTO rulebook.

There are also broad exemptions one can invoke in defending a policy against charges of being a WTO rule violator. While legal scholars debate the breadth of these exemptions in areas like health, public morality or security, that hasn't stopped members from invoking them. From 2018 the United States began relentlessly invoking the security exemption to justify all manner of legally questionable policy action, relying on the broadest possible reading of that exemption's text which amounts to, 'Vital security interests are exempt and vital security interests are whatever we say they are, shut up.'

'We don't need free trade agreements or regional integration, we can trade on WTO terms!'

I suppose this could theoretically be true, but it probably isn't. The World Trade Organization rules represent a baseline: the bare minimum of equitable treatment all its 164 members have agreed to offer all the others. Free trade agreements and regional integration build on that baseline precisely because that baseline is often quite poor. Put another way, if you are exporting to someone under WTO rules you are doing so under the same restrictions as those they put in place against the foreign supplier about whom they are most paranoid. You may be lucky and find that all the products you want to export just happen to be those without barriers, but you're probably not that fortunate. Moreover, your exporters will have to compete at a disadvantage against those from foreign countries which do have a free trade agreement.

The reason various trade agreements and regional integration schemes have proliferated is that even when the WTO stalled on agreeing new tariff cuts or new agreements, clumps of countries decided they could go further. They found ways to offer better terms to one another, precisely because they could do so without having to extend those terms to everyone in the WTO or wait for their consensus.

'The WTO is just the neoliberal puppet of big corporations!'

It wishes. If major corporations were still so invested in the World Trade Organization and its work that they spent the vast resources required to subvert its processes and bind the organisation to their will, that would probably be a win for the WTO on relevance grounds alone. It would mean that big business still considers the conversations taking place at the WTO to be vitally important – something top executives at major firms will state if asked, but often with all the enthusiasm and spontaneity of a political candidate attending their 93rd community town hall visit in three months. Large corporations certainly benefit from there being a rules-based trading system, but most are largely tuned out of it.

Many would be shocked to learn how few trade lobbyists there are in Geneva - compared to Washington D.C. or Brussels. The shadowy corporate overlords one imagines pulling the strings on the world economy tend to 'cover' the WTO by having someone in

Brussels or London spend about 1 per cent of their time on it. Such part-timers turn up once or twice a year to attend major events with the bemused and mildly horrified 'what's all this then?' air of an English constable arriving on the scene of an out of control food fight at the local clown college.

This is not to say that corporate interests aren't pursued by the WTO. Given the choice most corporations would prefer a stable, predictable global economy and the multilateral rules are a step in that direction. While there are likely to be corporate interests on both sides of any individual proposal at the WTO, the underlying thesis of a world where protectionism is restricted and trade policy is predictable is broadly attractive to business. Governments certainly had this in mind when they negotiated the rules in the first place.

There is also something to the argument that businesses are more effective at lobbying governments on WTO issues, and trade generally, than civil society. Most WTO issues move painfully slowly, are intensely legalistic and require a great deal of technical expertise to understand. This favours big corporations with deep pockets that can afford to hire advocates who speak the WTO's language, can maintain sustained engagement and know how to formulate proposals in ways that won't fall foul of laws or norms. With the possible exception of large and well organised labour unions, most civil society organisations simply can't match that. To the extent that corporations are effective in impacting the WTO's agenda however, it is primarily because they can shape the conversation on trade in major capitals – not because they're whispering into the ear of the Nepalese First Secretary on her way into the Committee on Trade in Goods.

As an organisation with very little power or authority, the WTO is primarily the venue, conduit and facilitator for discussions among the state membership. As such it is a puppet of neoliberal corporate interests to pretty much the same degree as national governments –

perhaps less so because the consensus requirement for its decisions means even a single member can thwart a corporate agenda in a way that may not be possible nationally or regionally.

Chapter 10
Trade Integration: Customs Unions

The process of regionally integrating economies, creating customs unions or even single markets, aligning regulations, signing a web of treaty obligations and creating processes and even courts to manage them is constant. Always controversial, it raises questions about democracy, national sovereignty and the benefits of collective action versus competition. To name just one example, the referendum in the United Kingdom on whether to leave the European Union, and the subsequent negotiations over the future trading relationship, dominated public debate in the UK for years.

I don't think it's useful to relitigate the Brexit debate in these pages as it is both a moot point at this stage and inseparable from the personalities, past positions and current ambitions of the main actors within Britain's cavalcade of political weirdness. What is more valuable is to try and explain, as neutrally as possible, the reasons some governments choose to pursue trade integration, what that entails, and why it raises concerns about sovereignty and democracy.

Over the last few chapters I have tortured you with the description of – and motivation for – government intervention in interstate commerce. In addition to lasting regret that you picked up my book instead of a murder mystery, I'm hoping you came away with both an appreciation of the complexity of trade bureaucracy, and of the incentives governments have to maintain its complexity. I suspect you also came away with an inevitable conclusion: that all this adds costs. Because it does.

Every time a product has to cross a border, with its inherent hefty bureaucracy and potentially tariffs, someone has to do the paperwork and pay the taxes required. The more border crossings a final product's components had to undertake, the more those costs burgeon. This is a problem because economics tells us that the smartest way to allocate resources is for different places to specialise in making different things, leaning into local advantages and producing at a more efficient scale. This encourages building a complex supply chain across multiple countries, but any efficiencies can be lost if the costs of moving components across borders exceed the savings gained.

Really big countries can replicate some of these benefits without trading. The United States can combine raw materials from the Rocky Mountains with machining in Detroit to build designs created by hipster artists in Portland, fill them with chips made at Intel's Oregon factory, parts from all over the Midwest and finance it all by raising capital on the New York Stock Exchange – all without crossing a national border. Yet most countries aren't nearly as large or internally economically diverse as the United States, and must therefore choose between limiting their supply chain to whatever is available domestically, or absorbing the costs of sourcing higher value products abroad.

So what can be done? If the problem is the cost of borders then the obvious solution would be to reduce those costs. If there are no regulations to navigate, tariffs to pay, or forms to fill in, then all the associated expenditures in time and money cease to be an issue. Except as we've discussed in the previous chapters, it's not so simple. Nation states often insist upon tariffs, checks, paperwork and regulations, and have good reasons for doing so.

The answer many governments around the world have arrived at is regional integration – projects like the European Union, Eurasian Economic Union, Mercosur, and the African Continental Free Trade Area. These are gradual, imperfect and not always linear attempts to replicate in a multi-nation region the ease with which a large country like the United States allows goods to circulate, harnessing the competitive advantages and specialisations of its diverse regions without the hassle of border crossings.

More than a Free Trade Agreement

Modern Free Trade Agreements have grown to encompass many supplementary topics, from women's economic empowerment to environmental protection, and we'll take a look at these in subsequent chapters, but at their core they remain about market access: cutting tariffs. They were designed to address a very specific need – countries wanting to exchange lower tariff access among themselves than they were willing to give the rest of the world. That has its limitations.

In the *Moving Goods Across Borders* chapter we identified a number of pain points for traders. The tariff that needs to be paid to the importing government, while potentially a serious or even insurmountable barrier, isn't the only one. Free trade agreements don't eliminate the need to register as a trader, to manage export restrictions and sanctions, or to correctly classify your products in accordance with a hideously complex tariff code system. In fact, for those traders looking to take advantage of their tariff benefits, they actually make the paperwork burden at the border more onerous by requiring Rules of Origin documentation which demonstrates the provenance and eligibility of the goods for a trade agreement's lower tariff rate.

As lower tariff rates globally have made the cuts delivered by a trade agreement sound less impressive, politicians have started claiming that modern agreements are about cutting regulatory barriers. But the extent to which they can smooth the regulatory compliance step is often limited. For the vast majority of traders, regulatory compliance under a free trade agreement looks pretty darn similar to before. Put far too simply: trade agreements are primarily about cutting taxes at the border. Regional integration, by contrast, is about reducing the need for a border in the first place.

There are two primary ways regional integration efforts go about this mission, one focused on tariffs and all the paperwork requirements around them, and one focused on regulations and the need to test or otherwise prove compliance with them. If you can get these two right with your neighbour, you can vastly reduce the formalities of international trade to the extent that you no longer need to consider goods going to them to be exports. This is the case inside the EU, for example. Yet the road to get there is long, arduous and comes with sacrifices – economic, political and sovereign. In this chapter we'll look at the tariff and tariff paperwork half of the equation: customs unions.

Removing Tariffs and Tariff Bureaucracy from the Equation

If my country and your country signed a free trade agreement eliminating all tariffs on every product type without exception, we would still need customs declarations and full tariff classification on goods moving across our mutual borders. Why? Because I can't trust that goods entering your market and then making their way into mine paid the tariffs they would have paid if they had entered my market directly – and I also can't trust that something crossing into my territory from yours actually originated there.

Let's conjure up an example. Your country has a long cultural history of growing papayas, a form of agriculture critical to the livelihoods of many of your citizens and their communities. You know there are cheaper sources of papaya abroad, but you consider the papaya sector so vital that you have imposed a tariff at the border to keep your own homegrown papaya sector competitive. Your next-door neighbour produces only a few luxury papayas, so doesn't directly compete with your more egalitarian and commercially accessible 'people's papayas'. That's why, when you negotiated a free trade agreement with it, you agreed to eliminate your papaya tariff. Your neighbour's industry is no threat to the bulk of your producers and your high-end restaurants benefit from access to its more refined fruit.

Yet now you face a problem. Because your neighbour is much less interested in growing papayas than you, it slaps a much lower tariff on them. It is also far more relaxed about trading away that smaller tariff when negotiating free trade agreements with others, even if they are large papaya producers. This means that if you want to stop a flood of cheap foreign papayas entering your market via your neighbour, you need border checks to ensure that any papayas claiming to be from your neighbour were actually grown there. While eliminating the tariff, your free trade agreement hasn't eliminated papaya customs bureaucracy. It may even have made it worse.

Granted, governments could simply choose to ignore the risk of someone bypassing their tariffs through this kind of backdoor arbitrage, but both states would have to be comfortable with it or you would end up with a situation where there is effectively only a border one way. If you don't care if third countries are exploiting your free trade agreement to bring in stuff tariff-free, but the other country does, it will demand tariff declarations and Rules of Origin (even if you don't). That means your traders are going to find themselves at a massive disadvantage because they'll be the only ones facing border tariff paperwork. Effectively, both sides will have eliminated tariffs but just one will still face bureaucracy.

Moreover, the industries that your third-country tariffs were meant to protect are unlikely to remain silent in the face of suddenly finding themselves unprotected. Effectively giving third countries full liberalisation into your market without getting anything in return is a hard argument to sell to your furious large producers – who are probably politically potent and well-represented.

As a government looking to facilitate trade with a neighbour you therefore have two competing incentives: you don't want goods coming in from that neighbour to pay tariffs or deal with customs paperwork, but you're not ready to risk their territory becoming a backdoor into your market for products from abroad that you have tariffs on but they do not. The solution is called a 'customs union'.

A customs union is an agreement where two or more countries agree that they are all going to have no tariffs on one another, and the same tariffs on everyone else. You can think of it like rides at Disneyland. Once you have entered the park via one of the gates and bought a ticket you can wander about freely to all the areas and ride anything you want without being challenged for your ticket. Disneyland can do this because all the rides are included in the price of admittance. If every ride and part of the park had its own price, Disney would need checkpoints or turnstiles everywhere. A customs union works on a similar principle.

If every country in the customs union is applying the exact same tariffs, there's no way you can sidestep the tariffs of one customs union country by entering the union through another. This means there's no need for goods moving inside the customs union to prepare painful Rules of Origin declarations because any goods moving between countries inside a customs union either originated in it (and are tariff free), or paid all the required tariffs when entering the customs union.

Costs of a Customs Union

There is a price to pay for the benefits of a customs union. Having the same tariff across the entire customs union means that no individual member nation can unilaterally change its tariff regime or lower tariffs through free trade agreements. Any such decision has to be made collectively because as soon as one customs union member has tariffs different from the rest, the whole enterprise collapses. In practice, joining or being in a customs union could mean being bullied into an undesirable tariff regime by a bigger neighbour, or endless lowest common denominator negotiations as consensus is forged among peer powers.

Even the large, dominant player in a region that's trying to create a customs union has to deal with the strongest sensitivities of smaller neighbours. Germany and France in Europe, Russia in the Eurasian Economic Union, or Brazil in Mercosur have considerable sway, but even they can only push the smaller states so far before facing a revolt. That means the tariffs inside a customs union are never exactly what any one member would levy if they were in sole control. Similarly, if these blocs negotiate trade agreements they must do so collectively, based on an agreed compromise position. This can mean a trade agreement languishes at the negotiation stage because the niche sensitivity of one customs union member, unshared by the rest, clashes with a red line of the party the customs union is negotiating with.

Such collective decision making also inevitably raises concerns about democracy and sovereignty. A government that signs up to a customs union is effectively outsourcing a portion of its policymaking to an international collective. Any worthwhile customs union would include legally binding commitments by its members to avoid unilaterally adjusting tariffs or withdrawing from the union without providing ample notice. Decisions about a country's import taxes and free trade agreements will therefore be influenced by representatives not answerable directly or indirectly to the voters or interests of that country.

Theoretically of course, the sovereignty is still there. Not only can any country pull out of a customs union if it wishes, but a government could order its customs officials to set up checkpoints and start collecting tariffs on its borders. Diplomatically and economically, the consequences would be dire, and the country's courts might block or undo such a move... But the regional power bloc, such as the EU, wouldn't invade or dismantle the checkpoints by force – so sovereignty ultimately still rests with the government.

However, the legal, diplomatic and economic consequences of swanning out of a customs union are generally so significant that doing so over any one point of trade policy preference is virtually unthinkable and the operating assumption is that countries will want to abide by the treaties they've signed up to even if theoretically no one will force compliance at gunpoint. While you can play semantic games about what exactly constitutes a loss of sovereignty, it's more intellectually honest to admit that like any other international treaty, participation in a customs union entails limiting your own sovereignty because you judge the benefits to outweigh the costs. I myself am far more comfortable arguing that the decision to give away some of your sovereignty through a treaty is itself an act of sovereignty, albeit one that may limit the options of successor governments.

Sovereignty issues aside, governments that sign up to a customs union are also, inherently, outsourcing part of their customs regime to others and thus taking on some risk. If you're deeply invested in having car tariffs and your customs union neighbour is not, you have to trust that they will still vigilantly collect tariffs on cars from outside the customs union. Lax, corrupt or incompetent tariff collection in one customs union country creates a hole in the shared tariff force field of the union in ways that can be hard to detect or address because the errant officials aren't under your jurisdiction.

Recent history has also shown that a customs union can come under significant strain when geopolitics pulls the participants in different directions. The Eurasian Economic Union (EaEU) ran into difficulties almost immediately because sanctions and counter-sanctions between Russia and the EU did not extend to or weren't replicated by its EaEU partners. Belarussian exporters to Russia found themselves suddenly facing customs and border checks because they did not replicate Russia's ban on EU agricultural produce, making their country a prime destination for smugglers meeting the demands of wealthy Muscovites for French camembert and Italian ham.

Advantages of a Customs Union

For all their costs and downsides, customs unions have still proven attractive all across the world because they have several advantages. By eliminating the need to have internal customs borders between the customs union members, goods can be moved around more quickly and cheaply. Because there are no tariffs to pay and very little paperwork to do, a business can structure its delivery or supply chain with shipments or components crossing borders multiple times. This is especially helpful for the kind of mixed consignments that would ordinarily prompt nightmarish customs paperwork (imagine individually tariff classifying every item on a truck sent to restock a dozen supermarket shelves with a hundred different items). This should not only bring down prices for consumers on goods from within the union, but also allow individual union countries to specialise and harness economies of scale to compete more strongly globally. Finnish design utilising parts from Italy and Germany, assembled in Poland before being shipped out through the hyper-efficient port of Rotterdam makes for a far better value final product than if any of those countries tried to build and ship that product entirely in-house, or if that supply chain required each component to undergo customs procedures at every step.

When they undertake trade negotiations, customs unions also benefit from pooling their collective mass. In pushing for concessions from the other side, a key determinant of your leverage is how many potential consumers your own market access commitments will allow the other side to sell to at a lower tariff. All other things being equal, lower tariffs to a market of 300 million are simply worth more than those same cuts to a market of two million. By negotiating as a collective and thus offering up access to their combined markets, customs union members combine their bargaining power, allowing them to demand more from counterparties than any of them could individually.

Being able to stand down your customs officials and dismantle your customs posts on borders within your union can also have significant advantages. The Netherlands, for example, has over 1,000 km of land border with Belgium and Germany. Not having to worry about collecting customs duties on goods moving across those borders allows the Dutch authorities to focus their efforts on the few major ports where goods from beyond the union can enter.

Customs Unions – Are they Worth it?

Whether a customs union is a good idea for your country or not isn't for me to say. What's vital is that you have a good grasp of the arguments for and against, and a sense for when they may be overstated, exaggerated or fabricated. This is especially true of the more principle-based arguments around customs unions and sovereignty. There is no objectively correct answer to how much sovereignty it's worth keeping.

From the perspective of making trade easier to conduct across borders, a custom union may be a good choice if:

- You do a lot of trade with your neighbours in something other than bulk primary commodities, or you envisage supply chains running back and forth across the borders and want to encourage that;
- You think there may be a lot of trade in perishable or time sensitive goods that disproportionately benefit from clearing borders faster;
- You anticipate lots of trade being done by smaller businesses and individuals, which tend to have less capacity to handle complex border bureaucracy;

- You don't disagree so wildly on appropriate tariff levels with your neighbours that a unified customs policy will be untenable, impossible to negotiate, or too politically painful to sustain.

There is also a strong (trade) argument to keep a customs union if you already have one, and have had one for a while. Since leaving the EU, and despite signing a comprehensive free trade agreement with it, the United Kingdom has had to inch very slowly toward full border bureaucracy with the bloc because its supply chains, businesses and officials had developed around the Customs Union over decades. Whether leaving the Customs Union was ultimately worth the resulting commercial damage is a question beyond the scope of this book, but the difficulties UK traders face and continue to face at the border are certainly evidence of the disruption that can be caused by leaving a customs union.

Chapter 11
Trade Integration: Regulations and Single Markets

Regulatory Harmonisation

A customs union is a formidable tool for eliminating border bureaucracy, but as the name suggests it focuses exclusively on customs. That's something. Classifying goods by their tariff codes, paying the relevant tariffs, meeting and proving compliance with Rules of Origin requirements can all be massive headaches for business – sometimes so painful as to be prohibitive to trade, or fatal to competitiveness. There are, however, other barriers to trade around regulation and certification, and these customs unions alone cannot do away with.

My country's regulations are the rules it has imposed on what goods must be in order to be eligible for sale in my territory. If you want to bring goods into my territory, you have to satisfy me that they meet those rules. A regulation is generally there to prevent some negative outcome, like people getting sick or consumers being sold a defective product. The greater the negative consequence in terms of impact and likelihood, the more stringently the regulation is likely to be enforced and checked against. So for example, a regulation in Australia might be that all appliances sold come with a standard Australian power plug or adapter – however, as the consequences of something slipping through without one are comparatively mild (if annoying for the consumer), the Australian government can be somewhat relaxed about how much proof it requires each individual kettle meets that requirement. A regulation against importing a dangerous pest that could really damage Australia's delicate biome, on the other hand, would be much more rigorously enforced and tested against, because the potential damage is so much greater.

For a business looking to export something covered by a regulation (and almost everything is covered by at least one), that raises two questions. Does my product meet the regulation? What do I need to do to prove to the importing countries authorities that it does? This second question is where things get complicated. A government is free to determine what level of proof it will demand – balancing the risk that something gets through that shouldn't have against greater costs to the trader, and thus ultimately the consumer.

Imagine your country has a regulation banning a certain kind of growth hormone in beef. How would you enforce that ruling? At one extreme you could mandate that every steak or carcase entering your territory be individually trace-tested for this hormone by a government-run laboratory. This would largely eliminate the chances of beef with the troublesome hormone ending up on your supermarket shelves, but individual testing takes forever and the cost is likely to be high, whether borne by the taxpayer, or, more commonly, by the importer (and thus ultimately by the consumer). It's an option, but probably not a feasible one except in the handful of cases where the likelihood and severity of the risk make it the only option.

The other extreme is to forgo all oversight at the border and instead rely on either retroactive enforcement or a so-called intelligence-led approach. Retroactive enforcement means you don't check for the hormone at the border but importers know that if this hormone is later discovered on supermarket shelves, you'll come looking for who brought it in and punish them. An intelligence-led approach supplements this with a crime-prevention strategy whereby information and analysis on potential violators is used by customs to make checks at the border on only those shipments they have reason to believe may be flouting the regulations. This approach has downsides, too. When something inappropriate ends up on a supermarket shelf, neither the public nor political leaders have a lot of appetite for excuses about border efficiency, and even the best intelligence-led approach is going to miss things.

In between these maximalist and minimalist extremes is an entire spectrum of options, which regulators and officials can use to calibrate their precise risk-versus-disruption appetite on each regulation. For example, you may decide that you won't check for the hormone at the border, but only accept beef from slaughterhouses that have been inspected by your officials within the last five years. You could test at the border, but do so at the shipment level, randomly, with heavy fines to discourage importers from simply taking their chances. For one regulation you might accept test results from a foreign laboratory, for others you might insist the tests be done by your own. You might grant large, trusted operators with years of clean tests a presumption of compliance, or you might go in the opposite direction and exempt small shipments unlikely to pose a major risk.

Regulatory integration offers an additional path forward, albeit a far from simple one. The reason you need to check against regulations at the border in the first place is that every country has its own rules. The hormone you consider unacceptable may be fully legal in the country a shipment is coming from – or may be so laxly enforced there that you can't trust the local ban was actually followed. To forgo checks on goods coming across a border from a specific neighbour, you therefore have to be certain of two things: that their regulations and yours produce identical results, and that their enforcement is rigorous enough to give you peace of mind.

Baby Steps – Testing and Certification

The first halting steps toward integration aren't really integration at all. Instead, one side or both decide that they will accept testing or certification against their regulations performed by the other's officials or private enterprises. Everyone keeps their own regulations, and it is their regulations which govern what can enter their territory. The only difference is that instead of tests needing to be conducted at the border or by a visiting delegation of your own experts, you instruct your border officials to accept certificates of compliance issued against your regulation by the other country's officials or labs.

Imagine Peru has stricter standards on the energy efficiency of lightbulbs than Argentina. Argentinian bulb manufacturers would have the option of producing to either the domestic standard or the higher standard required to sell to Peru. If Peru wanted to minimise the risk of importing wasteful bulbs it could carry out tests at the border, or Peruvian officials could regularly visit and inspect Argentine lightbulb factories. An alternative would be for Peru to make things easier at the border and cheaper for its consumers by allowing Argentinian labs to self-certify that shipments of their bulbs bulbs meet the Peruvian standard.

For businesses, such certification schemes can be convenient and cut costs. If I'm producing something in my country for sale both at home and abroad, it's a pain having to certify compliance with two sets of regulations. However, this way I can at least get my testing done in my own time, at one facility that's probably closer and more accessible.

For governments, this approach is attractive for the control it offers. Not only is the underlying regulation still my own, but I can determine which foreign institutions I'll trust to carry out tests, set conditions for their retaining that trusted status and withdraw it if anything goes wrong. I can also change my regulations whenever I like, provided I offer the same information or training to these foreign certifiers as I would to my own testers at home. This kind of arrangement can be done unilaterally, without a binding legal instrument like a treaty, and it allows smoother trade despite both sides retaining their own independent regulations.

The downsides are convenience and risk. The regulations on both sides of the border remain different, as do their certification requirements. The only thing this has changed is the location of certifications. Having dental work done in the same building as your colonoscopy may be more convenient than having to drive across town between them, but both remain profoundly unpleasant experiences and (unless your physiology vastly differs from mine) fundamentally non-interchangeable. You are welcome for that mental image.

Equivalency or Recognition – Close Enough, Mate

If countries want to move beyond testing and certification, but aren't yet ready for true regional integration, the next intermittent step is called 'equivalency'. Simply put, this consists of declaring either unilaterally or in an agreement of some kind, that a specific regulation in one country achieves the same outcome as a regulation in another – even if the regulations are different. You have your regulation, and they have theirs, but both aim to achieve the same result and you believe theirs is stringent enough to consider the two to be equivalent. Therefore something entering your territory from theirs no longer needs to be tested or certified against that particular regulation, because the other country's own version is good enough.

Consider two countries with a shared objective of not allowing lead paint to be used on children's toys. In one country, this is achieved under the purview of the health ministry and enforced through a series of randomised inspections of all relevant imports and domestic manufacturing facilities. In the other, it's overseen by the industry department as part of a broader domestic certification scheme that checks against a range of requirements through carrying out rolling tests of randomly selected products. The regulations are worded differently, handled by different ministries and tested in different ways, but evidence suggests that both have a very high rate of effectiveness in preventing lead-painted toys from making it onto store shelves. One or both countries could therefore decide that they do not need to do additional checks on toys entering their territory from the other, because the sending country's regulations will have already ensured they're lead paint-free.

The benefits of this kind of regulatory ruling are an easing of border measures and the removal of redundant, duplicative checks. The US can probably rely on Canada to ban cyanide from baby formula, even if the exact wording of the relevant Canadian regulation is different to its own. Moreover, the US will probably be safe to assume that Canadian enforcement of its regulation will be strict and thorough, so baby formula cleared to circulate within Canada, either because it was made there or because it was legitimately imported, can be brought into the US market without additional checks. This is the logic of equivalency.

Businesses operating in a region where countries have granted one another's regulations equivalency benefit two-fold – they can situate themselves in the jurisdiction where the local regulations work best for them, while still being able to sell across borders without additional testing or certifications. Governments benefit from lower consumer prices without sacrificing public safety. It's a win-win, so why doesn't it happen everywhere? Like a lot of other things in life: effort and risk.

A determination of equivalence requires a pretty comprehensive mapping of your regulation, the other country's regulation, and how both are enforced in practice. That's a lot of work, especially when the regulations in question may be sub-national with regional variances in everything from wording to methodology to enforcement. Getting to the bottom of how another country actually goes about banning a pesticide, mapping that against how you do it, and reaching a determination that they amount to more or less the same thing is a huge bureaucratic undertaking – and you can't just do it once. Every time either side changes their regulations or procedures, a fresh check is needed to confirm the two haven't slipped so far out of alignment that they are no longer equivalent.

Then there's the risk. By granting equivalency you are trusting the other side to enforce its own regulations rigidly enough that you don't have to enforce your own. This may be a safe bet in many cases, but it's a bet nevertheless. If tomorrow people in your country get sick from a foreign shipment of radioactive prawns, the public may prove unwilling to accept your explanation that you didn't run a geiger counter over the crustaceans at the border because you thought the source country's nuclear-free-shrimp directive equivalent was sufficient.

The above example may sound contrived, but the fact is even very advanced economies often do not trust one another's certifications on more sensitive products. Medicines, cosmetics and pharmaceuticals are especially heavily regulated, with developed countries often requiring that drugs approved by their peer power go through an entirely new round of testing and approvals to qualify for distribution. The complexity of pharmaceuticals and the consequences of regulatory failure – with perhaps just a hint of protectionism and rent-seeking – have all combined to keep extensive equivalency in drug regulation a distant dream even between countries one would ordinarily expect to have no issues with one another's pharmaceutical competence. For example, drugs developed in Europe and fully approved by the European Medicines Agency must still be certified by the US Food and Drug Administration before being sold in America. There is no presumption of compliance, even though presumably Americans are pretty biologically similar to Europeans and the European Medicines Agency knows what it's doing.

The sum total of all this is that recognition tends to be a fairly bespoke, targeted affair confined to either very specific regulations, regulations where the risk is deemed low, or those comparatively few areas where the entire world has managed to painstakingly negotiate a common international standard.

From a democratic and sovereignty standpoint, recognition or equivalency poses two hidden dangers. First, by granting another country's regulations equivalence to your own you create a commercial disincentive to raise your own regulatory scrutiny. Any tightening of your standards has to be weighed against the consequences of tearing up the equivalency arrangement or risking your new regulations being undercut by goods of a lower standard entering your country. Second, once a large and lucrative market has granted you equivalency, they have effectively gained some leverage over you. At the stroke of a pen they could re-introduce significant border hassles for your exporters, potentially rendering businesses non-viable.

Beyond Equivalency – Alignment and Harmonisation

Some countries have decided that while equivalency and foreign testing are good policies, they're insufficient. These countries, along with their like-minded neighbours, have explored further aligning and harmonising their trade rules. If equivalency is about identifying regulations in different countries that achieve the same result, alignment and harmonisation are about jointly creating new identical regulations everyone will use, or modifying countries' existing regulations until they achieve the same level of protection.

If everyone in a region can come together and agree on a standard for maximum car emissions, and on how governments will ensure it's enforced, then the entire region has effectively built a new level of equivalency. Provided they trust one another to abide by what has been agreed, governments across the region can now stop checking that regulation on their internal borders in the confidence that any cars crossing them will have either been manufactured to the agreed emissions standard or been tested against it when entering the region from elsewhere.

This is all easier said than done, of course. Regulatory change is never simple and even where countries agree on the substance they may find it difficult to convince their legislators to pass the required acts or bills, or their regulators to surrender their future discretion. To make this more palatable for them, harmonisation projects sometimes leave a lot of flexibility around implementation, setting the standard to be tested against and the rigour of the testing, without specifying exactly how a government should go about ensuring compliance. This helps governments and regulators retain some sovereignty, and avoids having to agree every minor detail, but it's hard going nonetheless.

Making it Work

Integration can occur in a number of ways. In general, the deeper, wider and more complex the integration, the more structures have to be put in place to make it work.

The easiest forms of regulatory recognition and even equivalency are either unilateral, or reached through discussions between the regulators themselves. The veterinary authority of Paraguay, perhaps following a discussion with its Uruguayan counterpart, may simply decide that Uruguay's mad-cow disease rules are fine, and grant them equivalency. This makes life easier for Uruguayan exporters and hopefully reduces prices for Paraguayan consumers while having few implications for sovereignty or democracy, as the Paraguayan government is not in any way bound to maintain this decision any longer than desired.

In a bid to encourage regulators to act proactively, governments may decide to launch negotiations on a 'Mutual Recognition Agreement (MRA)' or to include an exchange of recognitions as part of a broader trade agreement. This is a little more complicated, both to create and in its implications, because unlike unilateral recognition, these require negotiations and trade-offs between the parties. Free Trade

Agreements can take decades to negotiate, and every aspect of them is a potential source of negotiating leverage. This could mean that they go further on recognition and equivalency than what might be possible unilaterally or through regulator-to-regulator discussions. It could also mean that equivalency and recognition are held up, or never granted, because the Free Trade Agreement that would have contained them is stalled for a decade over something completely unrelated like agricultural tariffs (it's almost always agricultural tariffs...).

There are sovereignty implications, too. By definition, Mutual Recognition Agreements and Free Trade Agreements are an interlinked balance of concessions. Once they are in place you can't usually pick and choose which of their elements you implement. If a government decides that it wants to withdraw one of the recognitions or equivalencies in an agreement, its options may be limited. Sometimes there will be provisions in the deal allowing such a thing under limited circumstances, but more often such a withdrawal would be a breach of the agreement and risk its dissolution (not to mention diplomatic and reputational consequences).

Moving even further down the integration path, toward something like the European Union Single Market, requires an ongoing process of integration, regulatory harmonisation and cooperation at every level. It means creating legal and procedural frameworks, joint decision-making bodies, and potentially even supra-national legislatures. An entire international architecture must be put in place, bringing together officials from all parties to advance and maintain a continuous and expansive regional integration process.

Any ongoing integration project inevitably manifests a tension between speed and unanimity. If ten countries are trying to integrate and nine of them agree on a new, common regulation, should the tenth be allowed a veto? A veto risks reducing progress to only the lowest common denominator issues, but in the absence of such a veto the project will face endless questions regarding its equity and democratic legitimacy. Voting among the members might be more democratic and agile than requiring full consensus, but how should the votes of large, populous states be weighted against smaller ones? Moreover, is there anything truly democratic about your citizens becoming subject to a rule or law neither they nor their elected representatives support?

Departing from a common approach can be commercially lucrative – with potentially significant consequences for both neighbours. If Lao and Vietnam agree to harmonise their carbon emissions regulations, but Lao is far less invested in the project then Vietnam, it can make its factories more competitive by looking the other way while they cut costs through releasing more carbon than permitted. Now Vietnamese industry is howling, but Vietnam isn't allowed to double check the carbon footprint of Lao's exports because on paper the two regulations are supposed to be equivalent. To keep the integration process from collapsing, Vietnam needs a way to raise such concerns with Laos, with some hope of getting to the bottom of and hopefully rectifying the situation without tearing up the regulatory harmonisation.

Managing such inevitable differences, even when it comes to the implementation of carefully worded language, requires pre-agreed frameworks and procedures. For example, all sides could agree that if they cannot resolve a disagreement through diplomatic talks or in committee, a court or dispute settlement system will be able to examine the case and issue a binding ruling to all parties. This creates a pathway to resolving arguments through legalism rather than power politics or horse trading, but means a panel of judges potentially ruling the actions of a sovereign legislature illegal. On the flipside, leaving questions of interpretation and dispute resolution exclusively to diplomatic negotiation risks the perception of injustice, and that the rules are merely optional or unenforceable.

Despite these and other murky waters, the potential benefits are considerable. The European Union Single Market, while imperfect and incomplete, has achieved levels of regulatory harmonisation and trade facilitation exponentially beyond even the most ambitious trade agreement. By some measures, the EU has fewer internal barriers to trade among its member countries, especially in services, than the United States does for trade among its 50 states. Moreover, the EU has successfully leveraged its market size to push its regulatory approach beyond its borders. Even firms outside the EU must at times bite the bullet and operate in line with the EU's regulations in such areas as internet privacy, because to do otherwise would be to risk fines or loss of access to comparatively wealthy EU consumers.

However, because of the difficulties and tradeoffs required for this degree of integration, the EU remains the only example where more than a handful of countries has achieved anything like a single market. While other regions such as the Economic Community of West African States, Latin America's Mercosur or the ASEAN have made significant steps toward integration, they remain leagues away from the depths of complexity of the EU Single Market. By and large states around the world have proven unwilling to invest the vast resources and sacrifice the policy flexibility required to build anything like the EU in their own region. This does not make them lazy or the EU a democracy-sucking lizard. Like everything else in policy, it is simply a reflection of choices and priorities which reasonable people can disagree on but should at least understand.

Part 2

Trade and the Things You May Actually Care About

Chapter 12
Trade and Jobs

Work Hard, Trade Hard?

Having treated (or subjected) you to a few thousand words about what trade policy is and how it works, I want to spend the rest of this book looking at how trade policy intersects with some of the areas of public life you're probably far more interested in than trade itself. It is often here, in trade's impacts, that the most interesting conversations and the most pernicious lies can be found.

Let's start by talking about the relationship between trade and jobs. We know trade as a whole creates jobs. But how trade policy affects jobs is harder to unravel and this complexity provides cover for all sorts of bad faith political actors to make grand claims or dire predictions with few connections to reality.

Politicians from Our Party Create Jobs

Three things governments in the West generally believe are that:

1. Businesses create jobs.
2. The government deserves full credit for every job created.

3. The government bears no responsibility for any job losses.

(Curiously numbers two and three have a funny habit of reversing themselves the moment a political party enters opposition.)

The unemployment rate is commonly seen as a proxy for economic competence and performance. Politicians are ready with a thousand excuses for why it might be high when they're in charge and are ready to insist that any opponents deserve the chop if it rises while they are in power.

Alas, governments have few mighty levers to pull to lower unemployment in the short term. Cutting interest rates might spur some economic activity, but the decision to do so is often in the hands of a quasi or fully independent central bank more concerned with inflation than popularity. Massive government investments in infrastructure, the civil service, or the military can directly create jobs, but generally these spurts are only temporary – and worsen public debt. Long-term investments can work wonders, but they have a nasty habit of manifesting their benefits a decade later when the politicians who made them may be out of power. Tax cuts or regulatory relaxations can also encourage investment and growth, but neither are instant, guaranteed, or bottomless wells one can exploit every time the employment figures dip – and both come with their own complications.

A national employment market is, in truth, a complex mix of domestic regulation, labour skills, credit availability, demand at home and abroad, consumer sentiment and countless other factors that do not lend themselves to large, dramatic gestures by a government eager to show off its job-creating virility.

Enter our hero(ine): trade policy.

Take a Bow, Trade Policy

Almost any action taken by a trade ministry can be sold by its proponents or attacked by its detractors as affecting 'jobs'. The starkest example is the free trade agreement. Every trade agreement in the history of human civilisation has been advertised by the government that signed it as a jobs bonanza that will open up lucrative opportunities to sell goods and services abroad. Every new trade agreement has also been attacked by opposition politicians as a potential job killer, removing the protections local firms need to compete 'fairly' with foreign producers.

As proponents wax lyrical about the glorious opportunities that will rain down upon the citizenry the moment a trade deal is signed, opponents utter dark warnings about factory or farm closures, job losses, mass layoffs and destitution. What often frustrates economists and trade experts about this hullabaloo is its framing of exports as good (job creating) and imports as bad (job threatening). The reality is far more complex, especially in an age of global and continental value chains. To give just one example, the ability of a widget factory to import a component, hire consultants with unique skills from across borders, or raise capital on foreign markets, may be the only thing keeping it internationally competitive and its workers paid. Erecting barriers to keep out foreign parts, people or money may simply close a factory's doors, instead of causing it to procure, hire and raise capital locally.

Yet even in that example, you can see the focus inevitably returns to jobs. Those who champion international trade will often talk about 'productivity gains' rather than refering directly to employment, but the underlying meaning is the same. Jobs. More jobs. Better paying jobs. More reliable jobs.

Jobs, jobs, jobs.

For trade ministers, this imperative is even stronger. The trade portfolio is rarely sexy on its own terms. Unlike a treasury minister who gets to write the budget or a health minister who gets to cut the ribbon on new hospitals, trade ministers really do have to make their own fun if they want to have a list of easily marketable achievements to their name when they scramble up the greasy pole of politics. This puts pressure on the departments and ministries they run to project even the most modest international diplomatic advances as groundbreaking achievements with dynamic impacts on the job market. Many a trade expert has clutched their head in despair reading a trade ministry press release hailing as momentous a non-binding handshake agreement to hold future discussions about a niche market, especially when it's written in language that would eclipse the Epic of Gilgamesh.

Trade expert headaches aren't really a problem for governments though, at least not a big one. Neither is the verifiable truth of their claims about the impact of a trade agreement. Predictions are always considered guesswork and changes in the job figures are so clearly multi-causal that there is bound to be an external event that can take the blame for why promises failed to materialise. Even setting bad faith aside, it's monstrously difficult to work out just how many jobs an existing trade agreement created, let alone forecast the impact of a future one. That does, however, pose a problem for anyone who wants to know what a trade agreement might actually mean.

Is This Deal Going to Help You?

Let us say you have a company that produces washing machines and would like to start selling them in the European Union. The EU has hundreds of millions of customers, and many of them starting to buy your washing machines would create lots of wonderful jobs. Can trade policy help?

The best answer is, unfortunately, a narrow 'maybe' – heavily dependent on a set of circumstances unique to your product, your brand, and market position.

Why so narrow and why so qualified? Because trade policy can only help if the reason you're not currently selling into the EU is:

a) Primarily Due to a Government Policy

International trade policy is about governments talking to other governments about government policy. That's it. For a trade negotiation to help you, the root of your problem must lie with government policy. So, for example, if the reason your washing machines aren't currently in EU shops is because the EU has a tariff on them (making them more expensive than locally made machines) or because the EU has a regulatory standard that discriminates against machines like yours, that's something a negotiation could potentially fix. Similarly, if your own government has policies that are hurting your business (like tariffs on the parts you need, or an insufficiently rigorous copyright regime which allows knockoffs of your products) a negotiation could end up fixing that, too.

b) That Government Policy is Open to Negotiation

Not all a government's policies are going to be on the table in a trade negotiation. Just because you can identify a law or regulation on the books that's hurting your washing machines, doesn't mean that the government will be able to negotiate a change. Most trade negotiations end up leaving the vast majority of rules, procedures and regulations pretty much as they found them.

There may be more important non-governmental reasons why the EU market is not working for you. Other washing machines in EU shops could simply be outcompeting yours on value. You may struggle to find distributors or retailers because all the major homewares stores already have the models they need. Your brand may lack consumer recognition or trust. The shipping costs from your factory to EU distribution hubs may be too high. You may not be able to match your competitors on after-sale service because the cost of establishing a network of repair and maintenance centres across the breadth of the EU is prohibitive.

All these reasons and more might explain why you're not competitive in the EU, and the overwhelming likelihood is that trade policy won't be able to address them because they don't stem from government policy. The EU can't sign up to a clause mandating that Belgians and Greeks prefer your washing machines to those of Bosch or Samsung, or requiring that shops in Paris stock your products if they don't want to. Even when government policy barriers are one of the challenges you're facing in a foreign market, it can be difficult to predict if they are the primary problem.

Why Creating Big Trade Deals is Hard

Even when government policy is the prime suspect for a firm's lack of success in an export market, there is no guarantee that trade negotiations will come to the rescue. As a trade negotiator, I know that sounds like the most desperate expectations management since my first sexual encounter, but it happens to be true. Many trade policies that obstruct market entry are there for a reason, and can be tricky to shift.

Remember the 'Why is Trade Policy?' chapter when we briefly talked about how governments switched from thinking about tariffs as a way to raise revenue to thinking about them largely as a way to shield domestic industries from foreign competition? This creates a considerable problem for negotiators trying to get rid of them. If the primary value of a tariff is the revenue it generates, a negotiator only needs to make the case that what they're offering will yield more money to the treasury. In practice, this is not so easy because treasuries tend to prefer the hard cash they are collecting today to hypothetical revenue tomorrow. Still, it is possible to make the argument successfully. In lobbying for governments to agree to the Information Technology Agreement[1], for example, advocates could argue that the ensuing entrepreneurial gains and company tax revenues from cheaper iPads, PCs and the like would quickly offset the tariff revenue previously collected on those items. So, while difficult, this is fundamentally an argument about money in and money out: quantifiable and tangible.

That is rarely the case when discussing the elimination of a tariff that exists to protect a chosen industry from competition, let alone a

---

[1.] Now two agreements between over 40 countries to reduce or eliminate their tariffs on a range of IT related products like computers and servers.

regulation or procedure designed for another purpose like protecting the public. Imagine you are championing your rice exporters and want to lower the exorbitant rice tariff introduced by a faraway land to protect its rice farmers from competition. What arguments can you make? Here are four:

a) Even without any tariff, your producers wouldn't be a threat to local producers;
b) Your producers may threaten local producers, but the competition will make them stronger;
c) Your producers may threaten local producers, but the benefits to consumers will outweigh that;
d) Your producers may threaten local producers, but the access you're offering in your own market will benefit other producers sufficiently that, on balance, it's still a good deal.

Arguing that eliminating the tariff wouldn't threaten local producers can be awkward, because the obvious retort is: 'If you're not going to sell us any rice anyway, why do you want us to get rid of this rice tariff?' It's very hard to explain why not getting something you claim will be insignificant is a deal breaker. Arguing tariff elimination won't increase sales also makes it difficult to claim back home that you've kicked open the door to a lucrative market, created a billion jobs, and ushered in a new golden era of prosperity.

If you're unable to credibly argue that eliminating the tariff won't increase competition or challenge local producers, you have to rely on the argument that 'You should still do it anyway'. In other words, you have to convince a country that the benefits of increased competition to their producers and consumers outweigh any potential job losses caused by competition.

This can be a tough nut to crack. 'More competition is better' is the sort of thing most business lobbies will say in the theoretical and abstract, but find a thousand excuses to push back on when it looks like it could actually happen.

Few domestic businesses will concede they are falling short on productivity and innovation, and fewer still will concede their foreign counterparts are outworking or outthinking them. In almost all cases, industries will instead point to a range of real and imagined factors as providing their foreign competitors with unfair advantages which the tariffs help to nullify.

Most businesses also loathe uncertainty, and the effects of losing their tariff protection certainly fall into that category. If protection is lifted, greater competition might spur a company to eventually improve its processes, marketing and products, and emerge stronger... but it might not. If on the other hand the protection remains in place, it can soldier on happily as it is and decide whether to invest to strengthen its competitiveness at its own leisure, bothered only by domestic rivals.

If instead of the productivity and competition benefits to domestic producers, you want to focus on consumers, you soon run into a big problem. We shall call it by its technically correct definition: diffuse versus concentrated beneficiaries. That sounds incomprehensible but it's a fairly simple idea in practice. Small benefits given out to a lot of people are rarely noticed, while big bad changes to a small number of people tend to cause a stink. You could watch any news bulletin to understand this, but let's take the example of slightly cheaper rice from abroad. Very few voters are likely to vote for you, canvass for you, organise their friends for you, or take to the airwaves to praise you, because you slightly lowered the tariff on foreign rice. In fact, they may not even notice you have done so. Tariffs are paid at the border on the price of a product before any of the additional packaging, transportation charges and retail markups are applied – meaning a 10 per cent tariff cut is likely be much smaller than a 10 per cent reduction in the final consumer price – and can easily get swallowed up by inflation or currency fluctuations.

By contrast, even a small change in prices at the border could make foreign rice more competitive than a domestic product, and a farming community which is suddenly priced out of the local market by competition from abroad risks losing their livelihoods... you can guarantee they are going to make a fuss about that. Worse still, when they make noise the story they tell will be about that most sacred thing: jobs. Jobs not just for themselves, virtuous food producers who toil on the land so that we might eat, but for all those who supply and work with them. An entire industry might be at risk. Maybe even an entire community. It's not something governments like to contemplate.

This dynamic also comes into play when discussing offset benefits, such as suggesting that any damage to employment in the beef business from your removing a tariff is going to be outweighed by opening up a market for your wheat growers, steelmakers or even accountants. Jobs, unlike tax revenues, aren't fully fungible (that is, interchangeable). A 57 year old rice farmer on a seventh generation paddy is unlikely to be able to switch neatly into producing lamb, let alone take up management consultancy. Neither is their community. Moreover, threats can often feel more real than opportunities. So you can fully expect the farmer to be more full-throated in opposing a deal that cuts their protection than the beneficiaries of whatever trade-offs you negotiated in exchange. While market openness abroad may create hypothetical jobs, for someone, somewhere in your country, in the future, any protection you lift at home now could threaten actual existing jobs today.

Regulatory Barriers

Trade negotiations aren't just about lowering or removing tariffs. Increasingly, businesses will tell you that their primary barriers are regulatory or procedural.

Consider a regulation which prohibits a certain kind of pesticide on tulips, backed by a procedure whereby an importer must pay for every shipment to be certified as pesticide-free by laboratories at the border. The tests these laboratories carry out are slow and costly, so by the time the tulips are cleared for entry, their freshness and value have decreased compared to local supplies, which are assumed to be free of the pesticide in question and so do not need to undergo testing at all, or not nearly at the same frequency.

Such a regulatory and procedural one-two punch might seriously hinder a product's ability to compete on value. Yet none of the arguments we floated above to try and get a tariff lowered really fit. The stated underlying policy motivation of the pesticide testing is to protect the public from dangerous chemicals. That makes it difficult for a government to abandon without either admitting it was previously over-cautious, at the expense of its shoppers, or that it is now endangering public health to bag a new trade deal.

A government may be able to get away with relaxing the procedure somewhat, or accepting the word of foreign authorities that their products are pesticide-free, but even that becomes a challenge if there is significant public focus and robust opposition. The technicalities behind something like establishing the appropriate level of tulip pesticide residue testing are hard for the public to understand, but easy for producers and politicians to demagogue into headlines.

Despite all of these problems, trade liberalisation does happen. The reason most countries have comparatively low tariffs, that your car is made with components from 23 international sources, that you can get your portrait painted overnight by an artist on the other side of the globe and that over 400 trade agreements have been signed around the world, is that the arguments for comparatively free trade are persuasive.

The challenge for governments and negotiators in the modern era is simultaneously defending the liberalisations achieved and liberalising the more contentious goods and services that remain unliberalised, where it makes sense to do so. Almost by definition, the products where the largest remaining gains can be made are now those where existing protections are either obviously necessary or most resolutely defended on a political level.

Depressing Press Releases

What does this mean for you, the consumer of news and checker of government press releases? It means you have to be sceptical as hell about everything you read, especially when it comes to promises of vast, treaty-borne job creation. It is very unlikely that a government has managed to transform an economy by signing a trade deal. Unless you are a tiny state whose exports can't possibly threaten anyone, a trade agreement that is going to create a mountain of new export jobs would mean the country you've done a deal with has fought and won a bloody internal battle against its protectionists for your express benefit. This is unlikely, so it either didn't happen, or it's legitimate to ask what your side offered that was so lucrative as to motivate its counterparts into the political trenches.

Government press release writers are wise to this and the unpredictable nature of jobs 'created' by trade agreements, so will generally avoid making any specific claims. Instead, they use rhetorical flourishes that would be generously described as 'marketing' and less charitably as 'bullshit'.

Example 1: This Deal Covers 98 per cent of Trade

This is a pet peeve of mine, because it's technically correct but designed to mislead.

In most cases, a government press release will say something like this when a new trade agreement includes commitments that theoretically affect 98 per cent of tariff lines, or more likely explicitly carve out 2 per cent of them. As you'll recall from earlier, tariff lines are basically a long list of numbered categories covering every good and product imaginable. Businesses (or their customs advisers) use them to find the right tariff for each of their products and thus the payment due. Saying a deal 'covers 98 per cent of trade' is almost always misleading nonsense, for several reasons.

First, especially in a free trade agreement between two developed countries, a huge percentage of those 98 per cent of tariff lines were already likely to have been set at, or close to, 0 per cent. The trade agreement may include a commitment not to raise them any higher, but that was probably never going to happen anyway (in fact, governments may have already given that commitment to all members of the World Trade Organization).

Second, unless we're talking about two gigantic economies like the US and EU, trade and potential trade is probably limited to relatively few tariff lines. A tariff reduction on something my country doesn't make or isn't export competitive in is only a theoretical benefit. Saudi Arabia lifting an import tariff on sand in return for Britain lifting one on beer is unlikely to make much of a difference to anyone's life.

Third, while 98 per cent sounds like an overwhelming percentage covering almost everything, that can be deceptive. There are, depending on the level of specificity you're operating on, either over 6,000 or over 10,000 tariff lines, with some being very broad and worth billions and others being incredibly specific and covering trade in products of marginal value. If the 2 per cent of tariff lines not covered include the 30 odd representing most of your potential export value, 98 per cent is not actually very impressive.

The trade agreement in question may well have eliminated some tariffs and may create some jobs, but the 98 per cent figure is designed to bamboozle you into imagining a far greater opening of a market than probably took place.

Example 2: This Deal Covers Trade Worth $11 billion Annually

This soundbite lets politicians drop impressive figures, but it's utterly misleading and deceptive. In virtually all cases, the headline figure is simply the total volume of goods and services traded between the two countries in the year before the agreement was signed. You can see why this claim is so infuriating. Every dollar in trade 'covered' in this trade agreement was already taking place despite whatever barriers may have been addressed in the deal. Every job that one thought this deal was 'creating' already existed.

A more helpful and honest version of this claim would be: 'A deal that we calculate may create up to $x in new trade within the next 10 years.' But that sounds both less definitive because it's derived from computer modelling and less impressive because the number is probably a fraction of total existing trade.

An even more nightmarish version of this trope is when politicians or their pet tabloids declare a trade agreement to be 'worth' the total gross domestic product of the other country. This is so stupid I hesitate to even bring it up, except that it keeps happening – a headline will claim a trade agreement is worth some bizarrely high amount which when Googled is revealed to just be the other country's GDP. For the avoidance of doubt, a free trade agreement with the United States is not in any way, shape, or form a '$23 trillion deal'.

Example 3: This Deal Slashes Red Tape

I mean... sure. Maybe. For some of them. A bit. I have already discussed why as a general rule, you should be sceptical of anyone vowing to significantly reduce 'red tape' unless they specify exactly how. The odds that a trade agreement has managed to find so many acceptable risk reductions or redundant processes that it can 'slash' anything is vanishingly small.

An interesting incongruity in international trade policy is that while businesses will increasingly tell you they are more constrained by procedures and regulations than they are by tariffs, trade agreements are pretty bad at tackling both procedures and regulations.

There are a number of reasons for this, but the easiest to understand is that tariffs tend to be within the gift of the trade ministry negotiating the agreement, while power over regulations and procedures almost certainly belongs to other government departments. That means a trade ministry seeking to cut tariffs need only negotiate with itself and its own stakeholders while one trying to change a regulation (the rule) or procedure (the way officials implement or check against that rule) has to go begging bowl in hand to a fellow minister, Cabinet, or the head of government.

Regulations are also just harder to shift. Unlike tariffs, they are rarely country-specific, which makes exempting one country from them difficult. A specific pesticide is either dangerous or it isn't. Declaring that it is only dangerous if it doesn't come from a country you recently signed a trade deal with is incoherent and plain weird. Trade agreements can agree that certain checks can be waived or minimised because a specific trading partner's safety regime or circumstances are sufficiently robust, but this tends to be on a case by case and product by product basis. Not so much slashing bureaucracy, then, as gently trimming it.

Indeed, historically, the majority of the commitments in trade agreements (including at the World Trade Organization) around regulations and procedures haven't been about cutting paperwork at all. Instead, they've introduced broad principles like not creating regulations specifically to be protectionist, or not requiring foreign products to meet regulatory standards your domestic ones don't have to meet. These underlying rules are important, but they're not smoothing existing procedures. They are about stopping future regulatory chicanery.

Governments have agreed mutual recognition in some areas – which can reduce red tape – and have laid the groundwork for greater customs cooperation and data sharing in others, which can also be helpful. But anyone imagining a post-trade-agreement utopia of bureaucracy-free trade has been misled. This is doubly true when you recall that Rules of Origin mean that any trader looking to take advantage of an agreement's lower tariffs has to brace themselves for an avalanche of paperwork to verify that their product is sufficiently local.

So Are Trade Agreements . . . Bad?

I live by the mantra that one should, wherever possible, reserve most of one's criticism and ridicule for those with power and status. In trade, where agreements are overwhelmingly negotiated by governments, that mostly means ministers and to a lesser extent the well-funded think tanks who advocate for greater liberalisation and deregulation. Yet they are not the only ones in this space, and not the only ones whose enthusiasm for their argument can lead them to make outlandish claims.

Much as proponents of free trade agreements have a tendency to exaggerate or fabricate their potential for job creation, their critics tend to get carried away with uttering prophecies of doom. Industries suffer and jobs are lost for many reasons, from automation to changing consumer preferences and flawed business models, and most trade agreements carefully restrict new market access from damaging economically or politically sensitive sectors. Similarly, while the nature of trade negotiations makes them unlikely to slash regulations, they are also unlikely to create a free-for-all that will lead to poison being stacked on supermarket shelves.

Additionally, trade agreements, including those making up the World Trade Organization, allow governments to reimpose tariffs in the event of an industry-destroying surge of imports or certain forms of 'unfair' foreign competition. Most international trade lawyers devote their careers to such reimpositions, known as 'remedies'. I won't torment you with even a taste of their intricacies, but suffice to say governments rarely find themselves completely bereft of fully (or mostly, or at least potentially) legal options when an unexpected flood of imports outrages domestic producers.

In parsing both the arguments of those praising trade agreements as miracles of job creation and those claiming they'll doom us all to unemployment, I would urge you to return to those basic questions I outlined in the second chapter of this book. Very simply:

How Do Things Work Now, and What Specifically Will this Agreement Change?

In most cases, you'll find a list of how an agreement will actually change things to be more than enough to gauge the likelihood of a trade deal transforming your local economy, for good or ill.

Chapter 13
Trade and National Security

Alongside climate change, national security currently most dominates the conversation on trade policy. National security can refer to the physical security of a nation, its citizenry, and its assets, or more broadly the preservation of its interests against any threat. Its protection is generally the foremost responsibility of any government, with leaders tending to prioritise it over most other competing priorities.

National security has at times been invoked to trump even basic protections such as civil rights and due process, even in countries that claim to hold such things sacred. It is therefore perhaps no surprise that trade liberalisation and trading rules are often deprioritised when deemed to present national security concerns.

But what are we actually talking about here? How can trade rules, and trade more generally be a threat to national security?

Answering this question requires going back a little to one of the core rules of the WTO: Most Favoured Nation. This poorly named principle obliges governments to treat all potential importers of the same product category the same. So while under the WTO you are allowed to use tariffs to discriminate between an imported potato and a homegrown one, you aren't allowed to have different tariffs on potatoes depending on which country they are from. This creates a level playing field and prevents countries from constantly adjusting tariffs to individual nations as part of diplomatic bargaining or to signal displeasure.

The primary exceptions to this rule, as we've discussed in earlier chapters, are free trade agreements and preferences, but these just lower your tariffs for a partner – they can't *raise* them for everyone else. Since most large trading nations already have very low tariffs or no tariffs at all on most non-agricultural products, free trade agreements alone don't offer a lot of scope to change global prices.

What all this means is that according to the WTO rules you should be allowing economics, and not politics, to determine where your goods and services come from. This could mean that some of your industries are either supplied by or outsourced to countries whose government you consider to be a competitor or threat.

There are a few questions national security thinkers might be asking themselves when considering this. Though it's not the only example, let's illustrate some of the primary ones using the US and China because their geostrategic competition looks set to define the 21st Century. At present the US and China trade extensively, with some supply chains actually bouncing back and forth between the two multiple times on the way to a finished product. So what are national security hawks in Beijing and Washington losing sleep over?

Question 1: Are we enabling our competitors to own the future?

Many policymakers incresingly feel that a country's strength will be determined by the extent of its homegrown scientific breakthroughs and innovative industries. When they say this, they are not talking exclusively or even primarily about military technology. How the US and Chinese 5th and 6th generation fighter jets stack up against each other is important, but not the clincher.

National security folks are looking at civilian industries like artificial intelligence, machine learning, battery technology, electric vehicles, renewable energy products, quantum computing, social media, aerospace, and many more. Not only do they believe that these will be engines of national prosperity, but also the critical tools of influence in tomorrow's world.

Of course you can't truly separate a country's civilian technological edge from its military one. Defence contractors and armed forces research institutes in the US benefit considerably from being next door to Silicon Valley, and thus able to recruit from a large pool of talented and experienced professionals. Building a giant quantum computer for the military is a lot simpler if your country has many experienced quantum computer engineers – and a lot cheaper if you didn't have to employ them all at government institutes to get them that experience.

It could be argued that by importing these advanced products from one another, rather than sourcing them domestically, from allies, or from neutral countries, the US and China are effectively financing the growth of these future high-tech industries on one another's territory. Moreover, by exporting high end components to one another, or partnering to manufacture or assemble such things on one another's territory, they are actively enabling the transfer (appropriation or theft) of technology and know-how that might otherwise give an edge.

Then there are the security implications from the increasing integration of technology and connectivity into products through the 'internet of things' and after-market service. Increasingly, everything from our cars to our watches and fridges is connected to the internet. Not to get unbearably 'old man yells at cloud server' about this but my electric toothbrush has a mobile app now and I'm frankly worried it's judging me.

Though the dangers of this can be overstated, it is hard to dismiss them. While it's unlikely that the US NSA or their Chinese equivalents at the 3PLA can flip a switch and cause your Google Android or Huawei phone to explode in your pocket, our homes and offices are full of devices capable of recording, transmitting data, and running code updatable by programmers in a foreign jurisdiction.

Beyond the espionage and data-gathering implications, national security experts are concerned about influence operations and narrative shaping. China of course strictly controls which US applications and websites are accessible to its general public, and at least once a month someone in the US proposes banning TikTok (on either espionage, influence operation, or national sanity grounds).

Question 2: Are we leaving ourselves vulnerable to economic pressure?

When discussing sanctions, one of the ways I suggested you think about them was as tools in influencing the internal calculus of a foreign leader. The more painful a set of sanctions might be if implemented, the more they or their threat might constrain that leader's policy options. They are tools a foreign country can use to try to change thinking and shape decisions – that's the definition of leverage.

In contemplating their dependence on one another therefore, a key question for national security experts is whether the existing trade relationship allows the other side to issue an effective ultimatum. Could your country bully my country into changing a policy or abandoning a plan by threatening to disrupt some aspect of our trade relationship?

An obvious truism is that the less dependent you are on exports to, and imports from, the other side, the fewer options they and their allies have to blackmail you with trade sanctions or export restrictions. But what constitutes effective pressure, how much will it cost to apply that pressure, and what might the countermoves be?

The US and China are entirely different political and economic systems, with their own stakeholders, sensitivities, strengths, and weaknesses. To name just one example, an economic hit which is negligible to the US economy as a whole but which costs a sitting US President two crucial swing states in the upcoming election could constitute an effective threat. A Chinese President may be more resilient to electoral pressure, but must balance the interests of their own set of stakeholders and powerbrokers. In either case, merely identifying a sensitivity and deploying an effective threat are two different things.

Even before we factor in retaliation, as we will in a moment, implementing a measure potent enough to hurt the other is going to carry costs for both sides. The US and China are massive markets, with annual trade between them exceeding half a trillion in USD. There is no such thing as a minor measure when it comes to interfering with such a large trade flow.

Take just one example – soybeans. China is the world's largest importer of soybeans by a frankly silly margin, importing over 23 times more of them in 2022 than Mexico, the second largest. Historically, many have been purchased from the US, which is the world's second largest soybean exporter after Brazil. In 2018, amidst rising trade tensions and following a wave of tariffs implemented on China by US President Trump, Chinese purchases of soybeans from the US dropped by 75 per cent almost overnight.

Though this is difficult to prove irrefutably because there was no official order published, just about all China watchers agree that what occurred was a quiet but very forceful suggestion from the Chinese Communist Party to the private sector that it should stop buying US soy. This must have come at a price. Abruptly barring your firms from accessing over a third of a globally traded commodity is going to have implications for everything from prices to logistics and contracting. It was a price the Chinese Communist Party was willing to pay, at least temporarily (trade has crept back up since 2018), but it's a price nonetheless.

Another example to consider is SWIFT, the Society for Worldwide Interbank Financial Telecommunication, a protocol used by banks to securely exchange financial information electronically. When I tell my bank to move money from my account into yours, both banks need a secure way to handle that request in a way that leaves no room for confusion. The SWIFT, headquartered in Belgium, provides that for over 10,000 banks worldwide, including in China.

When Russia launched its full scale invasion of Ukraine in 2022, one of the first sanctions involved removing major Russian banks from the SWIFT system. At a stroke, this made it significantly more difficult for businesses worldwide to do business with Russian companies, for Russian banks to offer their services abroad, and for Russian citizens to access their funds outside Russia. Elaborate schemes emerged as Russians struggled with what used to be basic banking functions like moving money abroad, with Russian citizens liquidating their assets in Russia, converting them into cryptocurrency, opening bank accounts in the United Arab Emirates and using them to convert that crypto into US dollars or euros again. An onerous, expensive and risky process.

For both the US and China, the SWIFT system and the dominance of the US dollar more generally dramatically raises the stakes. Ejecting China from SWIFT would significantly disrupt its businesses, and anyone seeking to transact with them. It would unquestionably hurt China and China knows it.

Yet at what cost? Throwing this kind of hand-grenade into the global markets is not something to be contemplated lightly. Not only would the resulting disruption in global payments hit many US companies too, but it would lend credence to those voices who have long been identifying US dollar dominance as a security vulnerability for the rest of the world. Todate, attempts to replace the dollar have mostly led to nothing, because the convenience, security and interoperability it offers as a global currency are unmatched. That's why China uses it and SWIFT in the first place. Weaponising it against the world's largest goods trader could change all that.

Beyond the immediate blowback effects of intervening in trade to limit a potential point of future weakness is the near inevitability of retaliation. China and the US are too large and significant to one another to not have any weak spots. In fact, the existence of such vulnerabilities is what this question is all about. In taking action to close one potential source of weakness, you will almost certainly hurt the other side and provoke them into retaliating by using another against you. Is closing a potential weakness that could be used against you in the future worth the immediate pain, and what other other weakness will be used to punish you for it? Policymakers have to carefully weigh these considerations.

Question 3: Could we survive if trade suddenly stopped?

How their country would cope if trade with the other side were abruptly and extendedly disrupted is a question that haunts national security advisers from Beijing to Washington. This could occur because a shooting war has broken out between the two sides, or, as a penultimate step, if two sides on the brink of military confrontation choose trade embargoes instead. It could occur as a deliberate policy choice, or because tensions are so high that freight carriers are simply unwilling to risk (or unable to insure) their vessels. Even just a credible expectation that a ban on imports might be imminent would reduce trade to near zero overnight, as few operators want to risk finding themselves with a haul of goods they cannot legally unload. The significant tensions in the Taiwan strait make this scenario far more than an abstract hypothetical, and some version of this could in theory be triggered by circumstances short of a full-scale attempt to seize control of the islands by mainland forces.

It goes without saying that such a Sino-American bust-up would be very bad for everyone, everywhere. The international trading system can be resilient, but it's just not built to withstand the two largest economies in the world abruptly disengaging from one another entirely. It's hard to imagine any kind of trading order that could. We can reasonably expect stock markets to go into a tailspin, investment to plummet and prices to shoot through the roof – not just in the US and China but worldwide.

For planners in the US and China, this becomes something of a siege mentality question. If trade between the two were to abruptly stop tomorrow, what are the imports either side couldn't live without, couldn't replace from elsewhere, and couldn't produce domestically? It is assumed that if things have gotten this bad, both governments are *in extremis* and thus willing to throw money, resources and effort at the problem – so what critical supply problems won't that fix?

Some of the obvious starting points here might be things no one else makes. These might be certain kinds of rare earth minerals, or processed rare earth minerals in which China has market dominance. They may also be certain technologies, such as the highest end chip manufacturing which the US and its allies Taiwan, the Netherlands and Japan dominate. The investments required to divest from dependency on these would be vast, and would have to take place over many years. You simply can't start producing processed rare earths or 5 nanometer chips overnight, no matter how much money you throw at the problem.

Then there's a broader range of products in which both sides could replace their dependency on the other within a reasonable timeframe, but not without a period of considerable disruption and significant expense. For example, China and the US are the world's top two exporters of intermediate goods, and the world's top two importers of them. Intermediate goods is a fancy name for components – the things that go into the things you make. Modern supply chains rely on obtaining them from all over the world and then assembling them into a finished product and no contingency plan or reserve is sufficient to withstand an abrupt end to the US $50 billion trade in intermediate goods.

Most of the components that would stop flowing under this scenario are perfectly ordinary parts like ball bearings, screws or laptop screens. If deliveries of any one of these products stopped, it would be a problem and potentially disrupt shipments but not something a concentrated effort and a good deal of money couldn't fix. The body blow to the economy occurs when instead of one supply chain being disrupted, thousands are. All at once.

Beyond the economic and productivity impacts, there are broader national security implications to consider. Important infrastructure may well partially rely on common components sourced from the adversary because they are the best value producer. This could be anything from water purification chemicals to medical equipment components to spare parts for road repair machinery. I doubt even the mighty Chinese bureaucracy has the resources to truly audit, down to a local level, the full dependency of China on US goods and services, or assess the implications of their withdrawal. I don't think US planners have a complete picture either – especially when you factor in the potential of a trade embargo hitting not just direct trade, but also the imports needed by your suppliers in third countries.

Finally, something I'll only allude to because it's outside my area of expertise, but the impact on financial markets, the cost of government borrowing, interest rates and so forth staggers the imagination. If goods have stopped flowing, it's almost certain that capital flows are heavily impacted as well and just intuitively, that does not sound like something that would spark joy.

Question 4: Have we lost the ability to mass produce arms?

It is taking nothing away from the heroism of the soldiers involved to say that World War II was mostly won by factories at home. Once the US, USSR and British war machines got going, they were able to produce tanks, vehicles, aircraft and ships in volumes Germany, Japan and Italy simply could not match. The war in the Pacific was especially emblematic of this, with the US producing two to three times as many carriers, fighters and bombers as the Japanese Empire.

The modern concern for the US (China does not lose sleep over this, for obvious reasons) is that in becoming more of a services economy and a manufacturer of high-end, low-volume technologically advanced equipment, the US may have lost the ability to rapidly switch gears and start pumping out millions of munitions, hundreds of tanks and scores of ships. Concerned observers point to the invasion of Ukraine and the difficulties both sides have had keeping up with the endless demand for artillery shells. They note the war rapidly depleted NATO's reserves of certain kinds of equipment like infantry portable anti-tank weapons, and that Western defence manufacturers quote long multi-year timeframes to replace depleted stocks.

There are two reasons advanced for this slowness. The first is that the US military's focus on slowly producing fewer, more expensive, high-end weapons has atrophied the muscles of US arms manufacturers when it comes to churning out huge volumes of cheaper weapons. They archly note that in World War II German tanks were sometimes the most advanced on the battlefield but ended up being overwhelmed by a USSR capable of throwing four T-34s at every Tiger.

The second is that as mass production has moved overseas (notably but not exclusively to China), the US has lost the ability to produce the inputs a vast military production effort might require, and has too few factories and shipyards that could be converted from civilian to military production in a crisis. The logic goes that it is far easier to take a factory currently making tractors and convert it to making tanks than it is to build a brand new tank factory, or undertake that same conversion with a small high-tech workshop building state of the art radiological equipment.

The trade angle here is that the availability of cheap imports is blamed for this change in the US manufacturing footprint. With liberalised trade and decreased global shipping costs, countries like China could use a combination of cheap labour, vast economies of scale, good logistics and state subsidies to outcompete US producers in mass manufacturing. The logic of the market saw US firms respond to this by pivoting into the areas where the US had advantages, which tended to be higher-end, lower-volume manufacturing and services. This has probably been a boon for US technological development, but might leave it without the inputs or solid foundation it needs to ramp up production of military materiel in an emergency.

The extent to which this is all a problem is contested among military thinkers. Sceptics might argue the US military, with its overwhelming air power and combined arms tactics, should never find itself fighting the kind of static artillery war seen in Ukraine – a war which looks the way it does precisely because neither side has access to significant quantities of genuinely modern weapons. They might point out that both China and the US are nuclear powers, so any conflict would probably escalate into a world-ending exchange of intercontinental ballistic missiles long before a steel shortage or lacklustre artillery shell production became an issue.

Finally, they might express confidence in the ultimate adaptability of US (and allied) productivity, noting that the failure to adequately supply Ukraine is occurring for a range of reasons other than an underlying lack of capacity (political constraints, a lack of true urgency, a mismatch between NATO munitions and what Ukraine's Soviet-era weapons fire, and so forth).

Trade Policy with National Security Characteristics

Underlying all four of the concerns described above is that too many of the factories, laboratories, patents, data servers and digital products (I'm going to use factories as shorthand for the rest of this chapter) you might need in a crisis are located either abroad, or worse within a geopolitical adversary. The implied remedy is to somehow move or create suppliers on your territory, that of your allies, or at the very least that of unaligned countries whose continued supply you can count on if things get ugly.

Trade theory tells us that if your country doesn't have a specific kind of factory, it's because you couldn't produce or maintain a competitive market position in that type of product. You could not, at an acceptable cost, compete with the value of products being offered by others and so your private sector is doing something else instead. Probably a craft brewery or some Software as a Service offering the purpose of which the company can't adequately explain but which was valued at $2 billion anyway.

If you want to change the above dynamic through government intervention, you have to change the equation under which domestic production is being outcompeted. There are a number of ways you might go about this, all of which fall under the newly rediscovered banner of 'Industrial Policy'.

First, you could try to improve some of the things which make a country attractive as a manufacturing hub. This could mean lowering taxes, improving infrastructure, easing planning permission and other approvals, zoning more land for the type of commercial activity you want to encourage, reducing the regulatory burden, weakening labour protections, and tolerating greater environmental impact.

All of these ideas come with their own costs, trade-offs and opposition. Many of the most meaningful improvements are also not the sort of thing you can do overnight or even over the course of a year or two. Massively upgrading freight infrastructure across the US or doubling the size of the Port of Miami would probably make a difference, but these are projects that take decades not months.

Some elements of an improved business climate may also be incompatible with other national priorities. The strict social and political controls exerted by the Chinese Communist Party on businesses within its territory, for example, probably have a chilling effect on investment, but are clearly part of a broader agenda that currently takes precedence. Similarly both countries would have to balance any easing of carbon or environmental regulations against their climate and sustainability objectives.

In both the US and China, some of these variables are controlled at the subnational level which may limit the ability of the federal government to alter them. It is also never certain that general improvements in the business climate will attract the kind of activity you're looking for. Unless carefully targeted you may simply find your intervention leads to businesses doing more of what they were already doing. In general, improving the business and investment climate is something many governments strive to do, but sweeping changes often run into the familiar public policy problems of unacceptable trade-offs, implementational complexity and entrenched stakeholders.

Second, you could provide subsidies and direct government incentives specifically for the kind of business activity you're hoping to foster. If the cost of production for a given product on your territory is too high, the guarantee of a long-term subsidy can make production commercially viable anyway. Subsidies can take a variety of forms, from direct cash transfers to tax incentives, but all fundamentally aim to tilt the cost of production equation in a favourable direction through the use of government funds (direct or forgone).

Subsidies sound nice in theory, and taxpayers may even be comfortable with government money being channelled to support local industry, but that doesn't mean they are easy to introduce. Opening the door for the government to identify individual industries or even firms to receive significant largesse from the treasury encourages parochial politics, cronyism, corruption and populist headline-chasing. It can reward businesses with connections to ruling elites, an effective lobbying apparatus, or simply those that resonate within the public imagination. Other countries, including your allies, are also likely to baulk when they discover themselves competing with firms that have the wealth of your government behind them.

Third, you could limit through tariffs or other restrictions at the border the availability of the imports you're being out-competed by

– or use export restrictions to deny the other country the inputs they need to be competitive. By artificially raising the price or limiting the availability of products, you will raise the competitiveness of other alternatives.

Tariffs and export restrictions of course come with their own downsides. At the very least in the short and medium term a tariff will raise prices for your consumers and those of your producers that rely on imported components. There's also no guarantee they'll spur your businesses to improve, expand and innovate rather than simply coasting while lobbying to keep the tariffs or export restrictions.

As with subsidies, there is also the ire of other nations to consider. Many products are traded on a global market and so applying tariffs on a product from a single source might simply lead to a reshuffle. You make it harder for Sweden to sell you apples, so they sell their apples to Peru instead, which means Peru no longer needs to buy New Zealand apples, freeing those up to flow into your market. If your goal was to encourage your own domestic apple growers, rather than simply becoming less dependent on Sweden, you're right back where you started from. There is also the very real risk of canny Danish operators importing Swedish apples and trying to sell them to you as Danish produce as a way to get around your tariff wall. To deal with these challenges, your tariffs may have to apply broadly, irrespective of origin. This will inevitably lead to tensions with, and potentially retaliation from, your trading partners whose industries will demand action.

Export restrictions, whereby you make it illegal to sell a country something its industry needs, could also lead to an endless game of cat and mouse as your components find their way into the restricted market through other places. Alternatively they could spur the other government into throwing a wave of resources into producing domestic alternatives so that your measure hamstrings them temporarily but ultimately leads them to become more independent of you as a supplier.

Fourth, you could attempt to create the factories and industries you want to see through direct government investment and the establishment of state-owned enterprises. A factory run by the state can survive even if not profitable, doesn't need to make decisions on purely commercial grounds, and can focus on objectives like the development of large-scale industrial capacity or supporting local producers further down the supply chain.

This could be an option but it's rarely an attractive one. Governments are generally reluctant to take on full responsibility for running a business. Though as a former civil servant I think people can get carried away gushing over the comparative efficiency of the private sector, it is undeniable that running large for-profit organisations is not within the skill set of most bureaucracies. Additionally, other firms may look askance at the prospect of competing or even negotiating with a business that is backed by the US government or Chinese Communist Party. A business that does not have to answer to the realities of the market or the value of its shares may not be properly incentivised to maximise efficiency and productivity.

Identifying which business to turn into a national champion or state owned enterprise in order to address a national security concern requires a genuinely nuanced understanding of supply chains and national vulnerabilities... and nuanced understanding of supply chains is not something governments are typically famous for.

The sense that a state-owned enterprise that exports may be doing so with an unfair advantage may also make other countries look carefully at whether tariffs might be needed to keep their market fair. Even if the state doesn't directly provide any advantages to this kind of business beyond starting and running it, the very fact that it has the government in its corner allows it to make longer-term investments, borrow money at lower rates and generally operate without many of the risks that might hamper a fully private enterprise. Other states will be aware of this and may look to redress it at their border.

This All Sounds Familiar . . .

If you have read the earlier chapters of this book none of the options described above should surprise you – they are exactly the same forms of protectionism, with similar risks and costs, as those available to policy makers looking to create jobs by thwarting competition or boosting their own producers. Though the rationale in this case is national security, crisis preparedness, and global competition, the challenge governments are trying to address remains the same: how do you create or move factories, jobs and supply chains to the places you want them when the market currently prefers them elsewhere? It's protectionism in an army helmet.

It's also manifestly inseparable from the political temptations that drive more traditional job creation motivated protectionism. Even if both the US and China really are primarily rolling out these kinds of policies for geostrategic reasons, the leaders of both are not averse to the opportunity to use them to create some jobs by fiat at the expense of distant foreigners. President Biden for example has been unapologetic in describing bringing back 'good high-paying manufacturing jobs' to the United States as an explicit objective.

As I hope I've made clear throughout this book, just because something is protectionist or parochially motivated doesn't automatically make it bad. It is, however, worth fully understanding the trade-offs they will entail, the likely consequences they'll have on the international stage, and whether your political system is built to effectively implement them. There is simply too much money to be made, too many positive headlines to be earned, and too many interests to balance for selecting national champions or handing out bags of government money to be risk-free.

What Does the WTO Say About All this?

For what it's worth, there is an opt-out for national security in the founding agreement of the World Trade Organization. This states that nothing in the WTO treaties will prevent a member from enacting policies that are vital to its national security, and then lists several potential security concerns that could necessitate a derogation from the trade rules. This is obviously a sizable exemption, and for many years countries avoided ever invoking it so as not to give others licence to do the same. This has changed in recent years, and the US has now invoked this national security exemption several times to defend a range of policies that would otherwise not be in line with WTO obligations.

This has led to some legal controversy because not all members agree on how the exemption should be interpreted. Some believe that the examples explicitly listed in the text, which cover fissionable nuclear material, weapons sales and actions taken during war, should be treated as an exhaustive list, with the only acceptable derogations being those that fall under one of them. Other members have argued that the national security exemption is broader, but that any member that wishes to invoke it can be challenged under the WTO dispute settlement system and must explain to a panel the nature of their security concern and why their measure was an appropriate and minimally trade disruptive response. The US rejects both of these interpretations.

The United States argues that a country is entitled to self-judge a national security concern warranting invoking this exemption. A WTO member should be able to simply declare that they consider a non-WTO compliant policy necessary for their national security, without having to justify their reasoning to a panel and certainly without the possibility that panel may overrule them. Where WTO panels have examined arguments on this and failed to uphold the US position they have been promptly told to go jump in Lake Geneva by Washington's esteemed representatives.

I have no idea who is right on the legal merits. I'm also, with the greatest possible respect to my legal scholar friends, not sure it matters. For my money the only practical way forward that preserves as much of the system as possible is for the exemption to be treated as self judging, but for its invocation to be limited by a combination of self-restraint and peer pressure from other members. At the end of the day the entire system is unenforceable without the active consent and investment of the membership and forcing the world's largest economy to choose between the international trade rules and what it views as a national security priority will not produce a happy outcome.

Where is This Headed?

With the national security genie well and truly out of the bottle and global competition for the 21st Century between the US and China only likely to heat up, I think we can expect to see more intervention by governments in international commerce on security grounds. Even narrowing our focus exclusively to US and China, this is pretty much guaranteed by the importance of international trade to their rivalry, and the vastly lower costs of trade measures when compared to military action.

I think we can also fully expect some of the measures implemented under a national security banner to be nakedly protectionist, impurely motivated, and questionably effective even when measured against their own stated objectives. That is not an indictment of either the US or Chinese system of governance or any individual leaders in either country – it is simply the inevitable outcome of humans with competing priorities being handed a powerful tool to intervene in the market.

How disruptive all this proves to business, how damaging to growth and development, and how stifling to innovation and long term investment will depend on the restraint shown by both sides, the extent to which a cycle of policy action and retaliation becomes self perpetuating, and how other countries react from the sidelines. The US and China are also hardly the only countries on Earth looking at trade through an increasingly national security tinted lens. We can expect to see national security invoked in the fight against climate change, various industrialisation strategies across the developed and developing world, and the simple populist urge to bring jobs back home at any price. In other words, we're in for a wild ride.

Chapter 14
Trade and Climate Change

Climate change and the damage we're ceaselessly inflicting upon our long-suffering planet is a problem so vast and horrifying that the mind automatically retreats from its implications. Like witnessing an onrushing tsunami while holding a single sandbag, the magnitude of the challenge simultaneously demands immediate action and makes a mockery of any individual response. It is also a problem of staggering complexity, where unintended consequences lurk behind every noble act and new dominoes rise and fall seemingly without contact.

I appreciate I am likely not the first person to express the radical idea that addressing climate change is complicated. I do so, however, because it feels like often when the conversation turns to trade and climate change, our appreciation of all that complexity melts away like ice cream in an unseasonable May heatwave.

The human propensity for simplifying complex narratives is invaluable for communication but isn't always helpful when the facts do not support such reductionism. Similarly, our quest for clearly identified villains to fit into neat morality plays isn't necessarily useful when the blame is spread so widely and the motivations behind our sins are so human. To even begin to unpack the intersection of trade and climate change therefore, I have to (unfortunately) take a step back and talk about the discourse more broadly.

Uncomfortably Hot Truths

Climate change is fundamentally a production problem born of a consumption problem. There are now many of us – and we want to live well. With notable exceptions such as ascetic mountaintop mystics, survivalist forest hermits, and the Amish, the world's population mostly define 'living well' at least partially in terms of the quality and quantity of goods they can possess and services they can access. This incentivises supply, and in the absence of external constraining forces such supply follows the path of least resistance, consuming natural resources and releasing harmful by-products of production at ever more prodigious rates. We want stuff, so we make stuff, and we want it to be cheap and so we make it in the cheapest ways – which are often the dirtiest.

With improvements in technology and transportation, and the emergence of growing consumer classes outside of traditionally wealthier countries, this cycle of consumption and environmental degradation has become increasingly international. Critics of capitalism will argue that this shift abroad is driven by pursuit of greater corporate profits, and supporters of capitalism will argue it is driven by competition and pursuit of greater efficiency. Regardless of the motivations, however, the underlying cause has been growing demand to feed consumption.

This challenge of overconsumption is often presented as a Western phenomenon, and it's certainly true that the lifestyle of average US or French citizens is many times more energy-consuming and destructive to maintain, in the aggregate, than that of their counterparts from Benin, Argentina or Myanmar. The problem is that this likely reflects the economic constraints of the latter far more than their enlightened morality. It would border on the offensiveness of the noble savage myth to suggest that the average person in Benin has simply chosen to make the lifestyle sacrifices required to consume 1/16th the energy of the average American. It is unreasonable to expect the citizens of Porto-Novo or Cotonou to unilaterally turn down a kitchen full of white goods, a pair of cars in the garage or regular holidays by airliner – and certainly many of the wealthier residents of Benin who can afford to do so avail themselves of these.

Consider just one example: air conditioning. At time of writing India has an average annual temperature of 30 degrees Celsius, with extremes well above that. Both the average and the peaks are likely to rise as climate change exacerbates the intensity of summers on the subcontinent. At present, only 13 per cent of Indian households have air conditioning, but there are predictions that this could rise to 69 per cent by 2040[1], with increases on a similar scale predicted for Indonesia, Brazil and Mexico. For India, this would mean around 800 million more air conditioning users than it has today, even before factoring in commercial and public air conditioning.

This illustrates the dilemma. On the one hand, close to a billion new users of comparatively energy-intensive air conditioning could have a huge impact on climate change. On the other, absolutely no one has the moral authority to tell either the Indian people or the Indian government that they should not use commercially available technology to make the lives of their citizens bearable, especially when we in the West have been doing so for decades despite enjoying generally milder conditions.

The challenge we have as a species is therefore not only that decadent Westerners are living in ways that require significant environmental degradation to deliver using presently available techniques, but that at least somewhat increased consumption is desirable to most

---

[1.] tps://www.deccanherald.com/national/indias-ac-requirement-is-set-to-rise-steeply-shows-study-1049050.html

of the world's other 6 billion citizens. This is often left out of the conversation, in part because like climate change itself, the sheer scale of the challenge is so staggering that it risks inducing despair, and partly because it sounds like a call for letting the West off the hook for excessive consumption.

Unfortunately, a reality being daunting or open to interpretation in unhelpful ways doesn't rob it of veracity. Westerners reducing and adjusting their consumption habits in more sustainable directions is a moral imperative – if not yet a politically palatable one. Yet reducing Western consumption alone, even if it could be achieved, would not be sufficient unless millions in developing countries simultaneously forswore acquiring any of the finer but more energy intensive aspects of modernity – which cannot reasonably be asked.

Humanity therefore faces a near insurmountable challenge if it attempts to tackle climate change exclusively through buying less. First, the level of sacrifice required by those in richer countries is unlikely to be politically sustainable until the crisis is so bad that it's too late. Second, because even modest increases in the disposable income of the world's average developing country citizen, which no one can begrudge, would lead to trillions more goods and services being bought annually – with inevitable climate consequences.

In case you're getting nervous that this book is about to take a sinister turn, let me reassure you that I'm not about to call for a culling of the human race, an end to growth or the release of an Umbrella Corporation zombie virus. I reserve such policy proposals exclusively for when someone in front of me is walking too slowly. The only two points I'm trying to make are that the solutions to climate change have to heavily incorporate the supply and distribution side, and that delivering them will require venturing beyond comfortable narratives.

Climate Ain't Shakespeare

As humans, we are prone to seeking clear narratives with defined heroes and villains to help us understand the world around us. We like morality plays and feel comfortable when a negative consequence can be directly linked back to the misdeeds or hubris of a specific group or individual. When envisaging solutions to problems, we naturally prefer to see the malicious, negligent or greedy punished and the virtuous rewarded. The problem is that's rarely how big systemic crises work.

In 2008, the global financial crisis was interpreted by many through this morality play lens. Governments had been too profligate, borrowing and spending too much, and would now have to appease the market gods with austerity and spending cuts in the hopes of mitigating their vengeance. Of course, this was nonsense. The causes of the financial crisis were many and complex, but getting out of the crisis required more government spending and stimulus, not less. By putting ash in their hair, rending their garments and adopting the language of 'belt tightening', governments may well have extended the crisis and hurt millions of people.

As in the financial crisis, climate change looks like it will be unfair, in its impacts, who has to make sacrifices to adapt and mitigate it, and who will profit from the solutions. Any policies we consider have to be mindful of this reality. Justice must be central to anything we devise, not only out of a moral imperative but a practical one – prolonged injustice will invite resistance. At the same time, we cannot allow the pursuit of perfect justice to become paralysing – vetoing any and all action that does not perfectly balance past, present and future fairness. If we refuse to act because we want climate solutions whose costs exclusively fall on the 'guilty' or from which none of the 'villains' of climate change benefit, we will doom ourselves.

The unpalatable reality of our situation is that any of the solutions or mitigations we envision to deal with the climate crisis are likely to benefit many of the actors whose actions got us into this mess. Even if techniques and technologies like vertical farming, sustainable energy production, carbon capture and the circular economy are pioneered by small, socially-minded start-ups or independent scientists, they will inevitably be refined or appropriated for the market by large corporations or become such corporations themselves through investments by venture capital funds.

There is both an inevitability to this and a certain desirability. Climate change is a global problem and so the solutions have to be available in staggering volumes. This will require global reach to deliver and integrated supply chains to assemble at accessible costs. The capital, know-how and process complexity required to put an iPhone in the hands of 900 million users is also probably our best hope of disseminating more energy-efficient goods and production methods before it's too late.

This feels like a bitter pill to swallow. Many of the same firms and capital funds which recklessly but profitably disregarded environmental care in the past will now pivot in the face of changing regulations, customer expectations and government subsidies to continue making profits by mitigating the damage they (at least partially) caused. There will be little justice in the distribution of the profits of any green revolution, and it's likely those that were environmentally reckless in the past will be largely insulated from the consequences of their actions. Legally, because they weren't necessarily breaking any laws – and practically because their wealth will shield them from the worst of climate change. It's Macbeth, if he and his wife had reigned happily ever after having invested in some really good hand soap or a nice pair of gloves.

I write this not to depress you, but to drive home a tension at the heart of climate change and trade policy's intersection. Trade, at least in the popular imagination, is thought to be the domain of the megacorporation, and trade policy is thought to be dictated by their whims. For this and a range of other factors, many climate activists are wary of trade and inclined to be suspicious of it, often favouring more local production and the active intervention of the state in international commerce. This isn't necessarily the wrong approach, but things are a lot more complicated.

If we massively simplify things, trade policy intersects with environment and climate change in two primary ways:

1. **Generally** encouraging or discouraging the sale of goods and services across borders **which could have an environmental impact**; and

2. **Specifically** encouraging or discourging the sale of certain goods and services across borders **based on their individual environmental implications.**

The General – is More Trade Bad?

Let's start with the first one since it's marginally less complicated. Trade itself has a carbon footprint because we have yet to find ways to move goods or (most) services around the world without expending energy and emissions. There is a movement which argues that a more sustainable economy would be one where goods are sourced locally wherever possible. In addition to the purported environmental benefits this movement also sometimes makes arguments such as locally made products creating employment in the region, being fresher (where applicable), and more 'ethical'. Their argument is beyond the scope of this book, because it generally focuses on changing the choices made by consumers or retailers, rather than using the power of the state to change those choices through policy.

Yet policy can start to get involved here. Governments can legislate and regulate to force companies and retailers to be more transparent about where their products are made. Consumers who are specifically interested in local goods, whatever their reasoning, can then make choices about what they buy in the reasonable certainty that they're not being lied to or bamboozled. In the same way that some governments prevent cereal companies from slapping 'health food' on the side of a box of hyperactivity-in-a-box chocolate-frosted loops, so too can governments help to prevent environmentally misleading labelling.

More kinetically, those that argue that trade itself is bad for climate change because of its carbon footprint describe anything the government does to make trade with distant countries easier as problematic, and anything it does to make it harder as beneficial. One of the most common responses you'll see when a government announces a trade agreement with a country on the other side of the world is the criticism that this will only encourage more carbon-emitting freight journeys that could be avoided if people were incentivised to shop locally instead.

If a country has a prohibitively high tariff on a product, it is unlikely anyone will be able to afford to bring it in from abroad. Similarly, if a country refuses to grant visas to management consultants, then no such consultant will get on a plane to deliver their services in person. In both cases, the impact might be good for the planet, but is not necessarily. Producing the same product domestically might mean fewer economies of scale, decreased competition might mean less innovative designs and so on. Similarly, the foreign management consultant may have contributed to a greener, more sustainable project design that ultimately offset the carbon costs of their travel. Either scenario could mean an overall negative impact on carbon from the trade barrier. Also, stop snickering, it's at least theoretically possible that a management consultant would be helpful.

We should treat the idea of fighting climate change by limiting trade with some caution. While global logistics is a big emitter, the vast majority of carbon it produces is driven (sorry) by trucks and freight vehicles. Giant cargo ships emit, but they're just so darn big and carry so much stuff at a time that their ratio of kilometre-tonnes to emissions ends up being pretty good, at least compared to existing alternatives. In fact, our growing appetite for home-delivered goods, which at least at the moment are primarily delivered by diesel or petrol-powered trucks and vans, is likely to exacerbate the problem more than any liberalisation of trade.

There are also trade-offs to consider around economies of scale and efficiency. A single heavily optimised gigafactory might be so efficient in terms of energy use and waste management as to more than offset the subsequent emissions of the transport required to bring its products to distant markets. To put it very simply, a giant factory making washing machines in Seoul and delivering them to ten countries might generate less in carbon emissions than ten smaller, less efficient factories scattered around the world, even factoring in their shorter delivery distances.

If you think that sounds like a slightly too convenient defence of global supply chains and neoliberalism, you're not wrong. Engineers aren't always going to be able to squeeze out greater emissions efficiency, and as we'll discuss later in this chapter there is no guarantee that factories in far-off countries will be compelled to regulate their emissions at all. The only point I hope to leave you with on this is that, by itself, local production is not a guarantee of greater climate efficiency. Policies and consumer preferences cannot simply be predicated on the assumption that anything that travelled a greater distance is automatically the more climate-damaging option.

Other arguments might also be made in defence of trade – and freer trade. Any technology we invent, skills we learn or knowledge we uncover will need to be disseminated rapidly and globally if it is to have any meaningful impact. Though far from perfect, international commerce provides the incentive structures and frameworks to encourage this. While we can of course rely on altruism or voluntary transfers, my suspicion is that making it possible and lucrative to sell such creations abroad is the best way to support their spread around the world. You are well within your rights to call me a naive footsoldier for rapacious capitalism for this opinion. Let's face it, I deserve it.

Another point to consider is trade's contribution to resilience. As the impacts of climate change become more pronounced, wild weather effects are likely to proliferate. The ability to move crops and commodities to parts of the world where agricultural yields are temporarily depressed by drought, flood or natural disaster will become increasingly important, especially for smaller countries whose entire crop could be devastated by a single event. Providing financial assistance to allow a country that is already well integrated into global trade to buy greater volumes is easier than providing food assistance directly, especially to a country that has not traded much in the past and thus lacks the infrastructure or policy framework to absorb inflows. An efficient global trading system that can move goods and services around quickly and reliably may be a vital component of mitigating some of the acute disruption climate change is poised to deliver.

None of the above is an invitation to cease being cynical about trade's overall climate impact. If something is being shipped from half the world away, having been made in a place that may take environmental commitments less seriously than your own home, you can and should question why. My only plea is that you avoid easy, sweeping answers, often offered by those with incomplete information or impure motives. Trade is far too big an element of human civilisation to fit entirely and neatly into any box labelled 'good' or 'bad'. Ask the right questions, get specific, and be sceptical of anyone who claims you needn't bother.

Getting Specific – Climate Driven Trade Policy

Trade policy that specifically targets climate change is a bottomless pit of complexity and you may want to get a cup of tea before we deal with it. Climate change is such a large issue, and tackling it is so multifaceted that virtually every government policy and regulation can have an impact. The inverse of this is that governments looking to do so can centre climate change considerations in virtually every policy and regulatory choice. This book can't even hope to cover them all, and won't try. Instead, I'd like to look at some of the big umbrella issues so you can get a flavour of the debates that shape them.

Preventing Carbon Leakage – Legitimate Comparative Advantage

Much of international trade theory is predicated on the notion of comparative advantage: that it makes sense to buy things from places that can produce them more efficiently, and instead focus on producing the things you can make more efficiently. There are lots of ways a country could have a comparative advantage. Lower wages, a highly skilled labour force, good institutions, excellent infrastructure, frictionless borders with its neighbours, a location on or near major trade routes, particularly fertile soil or even the prevalence of a specific language, can all give one country a leg up over its peers in specific industries.

For the latter half of the 20th and the early 21st Centuries trade policy considered most of the above to be legitimate sources of comparative advantage. Yet not all forms of comparative advantage fell into this category. For example if your comparative advantage came because your government allowed you to employ slave or prison labour, or from having a government willing to pay you $1 for every $3 you export, thus driving down prices, that's not going to win you many plaudits for international trade fair play. Trade policy therefore created a distinction between legitimate sources of comparative advantage which you were supposed to live with, and illegitimate ones you were allowed to take steps to prevent or rebalance. That brings us to one of the key questions of the climate and trade debate: which category does climate negligence fall into? If my government lets me make things in a more environmentally harmful, and thus cheaper, way than yours . . . is that a fair way for me to be more 'efficient'?

Historically, there was no expectation that the country shipping products maintained the same environmental standards as you, provided their negligence wasn't making the product itself unsafe. If that sounds unfair to you, remember that the main proponents of this approach were probably not greedy corporations eager to poison dolphins, but developing countries concerned they'd be locked out of competing in lucrative Western markets by unrealistic demands. Developing countries were (probably rightly) worried that Western governments would weaponise environmental standards to justify keeping developing country products out of their markets.

'But wait,' you might be wondering, 'don't the greedy corporations benefit from cutting costs?' It depends. If you're in a really crowded, low-margin sector, then cutting costs by moving a factory overseas will only increase your profits if none of your competitors do so too. The fact that any of your rivals can also move their production abroad to find the same savings not only erases many of the profit benefits of offshoring but somewhat perversely, makes them obligatory.

Imagine you make generic black socks at a factory in Stockholm. They cost $3 each to make, and you sell them to retailers for $5, which is about the same as your rivals with factories in Manchester, Turin and Munich. If you had the option of moving your factory to North Korea, reducing costs to $1, you could keep selling those socks to retailers for $5 and make much more profit, but you would likely instead start selling them for $3 to corner the cheap socks market, vastly increasing your sales while keeping the same profit margin. Except of course, you're not the only one who knows how to move a factory.

Your competitors, upon seeing you move to Pyongyang, will almost certainly have to start looking for a cheaper manufacturing base of their own. Suddenly you're all producing for $1, all selling for $3, and everyone's market share is back to where it was. You've all now spent hundreds of millions moving factories to end up back where you started. From your perspective, it would have been far more cost-effective to spend a fraction of the money on a lobbying campaign to convince the government to ban, or slap high tariffs on, foreign-made socks to lock in the status quo.

This doesn't apply universally. Prestige or brand-name products which don't have to worry about direct competition on price benefit hugely from offshoring savings. No one is buying Gucci or the new iPhone because they are the cheapest offerings on the market, and it would be very hard to steal market share from Gucci or Apple by undercutting them on price. The segment of the market those two firms are going for is the one that specifically wants their brands. In fact, Gucci probably couldn't cut its prices significantly even if its production costs fell because it might deter consumers by diluting the prestige of owning a Gucci item. Therefore, when Gucci moves production abroad to save on costs, it can comfortably keep prices where they were and pocket the extra profits.

Though big brand names like Gucci and Apple are probably the ones we think of most often, they are the exceptions rather than the rule. The vast majority of factories worldwide are producing boring but critical components to feed into a supply chain, and there, price competitiveness is king. Firms like these with production in countries with stricter and thus more costly environmental regulations have historically grumbled about being made to compete with companies abroad in places with looser, cheaper rules. However with some exceptions, until climate change, they didn't have much success in convincing their governments to step in and rebalance things in their favour. In the past, the biggest savings from moving production abroad tended to be driven by lower wages (also economies of scale and the availability and affordability of land zoned for industrial production), which was where the political focus was, rather than laxer environmental regulations.

Now, governments are looking at differences between environmental regulations in different countries and exploring options to prevent these becoming a source of comparative advantage. In essence, governments are considering how they can use the tools at their disposal to 'level the playing field' for their companies against those abroad they deem to be 'cheating' by operating in markets that don't have the same levels of environmental regulation. One such tool is border adjustment

Carbon Leakage and Carbon Border Adjustments

Disclaimer: I am about to try to summarise for you in under 2,000 words a debate of such staggering complexity that people far smarter than I have devoted half a decade to researching slivers of it. I am going to zoom out to 30,000 feet and survey it in the broadest terms, so that you can follow the big issues, and perhaps, more importantly, recognise when a politician, activist or pundit is falsely claiming it's quite simple.

Despite sounding like something you might want to speak to a gastroenterologist about, 'carbon leakage' is a trade term increasingly used to describe fears about how regulations aimed at fighting climate change might be thwarted. Specifically, the scenario runs like this: a government introduces a carbon tax (or price or expensive regulation), which increases the costs of carbon-intensive manufacturing by businesses located within its borders. Instead of greening their processes, cutting emissions or raising their prices, the companies in question either move overseas to somewhere without a carbon tax, or just lose all their market share to competitors already abroad. The end result would be a lot of jobs lost domestically, but the same amount of net carbon in the atmosphere. A lose-lose-lose for government, local business and the planet.

At the time of writing, there is a fierce academic debate about whether this phenomenon has ever actually happened or is likely to happen at currently foreseeable levels of carbon taxation. In order to justify the expense of a move abroad environmental regulation or carbon measures would have to be high enough to offset the significant expenses of offshoring production. This may ultimately prove true for certain products, but there isn't a strong consensus it has yet, or will soon at current levels of carbon pricing and regulation.

Of course, as the title and hopefully the substance of this book makes clear, that doesn't necessarily matter. Human beings tend to lose all sense of proportion and perspective when they feel like they're being cheated, and even more so when they feel that cheating is being done by greedy corporations and scheming foreigners. Whether or not carbon leakage is actually happening, it certainly feels like it can or should be, so introducing measures to stop it has the unstoppable political force of intuitive obviousness. 'Why would they make anything here and pay a carbon tax when they can just make it abroad, pay no tax, and export to us?' is rhetorically powerful.

Consider this scenario: you've introduced a carbon tax, carbon credits or just particularly strict environmental regulations around carbon-intensive manufacturing. Not all your trading partners have done the same. Your businesses are howling. They share (or perhaps simply accept) your environmental objectives but now feel like they're being made to compete with polluters. They are demanding you even the playing field. You may suspect some of their motives, but their argument makes sense logically and is potent rhetorically. No leader wants to be painted as the sucker who regulated their own businesses out of existence while letting environmentally negligent foreigners gobble up their market share.

So what can be done? The most drastic option would be to simply ban imports from countries with more permissive regulatory regimes. This is difficult for a few reasons. First, even rolled out in a fairly limited way, it's likely to be economically disruptive and inflationary. Consumers and businesses would suddenly find themselves cut off from their suppliers for products for which there may be no local alternatives. Second, it would be an incredibly blunt response, almost certainly triggering strong retaliation and condemnation from trading partners. Third, it's blatantly in violation of your WTO obligations. The long term harm to the planet and thus your citizens from carbon emissions does not constitute the kind of threat to health or safety that, under WTO rules, justifies banning imports of any product from a country without carbon measures.

You could subsidise your own firms to offset the advantage their foreign competitors gain, but simply giving businesses back the money they would otherwise pay in a carbon tax is manifestly self-defeating – like if every speeding fine came with a hundred-dollar bill tucked inside. Of course, not all subsidies fall into this category. Government grants to help a factory upgrade its equipment and processes to reduce its carbon footprint are potentially sensible, but once the low-hanging fruit upgrades are made, you may find yourself paying more and more taxpayer funds for each per cent of emission reduction. There may also be products or sectors where meaningfully reducing carbon emissions is either entirely or practically impossible in any reasonable time frame.

The solution a growing number of governments are reaching for is to the introduction at the border of a rebalancing measure – commonly referred to as a Carbon Border Adjustment (or CBA). The logic is pretty simple. When a product from abroad enters my market, I'm going to charge it however much it would have paid had it been made here, under my local carbon taxation or pricing scheme. In theory, this shouldn't give my own businesses any advantage. It just takes away your ability to use the absence of a carbon tax in your country as anadvantage in my market.

Sounds Reasonable, Why are People Mad?

The theory of a carbon border adjustment is appealing, but there is plenty of room in the detail to hide many devils. As is often the case, it's easiest to wrap your head around these things by thinking about what will take place at the border.

Picture this: You have arrived at my border with a shipment of 100 shiny new machines. Let's imagine my country has an incredibly simple carbon tax under which any factory in my country has to pay $5 per kiloton of carbon dioxide equivalence (I picked this cost at random, don't send me letters). Since your machines were made elsewhere, if I want to apply this tax to them I need to know how many emissions were produced in their manufacture. Since I'm probably not familiar with the carbon footprint of every factory everywhere in the world, in practice, that means I need a document from you with that data.

Here we strike the first hurdle. Accurately calculating manufacturing emissions isn't straightforward. There are also some pretty strong incentives to cheat or undercount, as this will reduce at-border tax. When companies in my own country report their emissions, they do so at risk of audit by my authorities and within my jurisdiction where they could be fined or otherwise held liable for providing false or incomplete information. As a foreign producer, you're outside my jurisdiction and I probably don't have the resources to properly audit more than a handful of foreign suppliers every year. Producing documentation that is up to my standards, and that I trust, is therefore a major concern – especially for developing country suppliers.

If you don't provide documentation, or if I don't trust the documentation you've provided, I have to set some default level of taxation to apply to your machines. But where do I set that default? The most carbon-emitting washing machine factory in my own country? The most carbon-emitting factory in the world? My best guess of the most emitting factory in your country? If I set the default too high, I create an incentive for carbon-negligent producers to just keep taking the default forever. If I set the default too low, I risk punishing responsible factories doing the right thing but struggling to meet my requirements for paperwork or verification.

Things get even dicier when you consider a situation where the country which made those washing machines already has its own carbon tax. In theory, if you've paid $5 per kiloton at home, there's no need to tax you at my border. However, in order to be comfortable with that and grant your local tax an equivalency ruling under my system I need to trust your evidence that you have such a tax, how much it charges, on what, and that it was actually collected. If I think your country has a vastly lower tax, a similar tax it doesn't enforce, or a tax you can get out of paying with a quick bribe in the right pocket, I may not be willing to just accept that you don't need to pay mine at the border. And that's just the situation when we both use a tax approach to control carbon.

What if your country has a complex carbon credits scheme where you were allowed a certain amount of 'free' emissions and then had to bid for the rest in an auction system with fluctuating prices? How do I work out if that system is equivalent to my own tax – and therefore whether you should be charged extra at my border?

None of the above are insurmountable problems. A carbon border adjustment, designed in good faith, with purely environmental objectives, and genuine consideration given for the practicalities for producers outside of wealthy countries, could be fair and feasible – especially if its administrators are open to feedback and amending how it works.

Much of the pushback, however, arises from the suspicion among trading partners that when designing carbon border adjustments, countries may have motivations other than the purely environmental. Domestic industries, especially those not massively reliant on foreign components, have strong incentives to lobby for a maximally restrictive carbon border adjustment. Meanwhile, foreign firms know their plight is a low priority for the implementing governments. The concerns therefore are both that these border adjustment mechanisms will acquire a protectionist flavour and that bugs, inequities, and paperwork difficulties will linger unaddressed for years because they do not agitate any domestic constituency.

There's also a fairness issue. To date, the agreed international framework for reducing global carbon emissions has relied on national targets and reductions agreed under the UNFCCC framework through treaties like the Kyoto Protocol and Paris Agreement. These focus on the country as a whole, and are agnostic about how emissions reductions are reached. A country could have a sector that is very emissions intensive, but still comfortably reach its Paris targets if the rest of its economy is more responsible. The Paris Agreement and climate negotiations generally also have a core principle of 'Common but Differentiated Responsibility' under which developed countries make greater commitments because of both their comparative wealth and their historic contribution to the climate crisis.

Developing countries argue a carbon border adjustment runs somewhat contrary to these principles. A load of washing machines will be taxed at my border on its own carbon footprint, irrespective of how much the producing country is emitting overall, its level of development, or its historic contribution to carbon in the atmosphere. Defenders would argue that this is as it should be, because the goal is to eliminate climate recklessness as a form of comparative advantage, and that must by necessity take place at the product and not the national level. Yet it is understandably galling for a developing country with a tiny and perhaps even shrinking carbon footprint to suddenly find its one emission-intensive industry facing border barriers when entering a market with a vastly larger share of the current and past blame for climate change.

None of these objections are likely to mean carbon border adjustments aren't happening. They almost certainly are, and the first ones are slowly coming online even at the time of writing. The debates about their fairness, design, implementation and interoperability, however, are going to continue for decades. I also suspect that they will be weaponised politically, whether to blame them for higher prices on shelves (very unlikely), or claim their impotence or absence is behind every job lost and factory closed nationwide (also probably not true). Hopefully the above has given you at least some sense of why the inevitable sweeping statements you'll hear on the campaign trail at home or around the world bely this complexity.

Regulators – Mount Up!

Before we looked at carbon pricing/taxation, I briefly talked about the role of regulators in levelling the playing field when it comes to the environmental impacts of production. This is worth exploring further. There has been a fierce debate in trade law circles (read: 20 people worldwide have written articles at one another in prestigious academic journals and then bickered about them on Twitter) about whether it is within the spirit and letter of World Trade Organization rules for regulations to target how a product was made, rather than its completed state when it crosses your border. Trade geeks call this discussion 'Process and Production Methods' (PPMs).

The argument in favour of PPMs is that we, as a society, should be entitled to ban from our markets goods whose production we find morally or ethically objectionable, even if the harms they cause aren't directly to our citizens, flora and fauna. A bar of steel created with power from enslaved pug puppies on a water wheel may be functionally identical to one made with solar energy and pose no threat to puppies in the destination country, but we should be allowed to ban it.

The argument against PPMs is that once we open the door to arbitrating the production methodologies of other countries, the temptation to deploy them to advantage our domestic industries will become irresistible. Tit-for-tat exchanges, protectionism and moral panics will run rampant as politicians invariably choose the (comparatively) easy road of hurting foreign exporters over pushing back on public demands around emotive topics.

On environmental issues, and especially on climate change, the debate is even murkier. Like my slave-puppy-produced steel, a product made in a carbon emissions intensive way is not, in most cases, itself dangerous to the environment or morally problematic. It's just a bar of steel. However, unlike the pug-puppy watermill, carbon emissions on your territory can be thought of as a threat to the health and safety of my citizenry – even if perhaps indirectly and over the long term.

People have always argued, not without merit, that 'harm on your own territory' is an outmoded and morally lazy standard to apply. If demand for palm oil in my country fuels deforestation, habitat loss and eventually extinction for orangutans in yours, is that really not a legitimate concern for me? Is the extinction of a species a loss exclusively for the place where it lived, or a tragedy for the whole world? If, as the WTO rules do, we consider it appropriate for our regulators and officials to prevent our citizens from being sold goods made abroad with prison or slave labour, are environmentally reckless products truly substantively different?

Debates like the above have been raging for some time, and increasingly it feels like the movement in favour of Process and Production Methods as a valid cause for regulatory and tariff barriers is gaining ground. In following the controversy, keep your eye out for a few telling signs. First, is the discussion happening in the context of a Free Trade Agreement? Because a trade agreement is a bespoke deal that lowers tariffs below the levels agreed at the WTO, there really aren't any legal impediments to including any conditions the parties agree. Any producer that doesn't like those conditions can simply continue selling without benefiting from the trade agreement's reduced tariffs, exactly as they (presumably) were the day before the agreement entered into force. In most cases, I would argue this is not a big deal as it's not being done unilaterally, and it provides an optional path to better access without impacting the access that already exists. .

Second, it's worth asking whether the measure is general or weirdly focused. Choosing to focus on one product or type of product isn't necessarily a bad thing. You have to start somewhere, and there may be a low-hanging fruit to pick or an experiment to conduct. However, if the focus suspiciously aligns with a product made domestically by a vocal industry group, or the products chosen keep happening to be highly photogenic or emotive cases for which it's easy to fundraise, campaign and earn free media for, it's worth raising some eyebrows.

Third, as ever, consider the practicalities of meeting the new regulatory requirements, especially for suppliers in poorer countries. People in the developed world tend to assume that everyone else operates in a networked, digitalised and responsive bureaucratic context that can quickly and easily supply all required proofs and documents. That's not even universally true in their own countries, let alone abroad. Proving you meet requireements can at times be far more difficult than actually meeting them, and that kind of discrepancy can destroy lives and communities.

Fourth and finally, be wary of performative but ultimately useless charades. I once heard a politician, in defence of a new environmental trade barrier, assure a crowd of trade wonks not to freak out because their analysis suggested it wouldn't impact anyone. Imports of the targeted product into the politician's country were so negligible that, even if the trade barrier proved insurmountable, no one would notice. The point they were trying to make was that all the hullabaloo was an overreaction, but it made me want to scream because I knew that in other public appearances, he was selling it as a bold and impactful environmental measure driven by vital moral imperative. He was lying to someone, and the fact that it was probably to the general public and not to me wasn't a great comfort.

Say Something Positive, Coward

Carbon Border Adjustment and Process and Production Method debates tend to suck up a lot of the oxygen, but I would be remiss if I didn't end this chapter by flagging up the vast amount of other work being done on trade, the environment and climate change. This is going to be a non-exhaustive list and so if you're out there in the trenches trying to save the planet and I don't mention your work, please forgive me!

- There is an effort to try and agree a lower of trade barriers to 'Environmental Goods and Services'. If we can make it easier and cheaper to bring solar panels, less wasteful water pipes and recycling technology across borders, we can speed up the global deployment of these vital technologies. Similarly, making it easier for companies with expertise in environmental fields to sell their services abroad is equally vital, especially as often that expertise is cutting edge knowledge that may not be available locally;

- A global negotiation is underway toward a treaty seeking to end plastic pollution through commitments on how it's made, recycled and disposed of;
- Experts and policymakers are engaging on what can be done to ensure that the vast amount of global subsidies governments currently offer in industries like agriculture are better targeted, encouraging a transition to more sustainable and less carbon intensive modes of production;
- The International Maritime Organization, an intergovernmental UN organisation, agreed a target of reducing shipping's carbon footprint by 20-30 per cent by 2030, 70-80 per cent by 2040, and to having freight shipping be carbon-neutral by 2050. This is just part of a much larger effort to reduce shipping emissions which brings together governments, the private sector and experts;
- In just about every sector imaginable, experts and policymakers are looking at how regulations and private standards can encourage environmental responsibility while avoiding many of the problems I discussed above. International cooperation is key here, because there is a real risk of fragmentation as a latticework of different regulations and standards covers the globe in a way that is all but impossible for businesses to navigate. The more regulatory approaches can be alligned, and standards taken up globally, the greater the likely impact and the less disruptive and inflationary the effects;
- The United Nations and a large coalition of think tanks, academics and experts are devising ways to support a more 'circular economy' whereby policies create incentives for products to be reused, recycled or repurposed rather than discarded;
- There is a challenge in moving greener technology, from cutting-edge wind turbines to more resilient plant varieties, from the institutes in richer countries where they are developed,

into the hands of those in the developing world. Where this isn't taking place on purely commercial terms, private philanthropy, government aid and corporate social responsibility initiatives are all working to close the gap.

This really is just a small sample of what is being done. As you will no doubt have picked up by now, nothing on that list is simple or without tradeoffs and competing interests. At least in the short term, the cheapest ways of doing things are often environmentally negligent, and pushing businesses away from them and toward more responsible paths must be done carefully. Still, the scale and scope of the global effort to address the myriad different facets of this problem is a cause for hope. This stuff is hard, but smart people are trying.

Chapter 15
Trade and Peace

Trade Prevents Wars Until It Doesn't

Trade and peace are often intertwined. If you reduce the discussion down to its most fundamental elements, trade provides an alternative to violence. From the very first time our Neanderthal forefathers realised that trading a share of the hunt for a place at a nearby fire was a more efficient, risk minimising and long-termist approach than bludgeoning the fire's owners, a path was opened for avoiding conflict.

We as humans are fundamentally covetous creatures (or more generously, aspirational ones), programmed by our genetics and culture to fulfil not just our basic needs but to improve our comfort and status, too. This applies to individuals, families, tribes, clans and entire nations. We strive for more than we have, and inevitably we soon reach the limit of how well we're able to satisfy our demands by drawing exclusively on our own resources. The forest on our land may provide all the lumber we need to expand our home, but we lack the quarry our neighbours can tap to build a solid stone foundation.

In the vast majority of cases, going to war to acquire what you want is not a cost-effective option. Setting aside the morality and ethics of the question, an army is costly to maintain during peacetime but becomes ludicrously expensive if you actually try to deploy it. For almost any commercial considerations, such as access to resources, there are generally cheaper, less risky and more morally and politically acceptable paths to the outcomes you're seeking.

This is not to say that trade has abolished armed conflict. It obviously hasn't. It is just that as the importance of farmland to an economy has decreased with the rise of international trade, the logic of waging a war to seize resources has diminished. When most of a population were farmers, and the wealth of the nation came from taxing their harvests, seizing more land was one of the few ways an ambitious monarch could meaningfully increase the kingdom's wealth. These days seizing more farmland is about the worst way imaginable to try to grow your economy.

One of those things international relations folks used to (smugly) say was that no two countries with a McDonalds had ever gone to war with one another. The implication was not, as you could be forgiven for suspecting, that saturating a society with cheap fast food will render the population too out of shape to contemplate military adventurism. Rather, it was the somehow even more sneering assumption that two countries that have so embraced capitalism and international trade that they host McDonald's franchises will have moved on from the possibility of warfare.

In a story in Asimov's *Foundation* series, a war with a militarily aggressive power ends swiftly when the economically and technologically advanced party imposes a trade embargo on the aggressor. This leads the latter's economy to collapse and forces them to sue for peace.

The point of these fantasy narratives is that if countries open themselves up to one another's commerce they will become too economically interdependent and culturally familiar with one another to wage war or to sustain one in the face of a trade embargo. It's the kind of idea that makes trade economists, who tend to believe that more integration is always a good idea, feel like they are creating a more peaceful world in addition to one that maximises the efficient allocation of resources. It's also just not that simple.

At the time I write this, though hopefully not at the time you read it, Russian tanks are rolling around eastern Ukraine in a war of conquest. Prior to the war, McDonalds had 110 restaurants in Ukraine and about 850 in Russia[1]. Unsurprisingly, the commercial availability of Big Macs in both Kyiv and Moscow did not prevent an invasion. I'm not just being glib. The economies of Russia and Ukraine were significantly interconnected, to the point where it took more than eight years from the start of hostilities in 2014 for Russian shipbuilding companies to start bragging about no longer being reliant on Ukrainian factories for their turbines[2]. It certainly caused some problems for Russia, but it did not ultimately deter aggression.

In a similar vein, economic embargoes have yet to become the doves predicted by Asimov. Entire books have been written about the effectiveness of sanctions, trade embargoes and export restrictions, but at least so far these types of measures have not magically ended conflict or military aggression. There is a link between trade and peace, but, despite what politicians and economists sometimes suggest, it can be broken or perhaps more accurately: overruled.

Is Trade Integration Peace-y?

If trade relations don't prevent hostilities outright, does greater trade integration at least make them less likely? Trade integration is when governments go beyond simply selling one another goods and services and begin to create enabling frameworks like customs unions, single markets and regulatory cooperation deals to encourage cross-border supply chains and collaborative production. Proponents of international frameworks and liberalism often argue that greater

---

[1] https://www.statista.com/statistics/1092618/russia-number-of-mcdonald-s-stores/

[2] https://theprint.in/defence/not-dependent-on-ukraine-for-engines-want-to-be-part-of-make-in-india-initiative-says-russia/1083903/

trade integration reduces the likelihood of armed conflict . . . but does it?

The challenge in delivering a straightforward answer to this question is that, at least in modern times, wars break out comparatively rarely and are driven by a range of unique factors. We also, for obvious reasons, have very little data on wars that did not happen but which might otherwise have done so without trade integration. Unfortunately for researchers, leaders are not in the habit of sending out press releases listing the military invasions they ultimately demurred from because of likely supply chain impacts.

Perhaps the most commonly cited example of trade fostering peace is that of the European Coal and Steel Community (ECSC), which integrated those industries across Belgium, France, Italy, Luxembourg, the Netherlands and West Germany in 1951, and eventually became the European Union. At the time, coal and steel were two of the primary commodities required for the waging of war, and it was thought that integrating them across borders would make future conflict, most notably between traditional antagonists France and Germany, impossible.

On the one hand, without a doubt, there has been peace in Western Europe since the establishment of the ECSC. France and Germany, which had previously waged war on one another pretty consistently, have not fired a shot in anger at one another for the best part of a century.

On the other hand, it's difficult to say with certainty that this peace can be explained primarily by the integration of coal and steel, or the grand trade integration experiment that is the European Union's much bigger Single Market. Germany's reaction to its defeat in World War II could not have been more different from the seething resentment that built up after 1918. Moreover, France and Germany spent much of the 20th Century united by the common external threat of the Soviet Union, and became militarily allied as part of NATO in 1955. Then, five years later, France tested its first nuclear weapon. We simply cannot say with certainty that it was trade integration which prevented another Western European war when there are so many other considerations. There is also the obvious null-case comparison in Japan - the other World War II imperialist Axis power that has behaved entirely peacefully for the last 70 years without anything like the level of regional trade integration seen in Europe.

We could consider other examples. The European Union's common market is credited with helping to enable the Good Friday Agreement, which brought peace to Northern Ireland by removing the highly sensitive question of where to put a customs border on the island. Judging by the flare-up of tensions since the UK's departure from the EU, in large part over that very question, it seems fair to assign trade integration at least a portion of the credit for the Good Friday Agreement's success. Of course, it is equally fair to say Northern Ireland is a unique context, with circumstances and international arrangements not found in other places – where the common market resolved a highly specific problem of how to avoid an overt demarcation of a border.

Another oft-cited example is the conflict-chilling effect of the economic interdependence between China and the West in preventing a direct military confrontation over issues such as Taiwan or territorial rights to the South China Sea. The argument goes that the prosperity that has helped China to lift hundreds of millions out of poverty depends on importing Western intellectual property and capital, and exporting goods. At the same time, Chinese manufacturing efficiency has kept the cost of living in the West down, and means Chinese elements are critical to many supply chains. In other words, the two sides need each other too much to risk open conflict.

There may well be some truth to this, but it is worth being sceptical too. A direct conflict between the West and China, featuring at least two but possibly as many as five nuclear powers, carries risks far greater than supply chain disruption. Moreover, it feels way too early to be triumphalist about peace. While we all hope the status quo holds, there are certainly enough clues in the actions of both sides to suggest that it is precarious.

Trade as a Weapon

Trade can be weaponised as a coercive tool of policy, either to force another government to change course, or to change its internal calculus when making choices.

That last part is useful to bear in mind: government decisions are the result of an equation with many variables. When we dismiss the leaders of unfriendly regimes as erratic or insane, we're often simply misunderstanding the variables their decision-making equation contains, or weights they are attaching to them. A paranoid leader may consider even the rumour of an emerging threat to be a prime concern, a foolish leader may discount credible warnings or chase fantasies, and a greedy or corrupt leader may prioritise personal enrichment above all other questions of governance – yet the equation is still there, and can thus be externally nudged.

How effective trade is at doing this nudging depends on the tools available to the nudger, the equation used by the nudged, and just how big a nudge is being sought. Despite deploying some formidable trade weaponry, the US embargo of Cuba failed to achieve its stated objective of regime change. That's not entirely surprising. It's really hard to sanction a country into changing leaders. It's even harder to sanction leaders into stepping down. Ultimately, there's just very little you can do to the 'international commerce' variable to make it outweigh the natural desire of a government to stay in power, and the natural aversion of a populace to take on the immense risks, hardships, and uncertainties involved in its removal.

Yet even with more modest policy influence objectives, the potential of trade instruments is still variable. First and foremost, in order for one's sanctions to be scary they have to be meaningful. You need to be a significant export destination for the other country's goods, or a source of imports they can't readily substitute from elsewhere, or perhaps a big investor in their various industries. The United States, with its massive consumer base, strength in key sectors, large well of investment capital and the investigative power to pursue sanctions violators, can issue threats that must be taken seriously by almost any country in the world. Even more so when, unlike in the case of Cuba, it is operating as part of a coalition including the EU, another giant that ticks many of those boxes. Conversely, a smaller power like Australia or Canada, acting unilaterally, would only be able to threaten a significantly smaller number of countries.

This actually brings us to another prerequisite for sanctions – willingness to accept the consequences for the sanctioner, not just the sanctioned. Almost by definition effective sanctions come between a buyer in one country who wants something, and a seller in another that wants to sell. Getting in the middle of that hurts both parties. For much of the 2010s and early 2020s, Australia and China have been very good examples of how this can be limiting.

The Australian economy is significantly reliant on selling a small group of products, primarily ores and coal, to China. At the same time, the Chinese construction sector, a key driver of its economic growth, is reliant on these imports from Australia. In the late 2010s and early 2020s, the two found themselves increasingly at odds on the international stage. Relations went from cool to arctic. Despite the signing of the China Australia Free Trade Agreement in 2015, China began rummaging in the trade policy toolbox to find ways to cause Australia pain. Yet it didn't reach for the obvious sledgehammer of restricting Australian iron ore, and instead settled for the still painful but far less devastating bamboo switch of messing with Aussie wine and barley. There's no great mystery as to why. China needed to buy Australian iron ore as much as Australia needed to sell it. The equation on the Chinese side just didn't add up, and so the scariest sanctions stayed in the box.

Another obvious example of this phenomenon could be seen in European energy politics in the early 21st Century. The EU, including its economic powerhouse Germany, bet significantly on a reliable supply of Russian oil and gas – believing that the prosperity the billions of euros would bring into Russia would improve its relations in the West and prevent it from doing anything that might upset the status quo. A classic trade-for-peace gambit. Ironically, everything we now know suggests Russian President Vladimir Putin was looking at the same set of circumstances and making a similar calculation – that a Europe dependent on Russia for its energy security would not intervene to prevent his military adventurism in non-EU countries like Georgia, Moldova and Ukraine.

It turned out both had significantly overestimated the strength of their hand. Putin, believing European energy dependence gave him impunity, grew more and more hostile abroad on the back of an economy underpinned by European purchases of its hydrocarbons. Eventually, his aggression culminated in a full-scale invasion of Ukraine and the attempted seizure by force of its capital, Kyiv. Initially, it seemed like Putin's gambit had paid off as the EU found itself in the humiliating position of slapping sanctions on everything Russian except oil and gas, which is a bit like boycotting all sports from Brazil except football. Far from convincing Putin that trade with the West was preferable to regional thuggery, Europe's apparently unquenchable and addictive thirst for Russian hydrocarbons made him believe he could act with impunity.

This too proved to be a miscalculation. Despite the centrality of Russian oil and gas to many of its members, the EU provided considerable support to Ukraine in money, weaponry and supplies. It also levelled increasingly damaging sanctions on Moscow and sought to lessen its dependence on Russian oil and gas in preparation for the day when the pipelines stop flowing. The full story is more complicated than I'm making it sound and well beyond my field of expertise, but I think most would agree with me that neither Europe's bet on oil and gas imports pacifying Russia, nor Putin's bet on his exports buying him Europe's neutrality quite panned out. In fact, the early stages of Russia's 'Special Military Operation' in Ukraine saw the somewhat absurd spectacle of Russia and Europe at each other's throats while transacting billions in trade daily because neither could yet afford to turn off the flow of hydrocarbons.

Getting Positive

It may feel from the above paragraphs that I am dismissive of the 'trade for peace' concept – and the truth is I'm not. I'm just wary of the branding and the propensity of many, including political leaders, to wrap themselves in dove feathers while cooing about trade rhetoric. As a species we do not have a good record on global peace, and we should be able to recognise where trade can help to mitigate these tendencies without exaggerating them or believing our own hype.

That trade provides policy options short of armed force or clandestine operations for governments that find themselves in a confrontation is welcome. The sanctions levied against Iran to try to stymie its nuclear program are bad for the Iranian economy and a source of genuine hardship for its people, but any attempt to enact the same outcome through armed force would be much worse. It is simply too much to hope for that in the absence of trade as a weapon, governments would simply do nothing.

Trade creates patterns and processes for resolving disputes amicably, or at least procedurally and legally. Human beings are prone to muscle-memory behaviours, and trade often breeds good habits like reaching for negotiation, mediation and arbitration when faced with a perceived injustice. Though structures like this carry their own challenges around access, fairness and universality, they are generally preferable to a bludgeoning by brute force.

It's also good that trade provides opportunities for mutually beneficial exchanges across borders, for improved understanding between cultures and for friendships to be made in the margins of commerce. One of the first ports of call for any government looking to motivate its people into supporting the sacrifices a war abroad entails is the othering and dehumanisation of the intended targets. Trade makes this harder (though as we've learned, nowhere near impossible) and that's important.

Finally, it's unquestionably good that the complexity and interdependence of modern supply chains add a significant negative to the scales of any policymaker weighing up whether to start a war. The trade implications may not prevent them from pulling the trigger, but they do raise the stakes and that's not nothing. 'It could leave our factories without the imported widgets they need' may not be the most comforting rationale for avoiding war, but given our record as a species it's worth having.

Crystal Balling

The flipside to the 'trade leads to peace' thesis is to consider when trade may be a cause of conflict – or at least a predictor of where conflict could arise. Exports are, almost by definition, lucrative. Anything you can sell competitively abroad despite the costs of packing, shipping and distribution in another country is probably fairly good value. Moreover, it's a product for which you must have some kind of advantage, else the locals in your destination country or rivals around the world would out-compete you. Perhaps the most common example of this kind of advantage lies in raw commodities – which is what makes controlling them so lucrative. If your territory has a lot of easily mineable and high-demand substances, you're in a great position to sell it to people who live in places that need them, but don't have them.

Controlling valuable, exportable commodities and distributing the ensuing profits is therefore an important element in any attempt to forge lasting, sustainable peace. A peace process which does not recognise that those with exportable assets are likely to grow wealthier and more prosperous, while those without them will have to work considerably harder to achieve comparable results, is setting itself up for failure. Division of resources is as important as division of acreage for ensuring a just peace.

There is also value in forecasting now, today, the valuable commodities of the near future and beginning to think about how to handle flashpoints arising from their scarcity. Though at times overstated as the driver of all US policy decisions, the importance of securing a reliable and plentiful supply of oil was clearly a factor in 20th Century decision-making, including on matters of war and peace. We are still interviewing candidates for the key commodities of the 21st Century, but already there are some strong contenders.

Energy resources like oil, natural gas and coal remain important despite recent advances in renewable energy. The demands of high-end technology for rare earth minerals, many only found in a handful of countries, continue growing. Some types of production, notably the smallest semiconductors and their supply chain, require levels of expertise and types of equipment so rare or narrowly held that replicating what they do might take even a highly resourced and motivated rival a decade. Looming behind everything is the prospect of fresh water becoming truly scarce, a notion so terrifying in its implications the mind instinctively dodges its consideration like a school of fish parting around a reef shark.

Trade and how we manage it is going to be integral to preventing competition for these assets from becoming violent. Today, we need to be thinking through how we are going to handle situations where competing interests, from global superpowers to neighbouring families, lay claim to scarce resources. Trade's greatest strength in the maintenance of peace is that it allows people to get what they want in a mutually beneficial way. Trade's greatest weakness is that such mutual benefit requires that there be a mutually acceptable price and a degree of equanimity among those who find themselves outbid or unable to meet a seller's asking price. When it comes to the vital commodities of the future, both won't always materialise.

Chapter 16
Trade and Investor State Dispute Settlement

Please Don't Hurt Me

Few things in modern trade discourse provoke the same level of instant outrage and paranoia as the dreaded Investor State Dispute Settlement or ISDS. For a former trade negotiator, it is hard to even bring up this topic without instinctively curling into a defensive ball or beginning to scope the surroundings for incoming tomatoes. When negotiating the Trade in Services Agreement (TiSA) our team met with a delegation of civil society representatives and had the following exchange:

> *Australian Chief Negotiator:* 'We're here to address any concerns you might have about TiSA.' *Civil Society Representative:* 'We are deeply concerned about the Investor State Dispute Settlement elements of this agreement.'

Chief: 'Ah, I have great news in that regard. There are no Investor State Dispute Settlement provisions in the TiSA. None at all.'

Representative: 'OK, but imagine **if there were...**'

Chief: '...'

Chief [to us, sub rosa]: 'Help.'

So what is Investor State Dispute Settlement and why is it so controversial? The vast majority of international law and dispute settlement is state-to-state. You have to be a government to take a case in an international tribunal against another government. ISDS is a provision first emerging in the 1970s and proliferating since then, primarily through thousands of agreements called 'Bilateral Investment Treaties' (BITs), but also occasionally through free trade agreements. ISDS creates a process under which an investor of one country can sue the government of another country for damaging its investments there.

It was created to give investors greater legal certainty to make big, long-term investments abroad. It was intended to protect investors from governments seizing, expropriating or invalidating a big investment without adequate compensation – where the local legal system is unwilling or unable to do so. ISDS arose in large part out of decolonisation, when Western firms which historically enjoyed preferential treatment from colonial administrations demanded additional protections against the decisions of newly independent governments. ISDS then went largely unused for decades but has recently become invoked far more often.

A large proportion of cases are where wealthy investors sue wealthy countries. However, as much of the most strident critique of ISDS revolves around the power imbalances it creates, let's take a fictional example involving a less wealthy country. Imagine you invest millions of dollars in building a gold mine in Belarus and the day it's finished, the National Assembly of Belarus passes a law saying all gold mines are now property of the government. No compensation will be paid to the former owners. You sue in the Belarus Supreme Court but find that the judges are either government stooges, have a gun to their heads, or have their hands tied because the National Assembly amended the law protecting business against expropriation before taking this step. In this scenario, ISDS would allow you to seek recompense through international law and with international arbitrators, not Belarusian ones.

To massively oversimplify, the way ISDS works in practice is:

1. Turkey and Nauru sign a trade agreement that includes an investment chapter with ISDS provisions.
2. The government of Nauru does something which harms a Turkish investment in Nauru, in a way the Turkish investor feels violates the investment chapter of the agreement.
3. (Optional) The Turkish investor sues the Nauru government over the matter in the Nauru court system.
4. The Turkish investor notifies the government of Nauru of their intent to take a dispute over the matter under the ISDS provisions of the Turkey-Nauru trade agreement.
5. The government of Nauru is obliged to enter into consultations with the investor to try to resolve the issue.
6. After a set period, if the two are still fighting, an arbitration panel is established. Generally this is a panel of three jurists, one selected by Nauru, one selected by the investor, and a third mutually agreed by both to chair.
7. The two sides present their cases to the arbitrators who then issue a ruling.
8. If the arbitrators find in favour of the investor, the government of Nauru is obliged by the treaty it signed with Turkey to pay any compensation the panel orders.

Why is Everyone Mad?

People object to ISDS for several reasons. First and perhaps most strongly felt is the concern that ISDS could be used to block, raise costs on or chill regulation and policymaking that is in the public interest. Depending on the wording of an ISDS clause, a corporation may be able to sue (or threaten to sue) in cases far less cut and dried than an uncompensated expropriation or nationalisation – such as if new environmental protection regulation renders a foreign-owned and highly polluting factory less profitable. Because ISDS cases can theoretically award millions in compensation, and because they can be exorbitantly expensive in legal fees for the state, even if it wins, there's a concern corporations could use the mere threat of ISDS action to bully governments into abandoning sound policies.

Second, there's an investor equity concern. Access to ISDS litigation is only open to *foreign* investors, not local ones – who must make do with the domestic legal system. By signing up to a treaty with ISDS, a government is effectively agreeing to provide investors in its treaty partners a broader range of protections than its own investors enjoy. A foreign investor protected by ISDS gets several bites at the apple, with options to challenge in either the domestic legal system, through international dispute settlement, or both.

Third, there is a 'Hey, why them?' question. ISDS specifically protects investors, not other groups like importers, exporters or civil society who might feel they are equally invested (sorry) in wanting to challenge government decisions they do not care for. ISDS puts investors in a special class, entitled to defend their interests through international tribunals even when their government is unwilling to fight their case..

Is ISDS Just Negotiators Dancing to the Corporate Tune?

The concerns listed above may justifiably make you question if ISDS is the sort of moustache twirling evil corporate scheme most commonly associated with Scooby Doo villains. You would be entirely forgiven for believing the entire notion was created exclusively to protect big capital and inserted into trade agreements through coercion, corruption or deception. The truth is a touch more complicated and proponents of ISDS do have a few points to make in defence of their system (beyond how much it enriches international lawyers). I'm going to lay out these arguments as best I can so that you know them – not because I endorse them. Please do not picket my apartment, you'll scare the dog.

The first argument ISDS proponents use is that governments want investment, investors want certainty, and ISDS is there to signal to investors the commitment of a government to provide them with that certainty. Investors considering pumping billions of dollars into a foreign market are very sensitive to risk – and some governments are perceived as riskier than others when it comes to potential expropriation, extortion or uncompensated nationalisation. ISDS strengthens the ability of investors to defend themselves against such things without relying on the country's own legal system and irrespective of whether the investors' home country wants to take up the fight.

The second argument in defence of ISDS is a classical legal one – those who don't break the rules have nothing to fear. The United States is party to ISDS provisions in over 40 treaties, has been sued under them more than a dozen times and has never lost a case. If, as opponents claim, ISDS makes any regulation that hurts corporate profits illegal, surely the US would have been sued thousands of times and suffered a few courtroom defeats. Proponents would say that the solution to any potential 'chilling effect' on regulation from the threat of ISDS isn't to stop regulating or to remove dispute settlement, but to ensure your regulations are in line with your treaty obligations so that even if you are sued, you'll end up winning.

So Who's Right, Then?
I have no idea. Like most of what's in this book, this is an area where legitimate disagreement in good faith is entirely possible – the only

people you should truly be wary of are those who would paint anyone who disagrees with them as either an amoral corporate shill or an ignorant alarmist hippy.

While opponents of ISDS can at times overstate the threat it poses to regulatory sovereignty, their critiques remain valid. I have certainly heard anecdotal reports of governments at least delaying legislation in areas like tobacco plain packaging while they waited for an ISDS case elsewhere to play out for fear of also getting sued. Similarly, while proponents of ISDS can be somewhat dismissive of the practice's very real downsides, it's hard to completely reject their assertion that governments entered into these arrangements because they believed them to be in their interest, that investors win fewer than 30% of ISDS cases, and that regulation hasn't exactly ground to a halt worldwide.

Ultimately, a lot depends on the terms of the individual treaty. What does it cover? What kind of penalties can it impose? What are the carve-outs in areas like public health or national security? Does the treaty allow the panel to force the plaintiffs to compensate the government for the cost of defending a frivolous or absurd case? Unfortunately, many of these questions are rather hard to answer without going deep into the detail, and so if you're looking for a shorthand you're probably pretty safe with: ISDS isn't generally quite as bad as people say it is but there's enough concern to be wary, and plenty of cause to ask the question, 'Wait, does anyone really need this?' Then just ignore the chorus of international lawyers yelling 'us!"

Chapter 17
Trade and More

Trade touches on almost everything, from professional sports to movie release schedules, and I had to make some hard choices about what I could cover, and what merited a full chapter. Still, I wanted to spend at least a few pages talking about a few of the policy areas where I think trade's impact is particularly interesting, salient or prone to political creativity where the truth is concerned. As always, if something in this chapter sparks your imagination or intrigues you, I encourage you to dive into the vast wealth of literature, popular and academic, devoted specifically to explaining the nuances.

Trade and Development
One of the most consistently controversial questions in international trade policy is how binding trade rules can and should interact with the planet-wide project of improving livelihoods in poorer countries. While trade can certainly at times be exploitative, and may entrench inequality, there is broad agreement that it is better for developing countries than autarky (refusing to trade at all). Exports bring in foreign currency while imports lower domestic prices and further

the spread of technology. Investment creates jobs and growth. There's general consensus that these things are conceptually conducive to development, even if there can be considerable challenges around implementation and the equitable distribution of benefits. Where there is significant disagreement is over the developmental benefits of government rules that restrict, boost or channel trade.

So let's say you're a developing country, looking to create good high-paying jobs, attract investment, achieve technology transfer and generally become a richer, more prosperous country through trade. In the 21st Century you're not doing this . Your country will be trading in a rules-based system of treaty obligations and liberalisations which limit what you can do as a government, in exchange for other governments being similarly limited. How to feel about this?

Officially, most developed countries say that the rules-based international system is inherently helpful to you in your quest to develop. They argue that your legal commitments provide certainty to investors and entrepreneurs, giving them the confidence to make long term investments in your country and to make it an important part of global supply chains. They also argue that having these rules will help you to push back against bad, protectionist ideas within your own system.

Not all developing countries are convinced by these arguments. They argue that the needs of their citizens, and the often nascent state of their industries, requires help and protection from the government. Given the scale of the challenges they face, they argue they should have the 'policy space' to intervene in the market to help shield infant industries, encourage specific forms of investment, and regulate in the ways they deem necessary. They allege, with at least some fairness, that developed countries used many of these protectionist tools to achieve their own economic dominance and are now promoting a system that would deny them to others.

A third position, balanced between these two though not necessarily more correct, argues that the rules, while constraining, are a price worth paying to avoid an escalating spiral of protectionism and subsidies with one's neighbours and competitors. This perspective argues that even if subsidies or a great deal of protectionism would help your industries, those benefits would be lost and even reversed if everyone else were subsidising and protecting too. It's a bit like how the Geneva Convention doesn't ban toxic gas because it can never be tactically effective, but because any advantages it might bring you are outweighed by the prospect of a battlefield where everyone is spraying toxic gas.

This argument about whether trade rules are always good, or too high a price to pay, is ongoing – and not merely philosophical. Every trade policy discussion involving a developing country inevitably returns to the question of so-called 'special and differential treatment'. How should the rules be different where developing countries are concerned?

The challenge for the international trading system is that your answer to that last question very much depends on where you stand on the earlier three options. If your position is that rules are inherently beneficial even when they constrain you, the role of special and differential treatment should be to help developing countries reach a point where they can reliably adhere to them. That means including things like phase-in periods before the introduction of rules, promises of technical assistance or capacity building, or slightly looser reporting and transparency requirements to accommodate smaller, overstretched bureaucracies.

Conversely, if you fundamentally believe that the rules aren't helpful, exemptions and limitations are the way forward. By allowing developing countries to do more of the kind of policies that the rules would ordinarily ban, you can give them a leg up and help them develop faster than they would otherwise – a level playing field with a built-in trampoline for the world's poor.

This debate has paralysed negotiations at the World Trade Organization, because one of the first questions many developing countries ask about any proposed new rule is: 'How will we be exempted from it?' and the instinctive reply of many developed countries is: 'We don't think you should want to be!' It is very hard to reach consensus on anything when half the people in the room believe they're negotiating for something good and the other half consider it to be bad.

Things get even more difficult when you ponder the question, 'What is a developing country?' This is one of the most charged questions in international trade, and the rules do very little to help answer it. In terms of formal categories of development level, the World Trade Organization rules include three: developed, developing, and least developed. The least developed category is a data-driven one, with formal criteria for membership and graduation, monitored by the United Nations Economic and Social Council.

Things get messier with the developing and developed labels. They are almost entirely self-designated. You can simply declare your country to be 'developing', and there's no legal or procedural mechanism for anyone to effectively challenge that label. WTO members who consider themselves developing but are not on the least developed country list include giants like India and Indonesia, all the way through to much smaller countries like Samoa. The challenge for negotiators, therefore, is that any flexibility, carve out or easing of the rules one offers 'developing countries' will be available to small traders with little influence on international markets and to vast and proliferate traders such as China or Brazil.

Developed countries argue that it is absurd to suggest that China, overwhelmingly the largest goods exporter in the world, needs any special treatment. Developing countries counter by saying that declaring themselves 'developed' when millions of their citizens are still struggling is politically and logically unjustifiable. They resent any attempt to introduce more criteria for defining 'developing' status, or to stratify the category into different tiers. In fact, recent talks have only been able to make progress through having large developing country traders unilaterally promise not to use the special and differential treatment the agreement would entitle them to, without actually forfeiting their developing country status. A difficult and shaky compromise.

To an extent, the system has survived this conundrum thus far because existing special and differential treatment is simply not beneficial enough for anyone to get too upset if a country they think is too rich to warrant access has it. By far the most commercially significant form it takes is a rule that allows WTO members to grant 'preferences' to developing countries – in other words, lowering tariffs for them non-reciprocally. Many developed countries, and some emerging economies, grant near full tariff free access to most least developed countries, and significantly reduced tariffs for many developing countries. This is a big deal, but it's voluntary. Richer countries can choose to do this, or they can choose not to, and they can choose which developing countries they offer such premium access. It's an advantage, to be sure, but one that relies on largesse.

Secondly, a more recent treaty called the 'Agreement on Trade Facilitation' allowed developing countries to self-determine a timeline for being bound by each of its provisions, and even condition it on receiving aid from abroad. A developing country could say, 'Paragraph 12b(i) will not apply to me for ten years' or 'Paragraph 21 will only apply to me if someone sends me a bunch of money to get me ready for compliance.' Understandably, many developing countries like this self-designation approach to international rules. It allows them to sign treaties that bind others, while ensuring they dictate the pace of their own commitments. This model is now frequently proposed by developing countries in new negotiations at the WTO.

This is just a flavour of some of the major debates circulating in trade and development, which is a vast academic and practical field. While almost everyone, including the UN through its Sustainable Development Goals, agrees that trade can support development, there is significantly less consensus about the precise role of trade rules. Whether special treatment for developing countries should be an on-ramp to the rules, or a fast lane that bypasses them, remains a central and unresolved question- – as does the challenge of deciding exactly who should be eligible for such ramps or bypasses. There is also an even larger and more complex conversation about how to equitably distribute the benefits of trade, to ensure they're not simply enriching a small minority or being funnelled out of the country, but this is well beyond the realm of trade policy and thus the scope of this book.

Trade and Intellectual Property

Intellectual property is the idea that it is possible to own, in a legally protected way, ideas, technological innovations, medicine recipes, creative works and even lines of computer code. It is one of the most highly controversial areas of trade policy, which since the Trade Related Aspects of International Property (TRIPS) Agreement was signed in 1994, has often involved the World Trade Organization.

The tension at the heart of the intellectual property debate is how to encourage innovation without creating rent-seeking monopolies that drive up prices for consumers. Medicine is perhaps where this debate is most acute. The research and development costs for new pharmaceuticals are staggering, and for every drug, therapy or device that makes it to market many prove to be ineffective, dangerous or simply outclassed by other treatments. Pharmaceutical companies argue that only by being the sole intellectual property holders of their successful new medicines for years after they go on sale can they possibly recoup all their investments and turn a profit. Only by enjoying a temporary monopoly on the drugs that work, they argue, can pharmaceutical companies afford to absorb the costs of finding them amongst all the ones that do not.

The implications here are far from comfortable. After all, the pharmaceutical company uses its temporary monopoly to charge a high price for the product that is many times the cost of production.

When the products in question are life-saving medications or treatments, and the ones paying the cost are the sick or infirm, one would have to have a heart of stone not to squirm at this.

Things get even murkier when you factor in international trade. The majority of pharmaceutical and medical technology patents are created by wealthy Western countries such as the US, the Netherlands, Switzerland and the United Kingdom. Not only are their citizens significantly wealthier than the global average, but they have robust and competitive private insurance markets and governments with the resources to at least subsidise the costs of accessing treatment. If you established a flat, global price for a new drug or treatment based on what you consider reasonable for the US, where the median household income is over $70,000 USD, you would price out of the market even countries like Thailand where the median household income is around $21,000 USD.

Basic human decency suggests a regionally variable pricing model, and there's almost certainly a profit rationale for one too. After all, a million people buying your product at a 10 per cent markup is a lot better than 5,000 buying it at a 300 per cent one. The problem, of course, is how you prevent someone from travelling to a place where your medicines are sold cheaply, and taking them back to a place where they are more expensive. There's also the question of how you prevent a foreign company, in a jurisdiction other than your own, from copying your formulas and flooding the market with copies of your drug that inevitably make their way back to the West. It is therefore protecting their profits in wealthy, developed countries, rather than squeezing every dollar out of poorer buyers in the developing world, that most animates pharmaceutical companies in enforcing their intellectual property rights.

There are two important things to understand about that enforcement. First, that original treaty, Trade Related Aspects of International Property Agreement (TRIPS) and the WTO do not themselves enforce intellectual property. They just make it an obligation that countries do so. So TRIPS commits all WTO members to creating domestic laws and institutions that will protect the rights of intellectual property holders, foreign and domestic. Let's take *Star Wars*. The WTO doesn't protect *Star Wars* in Cambodia, but as a WTO member Cambodia is obliged to have laws protecting the film franchise and an office that Disney can seek legal intervention from if someone in Cambodia decides to make a biopic of Obi-Wan Kenobi without Disney's permission.

Even then Cambodia's protection of intellectual property is probably motivated by factors beyond just their WTO obligations. Many trade wonks would love nothing more than for countries to take their commitments under the WTO so seriously, or to fear the wrath of a WTO complaint so much, that divergence would be unthinkable. That's not really how it works in practice. While countries do generally try to abide by WTO rules, few hold them to be holy scripture – and even before the WTO Appellate Body was (potentially permanently) crippled by a US veto on appointments, few considered disputes to be a terrifying prospect.

While the TRIPS Agreement created a common set of rules and expectations, the real enforcement mechanisms compelling countries to take intellectual property seriously have always been investment and diplomatic pressure. On investment, countries that have poor records of protecting intellectual property have to work a lot harder, and offer a lot more, to attract foreign investment and supply chains – which most governments want because they mean jobs and growth. On diplomatic pressure, the fact that the large pharmaceutical and medical technology companies tend to be headquartered in wealthy, powerful countries, has historically meant they have leverage with their own authorities. The US or European Union can and will take measures to protect the intellectual property of their firms abroad, and have the capacity to make life difficult for any government they feel isn't living up to their TRIPS obligations.

Waiving Covid

A useful illustration of just how complicated all this can get occurred during the height of the Covid-19 pandemic in 2020–21. As the first vaccines emerged, the most effective versions were made by Western countries which then hoarded or hoovered them up, at the expense of poor countries. A vocal civil society campaign argued that intellectual property protections were stopping developing countries from manufacturing their own versions of the vaccines, and supported a proposal from India and South Africa to agree to a 'waiver' exempting Covid-related medicine from the TRIPS Agreement.

The underlying debate here is staggeringly complex. Proponents of the waiver argued that leaving it in place meant the world was not producing vaccines as fast as possible, exposing poorer countries to a deadly pandemic. As well as arguing that IP protection fosters innovation, opponents argued that intellectual property was not what was holding back vaccine production, and that the TRIPS Agreement already allowed governments to effectively nationalise or expropriate intellectual property if doing so was vital for public health – provided they agreed appropriate compensation and did not subsequently export the drugs produced.

The issue was hugely emotionally charged, and understandably heavily politicised. Neither side necessarily covered themselves in glory, with hyperbole and accusations flowing in both directions. I'm not here to relitigate that argument, but I do have some questions for both sides that I think illustrate the complexities of the debate:

1. Was there a factory somewhere in the world that could have, and wanted to, produce Covid vaccines but was prevented from doing so by IP protections?
2. If intellectual property was the only, or principal barrier to vaccine production in a given country, why did those governments place fidelity to their TRIPS obligations over a pressing health crisis? While we hope that everyone will live

up to their international obligations at all times, it is clear countries derogate from them regularly and often for far less pressing reasons.

3. Do opponents of the waiver really believe that a more permissive IP regime would have prevented pharmaceutical companies from developing a vaccine, especially given the vast subsidies many drew upon to do so?

Ultimately public pressure succeeded in taking this debate from a conversation on a TRIPS Waiver, to the US coming out in favour of one in principle, to an impenetrably complex negotiation on the detail and finally to the agreeing of something only vaguely waiver-shaped in 2022. Far from the sweeping and broad exemption from IP rules the proponents sought, the final deal largely clarified existing language and marginally broadened the rights of developing countries to subsequently export Covid vaccines created as a result of expropriated intellectual property. The process of negotiating the actual content of a waiver, and getting the holdouts (primarily the EU, UK and Switzerland) on board with the concept at all took so long that the urgency and political pressure faded. Ultimately when the final agreement was reached, celebrations were muted. Make of that what you will.

Trade and Gender

Since the mid 2010s there has been a focus on what trade policy can do to support the economic empowerment of women. The argument runs something like this: women generally enjoy fewer economic opportunities than men in many societies, and face greater obstacles in accessing those opportunities. As well as being unfair, this holds back development and growth because half the adult population cannot properly explore entrepreneurialism or contribute to industry. Trade policy changes the state of play in an economy, and if it can do so in a way that increases opportunities for women, that will therefore be good.

When this concept was first becoming mainstream around 2015, championed by the likes of Canada under the then newly elected Prime Minister Justin Trudeau, trade negotiators faced a challenge: gender is hard to incorporate meaningfully into trade agreements. Even countries fully supportive of the idea struggled to find where exactly in a proposed agreement they were supposed to make commitments that might improve the livelihoods of women.

The difficulty negotiators faced was that the vast majority of trade-relevant legal language, from the WTO texts down to local implementing legislation, is already written in an ostensibly gender neutral way. A huge range of factors drives the decreased participation of women in profitable trades, but it's rarely an explicit government policy (and where it is governments are probably not going to be willing to address that as part of a trade deal). Women-owned business can struggle to access capital, can face discrimination bureaucratically, can find themselves relegated to the bottom of a supply chain or locked out of lucrative contracts. The list goes on, but few of the items on it are borne of explicit, legal discrimination against women of the sort gender language in a trade agreement might address. There's no law stating women can't get a small business loan, they're just not being offered one. Signing a trade agreement that reaffirms that women should be able to access finance would not end that unfairness.

Despite this, gender chapters that, all things considered, didn't really *do* much were included in trade agreements. The Canada-Israel Free Trade Agreement is a good early example. It has a chapter specifically on Trade and Gender, but this consists only of general motherhood statements (a somewhat ironically named term for treaty language which just reaffirms broad shared values but doesn't have any practical or legal force), some cooperation activities, and the establishment of a 'Trade and Gender Committee'. It does not change any aspect of the trade regime in Canada or Israel, nor create new limits on what those trade regimes can include in the future. It is what trade geeks call 'soft law' – not worthless but simply not in the same realm as crunchier commitments that materially impact commerce or policy.

Since then, negotiators have found one or two ways they could incorporate binding language on gender issues into agreements, such as committing not to use gender as the basis for denying a visa to a services supplier from abroad. Generally though, these are the exceptions. Moreover, these often consist of commitments not to overtly discriminate between countries who would never dream of doing so and where any such discrimination would be struck down by a domestic legal challenge long before international trade agreements became relevant.

This is not to say that these early forays into incorporating gender provisions into trade agreements were entirely worthless. The trade policy community tends to be fairly conservative, and quite sceptical of new concepts. Like frogs being boiled slowly, trade negotiators had to be accustomed to the idea of gender considerations being relevant to their work in gradual increments, lest they freak out and hop away. In less than a decade, speaking of trade and gender in the same breath went from the strange fixation of a hyper-progressive Canadian government to a mainstream concept. That could only happen incrementally.

Perhaps more significantly, the intense focus of exactly how gender could be incorporated into trade agreements generated a vast amount of scholarship, analysis and serious thinking.

Through the Gender Lens

The core idea of the Gender Lens is deceptively simple. Instead of looking to insert specific provisions related to gender in a trade agreement, consider everything in it at least partially through how it's likely to affect women's economic empowerment – prioritising elements that benefit women owned business and sectors that disproportionately employ women. So for example, if you are deciding which of the other side's tariffs to focus on cutting, choose the one where more liberalised trade will be of greater benefit to women.

Trade negotiations are fundamentally about choices: what to prioritise, which points to defend, and where to pick fights within your own system. In theory, adding the question 'What will benefit women?' when making these decisions sounds like it should produce results supportive of women's economic empowerment. As always, however, there are a few challenges.

First, the gender lens can get a bit cloudy. Statistics about where women are currently employed, and their exposure to foreign trade, aren't always readily available or perfect. Moreover, just because an industry currently features a higher number of women owned businesses or female employees doesn't mean this trend will continue after liberalisation. If a particular product becomes a viable export cash-crop for example, patriarchal power structures may reassert themselves and see women cast out, marginalised or exploited..

Second, trade agreement priorities aren't created through a detached and objective calculus. Most trade negotiators will confess, perhaps after some alcohol, that their national objectives and red lines often have more to do with the effectiveness of the relevant lobby group or industry association than they do with economic assessments or modelling. Sometimes much more. Making something supportive of women's economic empowerment a greater priority means moving other things down the priority list, and that may come at a political price.

Third, a lot of what can make a real difference to the experience of women conducting trade isn't a natural fit into trade agreement language. For example, good security, proper lighting and safe toilet facilities at border crossings are especially important to women who might use them, for obvious reasons, but fit awkwardly into treaty text. Similarly, women tend to benefit when more processes are automated and fewer bureaucratic hurdles are left to the discretion of officials. This is the sort of thing that might go in a trade facilitation chapter, but is hard to be too pushy about if the government itself isn't keen because accusing the other side's officials of being sexist or extortionate is hardly conducive to constructive vibes around the negotiating table

Finally it's fair to say that not all governments around the world share the same levels of enthusiasm for women's economic empowerment through trade policymaking. For some this is driven by religious, cultural or philosophical objections to empowering women. For some it's a slippery slope concern, driven by an apprehension about what may come next once the 'progressive policy through trade' barrier is passed. Finally, some object tactically, on the basis that concluding an agreement without at least a token gender chapter will be something the other side could make concessions elsewhere to avoid.

Despite some scepticism and opposition, women's economic empowerment has been fairly comprehensively mainstreamed in trade-thought. Just about every United Nations and affiliated development programme with a trade-related element includes gender as both a specific focus and something to evaluate their success against. Many donors make supporting women traders, women entrepreneurs and women dominated export sectors a key priority.

Trade and Government Procurement

A significant percentage of any modern economy is government procurement – the purchase of goods and services from the private sector with public funds. This can range from buying pens for the vehicle licensing office to buying fighter jets for the army, and from a construction company filling in potholes to a private military contractor providing security for diplomats overseas. Government procurement contracts can last many years and be worth billions of dollars, making or breaking the businesses that compete to win them.

Government procurement is also one of the few ways that a government minister can directly 'create jobs' – rather than simply trying to create the right economic conditions for them to flourish.

A hundred million dollar contract to produce furniture for the civil service is a huge boost to whichever local communities house the factories that now have huge orders to fill for the forseeable future. That probably means a photo opportunity with lots of smiling workers in hard hats outside a factory, with glowing coverage on local news and champagne all around. Moreover, unlike a subsidy which can be readily attacked as 'picking winners' or propping up a failing industry, government procurement is at least in theory simply a matter of buying what you need from a competitively bidding supplier. All very good and proper (I repeat: in theory).

Trade policy comes into this by either restricting or enabling foreign firms, and foreign owned firms, from competing fairly for a slice of this lucrative market. If your government procurement rules prevent you from even considering a mousepad made in my country as a potential way to solve your lack of mousepads, then that's a trade barrier – it's the government putting itself between a customer (in this case itself) and a vendor that may offer the best value. As with any trade barrier, that's a choice featuring trade-offs. On the one hand it might mean the government is receiving less value for the tax dollars it spends on mousepads. On the other hand it means the tax dollars spent are going into local businesses and supporting local jobs. You can make a case either way.

Depending on the good or service being commissioned there may also be other arguments for accepting bids only from local firms. You probably don't want to be buying your air defence network from a geostrategic rival, even if their missiles are value for money. Similarly a public television channel designed to promote local auteurs needs to be able to discriminate in favor of the young filmmaker next door because that's why it's there in the first place. Let the commercial channels run repeats of *Seinfeld* or *Bondi Vet*.

Initially, international trade rules erred entirely on the side of letting governments do whatever they want. Government procurement is explicitly carved out of both the General Agreement on Tariffs and

Trade, and the WTO's other founding treaties. The text of these specifically states that nothing in these agreements will constrain a government in how it makes procurement decisions. So in other words, even if you have to keep car tariffs at 0 per cent because that's what you committed to in your WTO Goods Schedule, nothing in the WTO rules obliged you to even consider foreign vehicles as an option when buying a new fleet for the civil service.

However, starting from the mid-70's there was a movement among a subset of the WTO's membership to negotiate and agree a treaty that would at least partially liberalise government procurement, at least among themselves. These negotiations took decades, but ultimately led to the signing of the WTO Government Procurement Agreement (GPA). This treaty is a so-called plurilateral because it only includes 49 WTO members, not the full membership. However, that 49 includes the US, European Union, China, Japan and indeed all of the world's top 10 largest economies except India and the Russian Federation.

The Government Procurement Agreement basically says that when a government procures goods or services above a certain value, then as long as what it's buying or the department buying it isn't on their GPA list of exemptions, then it has to give suppliers in other GPA members a fair chance of winning the contract. I hope by this late stage in the book your automatic reaction to reading a sentence like that is to ask, "Hold on, what does 'a fair chance of winning' actually mean?"

In practice, this comes down to three broad principles.

First, on covered procurements the purchasing government is not allowed to discriminate against a potential vendor just because they are foreign, or foreign-owned. What's absolutely critical to understand here is that the GPA bans discrimination on explicitly foreign versus domestic grounds, but not on the practicalities of how that difference might manifest. If you are a Japanese firm bidding on a contract to repaint every school building in Scotland, Scotland and the United

Kingom aren't allowed to discriminate against you just because you're Japanese – but they are allowed to pass on your bid if all of your painters are 20 hours' flight away and have no way of getting visas. If a firm being foreign owned or based overseas has practical implications on the value, quality or risk of their bid, governments are still allowed to take that into account in awarding a contract.

Second, governments have to be transparent and accessible in how they list contracts for tender. When the government is contemplating making a purchase covered by the GPA, they have to publish it online in a reasonable timeframe and with a clear procedure in place for tendering bids. This is designed to prevent defacto discrimination, whereby foreign firms are effectively prevented from bidding because to even hear about a contract you need to be attending the right dinner parties or industry forums in the procuring country, or because actually tendering a bid requires being on a first name basis with the undersecretary for transporation's personal assistant.

Third, and mostly as a way of keeping governments honest about the first two, procurement officers are supposed to keep records and be ready to offer explanations for why they went with one bid over another. If a foreign firm loses out on a contract, the awarding government agency or department should be able to point to the criteria that deemed an offering to be worse value than the winning bid. This not only provides transparency, but sort of retroactively imposes on governements the need to be structured, methodical and procedural in how they go about making purchasing decisions.

Now, those of you who have ever had anything to do with the government procurement process might be smiling ruefully at this point. The actual process of comparing bids tends to be a committee, reviewing documents that can run to hundreds of pages and then assigning each bid a value against a set of criteria. There is a huge amount of arbitrariness and subjectivity involved, and a minister walking past every half an hour to absently remark how nice it would be if the contract ended up with the struggling concrete plant in their district rather than some foreign outfit can absolutely put a finger on the scales in a way that would be devilishly difficult to prove in any subsequent review. To quote a movie paleontologist, 'Life finds a way.'

There are also of course the carve outs, thresholds and exceptions. The GPA does not force the government to publicly tender and accept foreign bids when buying a new box of pens for Gary in human resources. Nor is there any obligation to open up bids on your next big warship to shipyards in a hostile power. As part of negotiating the GPA, or joining it later, each member had to get the others to agree to their list of exempt products (say, nuclear materials) and exempt entities (say, the air force), to which the government procurement provisions wouldn't apply.

Beyond these exemptions, there are also a range of goods and perhaps more specifically services that foreign firms would really struggle to supply competitively – unless working primarily through a local office or with local partners. Running the cafeteria at the Department of Health and Human Services is just not something you can do on a long-term basis without a local presence and many local staff. At the end of the day, that contract is either going to a local company or to a company that is going to spend the vast majority of the revenue it derives from the contract on paying local staff and local vendors.

Despite not being perfect, and not covering every type of procurement, the GPA is still generally fairly well regarded and increasingly expanded upon in free trade agreements. Even if governments do sometimes nudge a process in the direction of a local supplier, just having most procurements publicly advertised is a big win, as is the absence of overt discrimination against non-local firms and the ability to at least query a losing bid. Ministers are never going to stop wanting to buy local applause by channelling government funds to local producers, but the GPA and government procurement clauses in free trade agreements at least force them to be sneaky about it.

Conclusion

Like Ferris Bueller wandering out into the hallway in a bathrobe at the end of the movie, I am pleased, flattered and above all surprised that anyone is still here. Trade policy is not most people's idea of a riveting read, and while I've done my best I don't think anyone is going to confuse this book with a Tom Clancy novel. Perversely though, I would be somewhat pleased if you found this book to be 'accessible hard work worth doing,' because unfortunately that's what meaningfully engaging with trade policy in the public square tends to be. There are few simple answers and every decision is a balancing act between competing interests, political forces and systemic implications. Trade policy makes you work, and most politicians are never happier than when voters stop thinking.

That's not an attempt to shame anyone. The world and the political sphere are so complex and all-encompassing that you can't possibly thoroughly research every issue being debated on any given day. Even trade ministries, ostensibly paid to do nothing but navigate the murky waters this book covers, will often bemoan the shallow way they make decisions. Most will tell you they don't engage with nearly enough stakeholders, inconsistently consume the academic literature, have little opportunity to understand the implications of various policies for actually moving goods and services around, and rarely get the opportunity to reflect back on whether anything they did produced the intended results. Understaffed, overworked and chained to the hamster wheel of ministerial whim, they have a tendency to paint with broad strokes and then hope any smudges work themselves out later.

My goal with this book was to equip you, as best I could, with an appreciation of the complexities in trade policy and the most common ways in which intuition and common sense can be misleading. If your sense after you turn the final page is that you understand the outlines of how trade works, and know enough to question bold promises or catchy slogans, then I'll have done my job. You don't need to be a veterinary gastroenterologist to spot bullshit when someone drops it on your driveway.

In trying to keep this book manageable in length, I have had to make some hard choices about what to include, what to dive deep on, and what to flag but not truly explore. I'm sure I got some of those calls wrong and I'm certain there will be many of you who wish I covered something in greater detail or didn't bang on so long about something else. I do hope, however, that the general rules which cut across virtually the entire book will serve you even on the subjects I did not cover:

1. Ask what a policy will actually change for those trading.
2. Don't be bamboozled by large numbers and billion dollar implications – they may not always be wrong but they're often misleading and there's always more to the story.
3. Treat any policy that claims to have no losers (or only losers) with extreme scepticism.
4. Remember that businesses prefer predictability over almost everything, and any policy that introduces changes must yield greater benefits than the costs of associated uncertainty and change.

5. Dismiss anyone telling you that an intractable or complex problem can be fixed by 'just getting on with it' as the charlatan they almost certainly are.

This is a time of profound global change. The post-cold-war global era is being replaced by a complex overlay of powers, superpowers and alliances. Every year sees temperature records broken, climate impacts becoming more pronounced and the debate around appropriate responses growing more urgent. Technology, having reshaped the workforce with the industrial, digital and information revolutions now seems like it may or may not do so again as remote work, and AI creeps into the white-collar, creative workplaces that may have previously been considered immune from the professional insecurity of outsourcing or automation.

Trade is never far from the conversation in any of these discussions. It is in many ways the frontline of the tensions between the major and emerging global powers, it is integral to both mitigating and minimising climate change, and it will inevitably be a part of corporate and national responses to the changing nature of our workplaces. Intervening in trade will only grow more tempting for governments – the impacts feel remote and far removed, the constituencies unbalanced in favour of intervention, and the rhetorical force of the simplistic tends to outclass that of the true.

I owe much of my career to having been in the right place, at the right time, with the right credentials to stand in front of the firehose of bullshit that was the public debate around trade policy in the late 2010s and cry, 'Um no, that's not how that works!' The secret to my (limited) success wasn't any unique insight or unparalleled expertise. I don't think I had much of either. I just got lucky because politicians and public figures were constantly, lazily and repeatedly misleading the public in easily provable ways.

Neither this book nor indeed anything I do as a communicator about trade can ever keep politicians, corporate lobbyists, or anyone else honest. There are too many rewards and too few consequences for deception or confidently pronounced ignorance. The liars and grifters aren't going to stop – but hopefully this book helps you make them sweat a little.

Index

Acknowledgements

The problem with writing the acknowledgements before your book is published and reviewed is that you don't know if you are sharing credit or identifying a list of people who share the blame. Thankfully in this case, the great many people who helped get this book into your hands are entirely blameless, and so I can praise them unreservedly and trust any ire will be reserved for me alone.

This book would not have been possible, and it certainly wouldn't have been readable, without Martin Hickman, Gaby Monteiro and the team at Canbury Press. With the patience of a saint, Martin shepherded me through the process of writing my first ever book, and every sentence his editor's quill touched saw a vast improvement from my own inept scratchings.

Thanks of a sort should also go to Ian Dunt, who upon completing his own book *How to Be a Liberal* with Canbury recommended me to Martin as a potential author, encouraging me to do it with the inspiring words, 'Writing this is going to be a terrible, agonising hell… you should totally do it.' He was correct on the first part, and I'll leave you to judge the second.

That anyone has the slightest interest in what I have to say on trade, or indeed anything, is testimony to the many times in my life that extraordinary people have taken a chance on me. I owe the start of my career to Jagjit Plahe, Chris Nyland and Danny Burrows, and my current success to Lorand Bartels, Richard Baldwin, Tamara Pironnet and Joost Pauwelyn. They and many others taught me a great deal, but also (knowingly or unknowingly) threw me lifelines when the waters were rising past my ears.

Much of this book represents an attempt to summarise the many lessons I learned working beside some incredibly knowledgeable, wise and kind colleagues at the Australian Department of Foreign Affairs and Trade. Andrew Jory, Deanna Easton, Tara Booth, Leslie Williams, Lliam Findlay, Nate Henderson, Pierra Shannon, Natasha Spisbah, Jo Feldman, James Baxter, Simon Farbenbloom, Hamish McCormick and far too many others to name. My doubtless irritating habit of wandering into offices for a trade policy chinwag may have damaged Australian civil service productivity but taught me most of what I know.

Since then I have been fortunate enough to meet and draw on the expertise of many of the finest minds in international trade policy, investment and finance. Many of them have, over the years, taken a frankly unreasonable amount of time out of their lives to walk me through their areas of expertise. George Riddell, Sally Jones, Peter Ungphakorn, Patrick Low, Jennifer Hillman, Chad Bown, Kimberley Botwright, Alice Tipping, Jonathan Hepburn, Anna Jerzewska, Emily Reed, Christophe Bellman, Simon Evenett, Carolyn Deere, Alicia Greenidge, Michael Roberts and dozens more have made me a smarter trade wonk. I will be forever grateful.

A number of very smart and generous people took the time to review individual chapters of the book in areas of their specialised expertise I wanted to especially thank Nicolas Lamp, Inu Manak, and Sam Lowe for taking the time to review my draft chapters and very politely inform me where I grossly erred.

Finally, I want to acknowledge my partner, my family, my friends, and my dog for their depthless patience with me as I spent the better part of 18 months cancelling social engagements to work on the book . . . or stressing out at social engagements because I knew I should be writing. With the book published I can confidently promise to only neglect you for *Dungeons and Dragons*.

Dmitry Grozoubinski

Dmitry Grozoubinski is a former Australian trade negotiator and current Executive Director of the Geneva Trade Platform think-tank. He has trained hundreds of government officials, corporate officers, students and activists all over the world on negotiations and how trade policy works. Quoted on trade policy issues in publications like the *Financial Times*, the *Economist* and the *New York Times*, Dmitry specialises in making complex debates accessible. Born in Ukraine, Dmitry grew up in Australia where he obtained a Masters of Diplomacy and Trade from Monash University. He resides in Geneva where he is tolerated by his partner and his Shiba-Inu.

More titles from Canbury Press

TikTok Boom
The Inside Story of the World's Favourite App
Chris Stokel-Walker
Technology

**'It is rare for a business analysis to read like a thriller –
this one does.'**
Azeem Azhar, Founder, Exponential View

More titles from Canbury Press

How AI Ate the World
A Brief History of Artificial Intelligence and its Long Future
Chris Stokel-Walker
Technology

'From ancient China to Victorian England, How AI Ate The World is the story of the characters, moments, technologies, and relationships that populate the rich history of artificial intelligence. A book about what is gained – and what is lost – amidst the steady march of a technology that now saturates our lives, How AI Ate The World grapples with what the age of automation means for the people living through it.'
Harry Law, University of Cambridge

Publish with Us

Our aim is to depict the world as it really is, stripped of spin.

Modern non-fiction from London

www.canburypress.com

info@canburypress.com